How We Lost the War on Poverty

*trans*action/**Society** Book Series

HOW WE LOST
THE
WAR ON POVERTY

Edited by
MARC PILISUK
and
PHYLLIS PILISUK

Transaction Books
New Brunswick, New Jersey

Unless otherwise indicated, the essays in this book originally appeared in transaction/**Society** magazine.

Second Printing 1976

Copyright © 1973
Transaction, Inc.

Transaction Books
Rutgers University
New Brunswick, New Jersey 08903

Library of Congress Catalog Card Number: 72-91471
ISBN: 0-87855-079-8 (cloth); 0-87855-574-9 (paper)

Printed in the United States of America

Contents

1

INTRODUCTION

Barely War

MARC PILISUK AND PHYLLIS PILISUK

Beginning with John F. Kennedy's historic visit to Appalachia in 1960, the war on poverty has continued for over a decade. Like other wars, it too was "an extension of politics." It was conceived to preserve the unholy alliance between northern and southern Democrats just when that alliance was about to be destroyed by the civil rights movement. It is difficult now to recall how political support spread when President Lyndon Johnson promised the emergence of the "Great Society" as the dividend on his budding war on poverty. The loose coalition behind these moves extended from Students for a Democratic Society (SDS) and the ghettos to the corporations and law firms that switched their pattern of campaign-giving in Johnson's landslide victory. The issue of race had been deftly defused and the Economic Opportunity Act was sure to pass.

But a few years later the ghettos were afire, then the campuses; Johnson resigned, and his party required an army of riot police to protect their staged political convention. The war on poverty had fallen—a victim of the war in Indochina, of American military priorities, of an economy of waste in a society unwilling to redistribute its wealth. The war on poverty—never a real war at all—has been lost. A review of its various battlefields gives us insight into the way in which reform in American society, rather than subdividing accumulated wealth, protects its concentration.

The war on poverty was more than legislation. It was a national attitude that built hopes and community programs, sent student organizers into Hazard, Kentucky, Cleveland, Chicago, Newark and Boston, and pressed for new legislation and new legal services to enforce the old laws. Dropouts could realistically hope for new careers, and corporations for an enlargement of the skilled labor pool and of the market of middle-class consumers. For convenience, we have divided the antipoverty effort into three components—indigenous organizing, professional and paraprofessional action, and social policy. An effective war on poverty would have required a high degree of mutual facilitation among these levels of action.

In the introduction to our previous *trans*action/**Society** Series book, *Poor Americans: How the White Poor Live*, we stressed the viability of various poverty subcultures, the fallacy of blaming the people of such cultures for their own economic deprivation, and the error of demanding a renunciation of subculture as the price for a low-level entry on the economic ladder. A richer model of change is necessary. Change is not easily come by, and both the cultures of poor people and the intransigence of the social order have been blamed for the slow rate of progess.

We take seriously the radical critique that poverty continues because it is a natural product rather than an accident of the economic system. In our earlier book dealing with white poverty, we noted that it was but a part of a larger malady, white affluence, and that the two are inextricably linked. Poverty will not disappear, therefore, without a revolutionary change in the economic system. We believe that such a revolution, if it is not merely to be a superficial reshuffling among those who are the privileged and those who are the oppressed and impoverished, must be accompanied by a revolution in values, freeing the quality of life from its ostensible dependence upon retaining wealth and privilege—freeing the process of change from the values of acquiring or retaining power. But how to activate these revolutions we do not know. This book deals, then, only with efforts toward fighting poverty, not eliminating it. This is not a statement of pure pessimism. We have learned from the generally discouraging effects of our past eight years of antipoverty effort that federal programs conceived as technical solutions (whether to housing, job skills, food distribution or income maintenance) run into trouble where they confront vested interests, and that an apolitical view of such programs is inadequate. We have learned something also of the limits of community organizing efforts, most particularly that a local power base can go only so far before it confronts the larger powers bent on resisting, controlling or co-opting it. We have learned also that programs based upon opportunities for small numbers of poor people to transcend their cultural origins are not only an affront to our professed respect for racial and ethnic pluralism but are also a collective failure. We can successfully train a black dropout to the point where he may replace a white worker in job competition, but without creating more jobs we have only made changes (and enemies) among those at the bottom of the economy.

Out of these negative lessons comes a more realistic appraisal of what can and must be done to make our future efforts more successful. We are proposing a model of the change process in which we can see three distinctive levels of social intervention. The two complementary intervention levels are sound policy and indigenous action. We conceive of an intermediary level of professional and paraprofessional service as a force facilitating or helping community action to attune its efforts to pending policy changes, pressing policy-makers to remain responsive to diverse community needs, and providing services under local community controls.

Such a model of coordinated effort is no magic lever, no Rosetta stone to uncode and translate directly into a set of enabling moves to eliminate poverty. This coordinated effort may, however, help us to move more quickly to alleviate some of the worst aspects of impoverished living—isolation, hunger, ill health and despair. The model includes not only money for the poor, not only people to give them services, not only indigenous community action, but all of these. We have learned from our experiences in trying to help minority communities that people do not want to accept fully developed programs that well-meaning reformers believe would be good for them. To relegate people to the category of problems to be aided, programmed or rehabilitated, without their early participation, is to invite the most debilitating personal accommodations. Poor people must have some voice in deciding what actions are most desirable and appropriate for them.

There is room, however, for professionals and paraprofessionals to work in poor communities: to help people to pinpoint their own needs; to help them see precisely where and by what means their interests are being sold short; and to help people organize themselves to express their grievances collectively. Individuals can be overlooked, but it is harder to ignore a rent strike or a demonstration of welfare mothers receiving an income too small to feed and clothe their families. And it is still harder to ignore a disruption of sanitation and transport services in a large city.

So the poor, with or without professional assistance, are themselves critical to certain antipoverty efforts. Wherever a program requires the sustained action of poor people, that program will be obliged to take into account the needs fulfilled by their existing beliefs and interaction patterns. These cultural facts have developed for their psychic and social survival value. When we recognize the values of existing arrangements or subcultures, it becomes easier to comprehend reluctance to participate in superimposed ameliorative efforts. Thus we can understand an individual's unwillingness to attend fruitless meetings with strangers, or to cut ties, change his vocabulary and manners or to reach out to some program which, though it may be called "Horizons Unlimited," actually offers him little more than a chance to be competitive in the lower levels of the labor market.

Clearly, the poor have an important role in the dynamics of change. It is a role that requires a strengthening of their own communities around issues of common concern. Through collective protest, and perhaps through no other route, the poor can open the channels through which they may be heard. The effort itself can be personally productive for the activists. A mentally healthy person must be able to take action toward goals that have positive meaning for himself and his group. Social action creates an opportunity to break out of the resignation and despair that are frequent components of the generalized culture of poverty. Indigenous action also provides the only genuine pressure that poor people can bring to bear on the political process. There is, however, an attribute of poor subcultures that offers both a potential for radical organization and a source of ambiguity regarding the direction such action may take. Oscar Lewis makes this observation:

> A critical attitude toward some of the values and institutions of the dominant classes, hatred of the police, mistrust of the government and those in high position, and a cynicism which extends even to the church gives the culture of poverty a counter quality and a potential for being used in political movements aimed against the existing social order.*

How this potential is used depends in part on the roles of the professional and of indigenous leadership. The professional has several roles in the change process. The most difficult and perhaps the most important is to permit communication across the cultures. To do this, we must learn to listen to the anguish and the anger.† We must be able to understand the symbols that give meaning to the lives of those in communities that are different from our own. It is a task that cannot be done without guides whose origins among the poor subcultures make them capable of reaching out to clients in ways rarely available to the typical professional. For this reason the paraprofessional takes on increased importance both as conveyor of communication from the poor and as a means for delivery of services.

Since no currently available services terminate the client's

---

*Oscar Lewis, *Scientific American*, 1966, 215:4:19-25.

†See, for example, Vols. I, II, and III of Robert Coles *Children of Crisis:* Vol. I, *Children of Crisis, a Study of Courage and Fear*, 1964; Vol. II, *Migrants, Sharecroppers, Mountaineers*, 1967; Vol. III, *The South Goes North*, 1967. Little Brown and Co.

poverty, the professional and paraprofessional must serve in non-traditional ways. Advocacy is an important example. No therapist in a mental health center or physician in a clinic, no welfare worker or teacher's aide can serve adequately in a community of poverty without becoming an advocate for more services of higher quality, for greater participation and control in the hands of the community. Even professional research should be more often on behalf of, rather than simply on, the client population. The poor should know as much about the predictions and controls of those powerful men who are the gatekeepers of their destinies as these gatekeepers are continually learning from social scientists about the behavior of the disadvantaged. The professional should direct the frustration from unmet needs to the seats of power where policy is determined.

So far, we have been dealing with community pressure and community change. This is the only locus of pressure that the poor communities can generate. Yet American poverty cannot be eradicated using only local community resources. Economic impoverishment is the product of an economic system that distributes wealth inequitably. The system is pervasive. Technological displacement, opposition to welfare for the poor, tax inequities, dependence upon unstable war industry, the use of efficiency criteria without regard to human costs, priorities directing federal monies toward the military—all are matters of national policy. Patterns of support for services are both state and national matters. Structural unemployment is the elimination of whole job classes for which no amount of poor people's mobility or local organization may compensate.

However, where jobs do exist or can be made to exist by legislation, poor people are still often excluded because of the supposedly necessary educational or skill requirements. Does an automobile mechanic really need a high school diploma? Does a sales representative of a large corporation need a college degree? Does a nursery school teacher need to complete four years at a university? Does a college teacher need a Ph.D.? This is just one of the ways in which poor people, who never quite made it on the educational ladder, are prevented from increasing their income.

At every level of employment, including the most professional levels of health or legal services, there is a crying need to grant people employment on the basis of the quality of the job they can perform (or can be trained for) and not on the credentials they hold. Such change will require a crystallization of demands from paraprofessionals as well as legislative action. And here, perhaps more clearly than in most areas of change, the professional can be most valuable by loosening up the garrisons of his own special privileges. Still, sufficient jobs must be available for both the old professional and the new challengers, and job creating is largely a matter of national policy.

The professional and the reform-minded legislator have a role here in the design of social policy. There are dangers and limits in this role. The dangers lie in creating policy that fails to respect the poor person's rights of choice and of destroying his culture without recognizing the needs it serves. Plans to draft all 1-Y rejects and give them a chance through military socialization are of this order. The Army's Project 100,000 is a similar model of resocialization by coercion. A guaranteed income, in contrast, could eliminate a good deal of squalor without demanding such a price.

The limits of legislative action are revealed by an understanding of which pressures are amplified through the legislative system and embodied into law and which are not. The essence of political participation by vested interests lies precisely in the constraints which such interests can maintain against incursions. Even good laws can be expected to lose much of their impact when relying upon vested organizational interests for their implementation. Professionals and agency administrators prevented the new careers program, for example, from turning over to nonprofessional workers many aspects of professional work and supervisory responsibility they could have performed more cheaply. It is the relatively stable subsidies allotted to defense industries, large farmers, oil companies, military and intelligence agencies that preclude subsidies for people who are unable to obtain a decent income through work. The professional policy planner and the reform legislator work within confines too restricted by unquestioned priorities to ease poverty. What they can do effectively is work at the fringes to change the balance among these subsidized priorities. It is our belief that at least some of these legislative actions must be geared to the creation and maintenance of bases for continued pressure from poor communities, just as the contracts to defense industries provide the funds for their lobbyists.

There is a strong interdependence between national policy and community activity in fighting poverty. Making gains in one without taking strides in the other invites failure. A community can start local programs, but without federal support for jobs or a guaranteed income, the community in isolation cannot sustain such efforts. One thinks of Head Start programs and the promise of increased success they offered to poor children. But this promise could not be met because the economic plight and deprivations of the parents of Head Start children remained untouched.

Conversely, a scientifically planned program of "jobs-for-everyone" will not succeed if there is no feedback from communities determining what kind of work the community's citizens consider meaningful. A push-button work force may be as alienated as an unemployed male provider. The professional's role in this model of change is that of a catalyst. He helps the community mobilize around its needs, and helps initiate legislation which could meet these needs. This loop from poor community, to social action, to helping professional, to social policy and back again to poor community is our model for the dynamics of changing poverty in America. It is a coordination model for modest reforms in the problem of poverty and not for the radical changes necessary to eliminate it completely. However, the absence of coordination among various antipoverty efforts, the depoliticization of indigenous efforts (i.e., adopt good work habits rather than build a strong union), and the paucity of available resources for poor people characterize efforts so far.

There is the hope that a few poor people will escape their ghettos and move on the road to middle-class standards of living, and perhaps to the shallowness of middle-class existence. There is little hope that poverty will disappear in this society. The various subcultures of white poverty—ex-miners, street gangs, the disabled, the aged—cannot even afford the luxury of the black illusion of a separate society. These poor groups are part of the same social order in which the distributive process gives some people great wealth and power at the expense of the poor and powerless. Poverty and affluence, as we have noted in our earlier book on *Poor Americans*, are symptoms of the same disease. Pockets of isolation and despair belong to the same order as great concentrations of political, economic and police power. Both must be made to surrender to a more humane society.

FURTHER READING

Life at the Bottom, edited by G. Armstrong (New York: Bantam, 1971).

UPTOWN: Poor Whites in Chicago, by Tod Gitlin (New York: Harper, 1970).

To Serve the Devil, edited by P. Jacobs, S. Landau and E. Pell (New York: Vintage, 1971), 2 volumes.

Poor Americans, How the White Poor Live, edited by M. Pilisuk and P. Pilisuk (Chicago: Aldine, 1971).

Battlefield Reports—
The Record of Attempted Change

MARC PILISUK AND PHYLLIS PILISUK

Richard Parker's essay "The Myth of Middle America," provides
an overview of changes resulting from the war on poverty. The
facts regarding the distribution of wealth in American society
remain dismal. There has not been substantial movement of the
impoverished into the mainstream of a more affluent middle
America, by any measure. Instead, there have been community
actions, programs and policy guidelines, all ostensibly geared to
eliminate poverty at local levels. These attempts can be conceived
of as either "of and by" the poor or "for" the poor. Projects of
and by the poor are those in which members of the poor
community take action themselves to better their lot. Such
actions range from lobbying to rent strikes, boycotts, demonstrations or riots.

Some time before the American poor were officially declared
to exist, Saul Alinsky was working with indigenous leaders of
poor communities, building a power base and pressuring for
constructive change. A host of community organizers picked up
and modified his methods because they generated not only
governmental antipoverty action, but also the genuine hope of

participation behind local leaders. This form of social action meant both a taste of democratic process, too rarely seen in our society, and an opportunity to break out of that sense of marginality and despair which immobilizes some members of poor subcultures. Direct action is illustrated in Lipsky's essay, "Rent Strikes: Poor Man's Weapon." Here he shows the intrinsic relationships between a sense of power and actual power, between actual power and social changes. Reissman's chapter, "Self Help Among the Poor: New Styles of Social Action," suggests the strengths as well as the limits of Alinsky's approach. Among his criticisms is the assertion that organization around local issues fails to build up a politically viable movement on a larger level that might act upon larger policy issues. Organization among the impoverished, even around local and immediate issues, is a slow and difficult process. Yet, without both local and national focus the poor are not likely to see programs attuned to the magnitude of their needs or to their life styles. Tod Gitlin's moving book, *Uptown*, describes the Chicago JOIN project. The project, started by SDS, modified the Alinsky approach, and spoke of organization of a more enduring and more radical force among the poor. The extremely harsh treatment JOIN received from Chicago authorities and the internal rifts which developed are testimony to the difficulties of building a movement from its roots.

The poor have no broker in the political system as do professionals, large farmers, unionized workers and management. Historically, disadvantaged groups in American society have not been able to develop entry into the pluralistic brokerage agencies of power without resorting to violent or disruptive pressures.* Among the poor, the organizational clout and finesse to effect policy change is limited by miniscule financial resources, by their fragmentation and isolation, and by the despair generated by poverty itself. Among paraprofessionals and professionals who truly seek both to serve and to represent the clients' interests, some are working with poor people to bring their demands for

---

Power and Discontent by William Gamson, Homewood, Ill.: Dorsey Press, 1968.

income and for services to the gatekeepers who control the flow.

Several chapters of this section deal with a form of social action, advocacy, that requires professional assistance. Because the society is not truly geared to providing the legal, welfare or political rights which it theoretically guarantees to all citizens, the professional in the role of advocate can assist poor communities in obtaining their due. If this means clogging the courts with cases usually handled mechanically, overloading the local welfare office with claims ordinarily dismissed, or inflaming the proprietary feelings of the school principal, supermarket manager or realtor, so be it. The advocate role is one that helps the poor obtain a foothold in the social system.

Cloward and Elman, in "Advocacy in the Ghetto," deal with the function of advocacy as a new form of social intervention. Carlin, in "Storefront Lawyers of San Francisco," examines advocacy in practice and speaks to one of the pervasive tensions in advocacy organizations, the tension between community control on one hand and radical change on the other. The two are often viewed as synonomous. They are clearly not. The people served may well prefer more immediate services—help with a divorce, with a son in trouble with the courts, than with a test case designed to oblige the welfare department to release general funds being held up for administrative reasons. To us, it seems that social change can go no faster than its popular support. If the power of poor people is to increase, the advocate will have to hear needs and convey them before he can hope to mobilize the forces of change. The advocate's position is therefore, at times, a lonely and precarious one. Primarily, he defends clients in small areas of their well-being. Beyond that, he stands as a link between them and remote centralized decision forces—as a bridge in the gulf created by a planning process which precludes participation by the poor. For greater effect, various advocates may need a greater connectedness—perhaps through a link-up of the radical caucuses now emerging in many professional societies.*

The move toward using nonprofessionals to deliver essentially

---

*Alan E. Guskin and Robert Ross, "Advocacy and Democracy: The Long View" *Am. J. of Orthopsychiatry*, 41 (Jan. 1971) 43-57.

professional services can be seen with school aides, free clinic "medics" and in social work, where Reissman indicates the revolutionary potential of opening a breach into the sometimes impregnable professional wall. The most systematic attempt to bring this potential to national fruition came about in the New Careers program. Yet this dream has failed to deliver on its promise to reform social services, to meet community needs, and in its plan to employ large numbers of the poor in jobs that give them alternative ladders to skilled or professional careers. The reasons for anticipating such failure are described in Alan Haber's essay, "New Careers: Issues Beyond Consensus." He suggests the relationship between the issue of poverty and the issue of who is in control of antipoverty attempts. When the poor do show the ability to manage the services and resources of their own communities, will the custodians of these services and resources move over? Alvin Green's essay, "New Careers in Mental Health Systems; Epilogue to a Survey," is the conclusion of a comprehensive study of new careers programs. The new careerist has generally been unable to find a new career commensurate with his skills. The poor person is effectively trained for useful work, but the larger systems fail to provide him with status and sufficient remuneration. The issue is critical, for it relates to the paradox we have suggested before about poverty. It is a part of a larger social system of wealth and power. Neither alone, nor with help, can the poor change the circumstances of their lives without major adjustments throughout the system.

The fourth group of essays deals with those changes in the circumstances of the poor that are generated by administrative and legislative moves in national policy. The section begins with an article by Miller and Rein, "Will the War on Poverty Change America?" Its summary of the Economic Opportunity Act of 1964 raises issues that are true, as well, of most of the legislation that has since followed this historic law: 1) it considers poverty to be defined by a fixed line rather than relative to time, place and possibilities; 2) it makes no overture toward a basic redistribution of wealth; 3) it treats the culture of poverty as a deficient system which would somehow disappear if skills and educational level were upgraded; hence, it emphasizes employability, but leaves the economy (and employment opportunities) untouched; 4) the focus of the Economic Opportunity Act is almost exclusively on youth. (The Moynihan emphasis has been to favor intact families, but this is still limiting.) The aged, the alienated, the disabled, the handicapped, the migrants are harder to reach. In fact, even within the selected target groups the effect has generally been one of skimming the cream, selecting the most gifted and the most probable candidates for a transition to the middle class and removing these potential leaders from their poverty subcultures.

"Social Action on the Installment Plan," by Miller and Rein, suggests the limitations of action through the legislative process and social planning. It is the view of the editors that the political process is best conceived as being amoral and without purpose. The political process responds to pressure alone and its response is its best effort to reach a compromise among conflicting pressure groups. The final decision reflects the relative strengths of the competing groups and the ease of their appeasement. The poor as a whole have been powerless. In the cases where they do have a professional advocate and an organization with the size and militance needed to press demands, they can be thrown the bone of a demonstration project. Such projects rarely create models that will be used nationally, even if they are found successful (although that promise is always implicit in their design). What they have done is to provide a temporary release for the pressure.

Many have suggested and several attempts have been made to go where the money is—to the corporations. The government has contracted with private industry to create jobs or services for the poor. But this tactic had limitations because it was directed essentially to the most employable group among the poor. In the process the contracting corporations took the opportunity to skim off their own profits and managerial costs before the advantages actually trickled down to poor people. The contracting of Job Corps centers to private industrial firms is an example of such abuse. The Litton Corporation fulfilled its contract by recruiting poor youth from all over the country to Pleasanton, California, with promises of training for high-level jobs. Using the facilities of an old army camp, its program sought to instill the discipline and the basic competence that could get these former draft rejects to the point of qualifying for military service. It then notified their draft boards, which provided a job placement, in many cases, the only available one.

The corporations' need to extract a profit for themselves was hardly a problem. With the decay of cities posing threats of underconsumption and of violence in the marketplace, enlightened capitalists sought to lend a helping hand toward the goals of jobs and stability. The risks, however, of marginal enterprises in deteriorated settings staffed by unreliable employees would not be borne by the corporations themselves. Through the development of the Urban Coalition, the lure for capital investment is in governmental subsidy. The actual workings of that attempt to develop black capitalism and of corporate antipoverty involvement are described by Wiley and Leman in "The Business of Urban Reform." The larger corporations have done reasonably well in managing to replace what few contracts they have lost from the defense sector with urban grants. Contracts have ranged in form from Job Corps centers to urban counterinsurgency work such as the Rand Corporation's work with the New York City Police Department.*

Stegman's essay, "The New Mythology of Housing," shows that we are failing to provide decent housing because simplified notions of the cause of the absence of housing lead to overly simplified (and overly modest) schemes for correcting these deficiencies. The current emphasis upon technical solutions seeks to create housing built by and for the poor without dealing with the power of construction unions or real estate boards. More important, technical solutions fail to furnish the income needed by poor people to maintain a living place which does not decay quickly and the power to design and run the programs which might provide the housing.

The one significant approach to poverty that does not hinge upon remolding the poor is the guaranteed annual income. Such

---

*A documentation of the extent of support for counterinsurgency work with urban policy may be found in Beverly Leman's *Social Control of the American Ghetto*, reprinted from "Viet Reports" in R. Perrucci, and M. Pilisuk, *Triple Revolution Emerging: Social Problems in Depth* (Boston: Little, Brown, 1971), pp. 550-560.

plans do not really speak directly to the provision of services or the need for power, and only indirectly to the despair of ghetto existence. They would not assure people an opportunity for a functional role in the society. But they could, if adequate, mean for most of the poor an end to hunger, victimization by welfare, and the reliance upon personally degrading or illegal means of sustenance. Christopher Green's examination of the various plans in his essay, "Guaranteed Income Plans—Which Is Best?" suggests the pros and cons of several models. The Nixon administration is moving in the direction of a system that maintains income, but at a level significantly below the poverty line. As we move to plans that assure both an adequate bottom and an economic incentive to work, we enter the realm of plans not confined to the poor. At the extreme, "social dividend" plans make payments throughout the population. There is already some Senate discussion about a universal child subsidy allowance—perhaps with an added incentive for the adopted child to counter any possible baby boom effect. Such programs are the most expensive, but also the most needed. They remove the stigma of welfare as charity, and their very costliness means that they will require either a curbing of military costs or a new taxation policy for the advantaged, or both. The target is an important one.

The final selection in this section, "Poverty Programs and Policy Priorities," by Rein and Miller, provides a comprehensive discussion of types of poverty programs and of aspects of poverty frequently overlooked: the lack of basic amenities, the facts of relative deprivation, the lack of mobility, the presence of external social control over poor communities, the lack of power and the denial of dignity. It lists the various goals and the various criteria for evaluating poverty programs and leaves us with the conclusion that basic value considerations, and not just technical considerations of efficiency, will have to play the predominant role in eliminating poverty. When we realize that those values which increase the wealth and power of the poor will decrease protected professional incomes, business profits, the availability of cheap domestic help, and the prerogatives of untampered governance within our unions, professional associations, real estate boards, schools and hospitals; when we realize that licensing or certification to run a business or provide a service may have to go with a stipulation to provide the service where it is most needed but least profitable—then the value question will be upon us. Wealth and power are relative commodities. When the poor gain, someone loses. Dignity, however, is of a different order. It is in the breakdown and redistribution of wealth and power that a gain in human dignity may be available to all of us.

The two concluding chapters, Eisenberg's "Poverty Professionalism and Politics" and Marc Pilisuk's "Toward a New War on Poverty," point to the lessons about our society which we have gained from our lost war on poverty. The program suggested is aimed not at the poor but at those among the affluent whose lives continue to generate poverty for others.

2

WHERE WE ARE

The Myth of Middle America

RICHARD PARKER

It was a tenet of both liberal and conservative dogmas following World War II that, economically, life in America was getting better all the time. Aside from the political flurry of McCarthyism in the early 1950s, the economy was everyone's favorite topic of discussion. After economists had predicted a major postwar recession, the American economy fooled them and began what seemed like a skyrocket burst. Between 1945 and 1965, the Gross National Product quadrupled, and disposable personal income increased two and one-half times. Postulating a "trickle-down" theory of income distribution, economists assumed that it was only a question of time before poverty was eliminated in America.

Suckled on the Horatio Alger myth and teethed on depression and war, the American public was glad to hear the news. Madison Avenue blared the New Affluence across front pages, and invited all of us to join the feast of consumption. The new symbol of

Reprinted, with permission, from the March 1970 issue of *The Center Magazine*, a publication of the Center for the Study of Democratic Institutions in Santa Barbara, California.

America was the suburb, the grassy, tree-shaded Eden of responsible Americans. There a family was safe and happy with its two cars, two children, dog and barbeque pit. Social science and the academy in general took over the affluence myth virtually *in toto*, declaring the end of scarcity, and with it the end of ideology, and the dawn of a new technocratic age where abundance, rather than scarcity, would be our bane. A Gallup Poll would most likely have found wide acceptance of David Lilienthal's views that "one finds the physical benefits of our society distributed widely, to almost everyone, with scant regard to status, class, or origin of the individual."

But the myth of the New Affluence was a cruel distortion of reality. Composed of half-truths, it closed our eyes, cut us off from a recognition of America, and blocked off political and social alternatives. Today, poverty in the midst of prosperity seems almost characteristic of mature capitalism. Moreover, deprivation also seems characteristic and, together with poverty, describes the living conditions of nearly half the American people. What once appeared to be a New Affluence, I contend, is in fact an expansion of the economy which has disproportionately benefited the upper and upper-middle classes, while it has left the poor and the deprived to gather what crumbs fall from the table.

Marx contended in *Das Kapital* and elsewhere that poverty was a normal condition of capitalism even in the best of times. He argued that even if workers' actual wages rose, the differential between their wages and the income of the rich would continue to increase. The issue was settled to the satisfaction of most American economists by the performance of their own economy after the Second World War. A number of them had their faith in capitalism shaken by the Depression, but the postwar boom quickly allayed most of their doubts. The original Marxian criticism that wages might rise but differentials between classes grow larger was lost sight of in the general euphoria of the 1950s.

The euphoria, moreover, was not limited to the traditional, or laissez-faire, economists. Liberal interventionists and Keynesians alike joined with conservatives to announce the death of poverty in mature capitalism. John Kenneth Galbraith, for example, claimed that by the late fifties American poverty was limited to "the insular poor" and "the case poor." The former were the inhabitants of areas like Appalachia and the rural South, where shifting employment patterns were causing "painful, but temporary hardship." The "case poor" were the alcoholics, invalids and elderly who could not, or would not, get ahead. Keynes himself (like Marx) had, of course, foreseen no such amelioration, even in Keynesian capitalism. As Paul Mattick notes in his book *Marx and Keynes*, "Keynesian interventions in the economy necessarily adjust production and consumption in favor of investments. Such adjustments cannot end the paradox of poverty in the midst of plenty, and are not designed to do so."

The problem of economists was to explain *why* poverty was disappearing at such a rapid rate. Census statistics indicated that families with incomes below $3,000 had declined from 28 to 14 percent between 1947 and 1966. But why? Obviously, prosperity in general and unionization in particular had improved the lot of the workingman. But raw data, as well as a few highly sophisticated studies, indicated not only that the economic pie was getting bigger but that a significant reallocation was taking place. It appeared that, for some poorly understood reasons, a real change was taking place in the economy. Arthur Burns, then an Eisenhower adviser, rejoiced: "The transformation in the distribution of our national income . . . may already be counted as one of the great social revolutions of history." Paul Samuelson spoke for the liberals when he said, "The American income pyramid is becoming less unequal."

Though still lacking an explanation, the economists' statistical foundations seemed eminently solid. Simon Kuznets' massive study, *Shares of Upper Income Groups in Income and Savings*, indicated a major decline in the percentage of personal income controlled by the upper strata of the society, a decline that "would continue." The late Selma Goldsmith and her associates showed that the share of personal income received by the top 5 percent declined from 30 percent in 1929 to 26.5 percent in 1936-37, and to 20.7 percent by 1944. Similarly, she showed that the share of the top 20 percent declined from 54.4 to 51.7 to 45.8 percent in the same periods. At the other end of the spectrum, the bottom 20 percent began to show some, if sizably smaller, gains.

Using these data, plus rawer data collected by the Bureau of the Census and other government agencies, economists postulated a theory for income distribution. According to the theory, income was slowly but irreversibly "trickling down" the income scale from the rich to the poor, to result finally in Samuelson's "flattened pyramid." It was presumed to be only a question of time before the last vestiges of poverty would disappear entirely; by the late fifties, Galbraith declared calmly, poverty in America was no longer "a massive affliction but more nearly an afterthought."

As a consequence, the study of income distribution as an economic discipline rapidly declined throughout the fifties. The university, like the nation at large, mesmerized by the new Affluent Society, was content to rest its discussions of poverty on clichés and rudimentary data. In economics, the new interest was in "value-free" econometrics; in the popular consciousness, it was in *The Organization Man* and *The Man in the Gray Flannel Suit*. Affluence was the presumed condition of almost all, and discussion centered on suburbia, martinis and psychoanalysis. Maladies were the result of too much rather than too little.

The "rediscovery" of poverty in America, then, came as a rude awakening to most. Michael Harrington's *The Other America*, which got widespread attention in the early sixties, provided graphic portrayals of the personal impact as well as the extent of poverty. It inspired a major reexamination of the country's goals. Harrington's estimation that one-quarter of the American people lived in poverty shattered not only national pride but also the sublime self-confidence of the economics establishment. To them, his words were heresy.

Discomfiture was not limited to economists. It spread through the social sciences. Two sociologists, S.M. Miller and Martin Rein, looking back on their colleagues' embarrassing mistakes, described the general theory that had governed sociological thinking in the fifties:

> The expansion of production and productivity resulted in a much greater economic pie. The graduated income tax,

expanded welfare services, and education were more equitably distributing this larger pie. Continued increase in aggregate economic wealth would invariably filter down, more or less, equitably, to all income groupings. Marginal economic groups, it was assumed, would in time "gracefully succumb" to continued economic growth and that small residual group not covered by expanded welfare and social security programs would be handily cared for by the public dole.

But even after Harrington pricked the popular balloon, air leaked out with surprising slowness. Those running the federal government's war on poverty (and many social scientists) agreed to define as poor only those families with annual incomes below $3,000. This swift bit of statistical legerdemain immediately shrank Harrington's one-quarter to a less frightening one-fifth. The effect was not only to minimize the poverty in America but to ignore the basic contradictions in the myth of prosperity.

A reevaluation of postwar prosperity leads to major second thoughts about "trickle-down" theories of income distribution. As early as 1957, Robert Lampman, of the University of Michigan, noted that initial gains by the poor to increase their share of the wealth had not only stopped but were reversing. By the early sixties, the rich were again increasing their control of the lion's share of personal income.

The premature optimism of economists like Burns lay in statistics that took no official notice of their unusual circumstances. During the war and shortly thereafter, the income of laborers and service workers increased almost twice as fast as that of professionals and managerial workers. But this was due chiefly to war-related factors that would be unlikely in a peacetime economy, such as full employment mixed with a shortage of nonskilled labor. By the late fifties, the lower categories no longer showed high-rate gains: laborers' and service workers' income increased only 48 percent while managerial income increased 75 percent. Joseph Pechman concluded in 1969 that "the distribution of income in the nineteen-fifties period may not have been very different from what it was in the early nineteen-twenties."

These gross figures, some would argue, are misleading because

of shifts in the labor market. Thus the small gains for laborers
might be offset by the diminishing number of common laborers,
or the high incidence of poverty among farmers offset by
decreasing numbers of farmers. But Herman Miller, an economist
with the Census Bureau, disagreed. Writing in a Bureau mono-
graph, *Income Distribution in the United States*, he concluded
that shifts in job distribution did not substantially affect patterns
of income distribution. "Of course it could still be argued that
the over-all stability of income distribution for the urban
population masks important changes which have taken place for
various subgroups within the population. But this hypothesis . . .
does not appear to be supported by the facts. Income distribution
within the urban population has not shifted even when that
population is further classified by labor force status of wife, age
of head, or size of family."

Miller, however, does underline one important trend: the
increasing number of families in which both husband and wife
work. "It should be noted that incomes are much more equally
distributed among families where the wife is working than where
she is not working; the sizable increase in the proportion of
families with working wives has therefore tended to decrease
income inequality during the past decade." Moreover, census
projections show that the proportion of women in the labor force
will continue to grow over the next two decades.

Yet even the increased family income provided by a second
earner was unable to offset the gains by upper and upper-middle
classes in control of personal income. Using census data as well as
studies by various economic agencies, Joseph Pechman acknowledged that the rich, but not the poor, had prospered in the
postwar era. He pointed out that the simplest census tables, those
most often cited, exclude capital gains and therefore grossly

Table 1

YEAR	Top 5% of Families	Top 20% of Families
1952	18%	42%
1957	16	40
1962	16	42
1967	15	41

misrepresent income trends in the upper fifth of the economy. For example, the Table 1 shows the standard before-tax income shares of the rich, according to census data.

What this table indicates obviously is confirmation of Burns' "great revolution." But are the figures accurate?

Tax data are needed to push the analysis further. These data are more useful, because they show the realized capital gains of these families and net income after federal taxes. The salient observation here is that, contrary to another popular myth now also on the wane, the federal income tax is *not* progressive in its effect. Computing total disposable (i.e. after-tax) income, we find the following:

Table 2

YEAR	Tax Units Top 5%	Tax Units Top 15%
1952	16%	30%
1963	17	33
1967	17	34

However, this table itself can only be considered an estimate that falls to the low side. Since the Second World War, innumerable tax benefits and payment forms have grown up which benefit only the rich. Pechman names tax-exempt interest and depletion allowances as sources of income, then adds: "During World War II, methods of compensation were devised to funnel income to business executives in non-taxable forms. The devices used are well known: deferred compensation and pension plans, stock option arrangements, and direct payment of personal consumption expenditures through expense accounts." Having listed these varieties of unreported income, he prefers caution, and concludes, "Little is known about the impact on the distribution of income."

Gabriel Kolko is not so timorous. In *Wealth and Power in America*, Kolko announced that "the impact of the federal income tax on the actual distribution of income has been minimal, if not negligible." Drawing on a number of sources for his data, he deduced that adding the uncomputed income of the upper classes would raise their total disposable income two or three percentage points above Pechman's own figures. (Thus the top 5 percent received about 20 percent of the personal income, and the top 1 percent about 10 percent of that income.) Since 1952, the effective federal tax rate on the upper 1 percent of the population has *dropped* from 33 to 26 percent.

What may be said of the federal tax structure can be repeated *ad nauseam* for state and local tax structures. The impact of property and sales taxes is clearly regressive, and, as one economist put it, this is "disturbing because the state-local tax system is the growing element of the national system." Federal tax revenues have remained fairly constant as a proportion of Gross National Product, hovering around 20 percent since 1951. State and local taxes, by contrast, have risen from 7.1 percent of the Gross National Product in 1951 to 11.9 percent in 1968. "Assuming that state-local taxes respond more or less proportionately to the rise in the national product ... the states and local governments must have increased rates by sixty-eight percent in these seventeen years to push up their tax yields to current levels." The motivation is obviously not simple greed, but a reflection of increased demand on public services and increasing population concentration in metropolitan areas. Nonetheless, the burden of these social changes falls most heavily on those least able to pay.

The Economic Report of the President, 1969 shows the following:

Table 3

INCOME CLASSES	STATE AND LOCAL TAXES (PERCENTAGE OF INCOME)
Under $2,000	25%
2,000 – 4,000	11
4,000 – 6,000	10
6,000 – 8,000	9
8,000 – 10,000	9
10,000 – 15,000	9
15,000 and over	7

Analysis of income alone, in the case of the rich, obviously also misrepresents the actual concentration of economic well-being in the country. Affluence for the rich, unlike income for the middle and lower classes, is rarely limited to wages and salaries. Rents, dividends, interest—all go into the total wealth of the upper class. James D. Smith, of the Office of Economic Opportunity, in analyzing data of persons with gross assets in excess of $60,000, found a highly concentrated wealth structure. This group, representing the top 1.5 percent of the wealthholders in the country, received the following amounts of income:

Table 4

TYPE	Billions	Percent of Total (each type)
Wages and salaries	$25.9	10.8%
Dividends	8.0	74.8
Interest	3.1	27.9
Rent	6.4	52.5
Capital gains	57.6	71.4

Furthermore, this table is an understatement of concentration. It excludes $1.7 billion in dividends paid to trust funds and nonprofit foundations; it assumes only average yields on assets, rather than optimum figures to be obtained through the advice of investment counselors; finally, its data are for 1958, and all subsequent information shows increasing pyramiding of the wealth structure.

Gabriel Kolko also contributes significant figures on the concentration of total wealth in the upper brackets which supplement Smith's own research. For example, in 1960 the top 10 percent controlled two-thirds of all liquid assets, while 51 percent of the spending units headed by unskilled or service workers had no assets. Other, more shocking data suggest that between .2 and .3 of 1 percent of the population control 22 percent of the personal wealth and 60 to 70 percent of all privately held corporate wealth.

What in fact was the condition of the poor through the fifties and into the sixties? First of all, we must have a definition of poverty. The federal government has chosen the income-line method, with all families falling below $3,000 (now $3,700, because of inflation) defined as poor, and therefore eligible for charitable assistance. Before 1962, little was known about this group; since then, a veritable antipoverty industry has dredged up quantities of information about these people, from their illiteracy rates to their reproduction out of wedlock.

Given all this information, what have we learned? First of all, the income-line method is misleading. It fails to account for assets, temporary impoverishment and several other factors. Second, and more important, the $3,000 has been recognized as ridiculously, if not criminally, low.

How in fact was the government's poverty budget originally arrived at? Politically, several factors interacted; methodologically, the explanation is simple. An annual food budget was prepared, and then that figure was tripled. The budget followed Department of Agriculture guidelines that included the notion that food occupies about one-third of normal expenditures. But simple methodology belied the gross underestimation of need. Oscar Ornati, in *Poverty Amid Affluence*, summarized a typical 1960 "adequate minimum" budget for a family of four:

It provides for simple clothing to protect against the weather and maintain cleanliness. A woman's coat, for instance, must last five years. Leftover food must be retrieved. A cup of flour spilled means no thickening that week; a blown bulb, no light for that month; and a chair broken in anger cannot be replaced for a year. The meat budget allows for stewing lamb, beef liver, or heart, picnic shoulder, fillet of haddock, or perhaps a boned veal roast. No frozen foods are provided for. It allows nothing for an occasional glass of beer, tobacco, or telephone calls. The budget assumes a small rented five-room flat. The family living room might have two chairs. A mattress and spring on legs may serve as a couch, a dropleaf table for eating; two straight chairs may also be there. Linoleum may cover the floor, and there can be a lamp or two. An electric refrigerator and iron are allowed. The family may listen to the radio an hour a day, but television is not included in the budget. There will be money to buy aspirin but none for "miracle" drugs. The husband may get a haircut once a month, and the wife a home permanent once a year. She can use a self-service launderette. There will be no money to buy the children candy or ice cream, or to go to the movies, or to offer a visitor a cup of coffee.

The government's budget is unrealistic on other scores. It fails to take account of the overpricing and shoddy quality of food in poor areas, as documented in books like David Caplovitz' *The Poor Pay More*. It ignores the high cost of other items such as housing and furniture, etc. (usually 10 to 25 percent overpriced, according to one Bureau of the Census economist) that drives up maintenance costs in the other two-thirds of its budget. In farm areas, it still relies heavily on the presumption that the rural families produce much of their own food, although as a percentage of the total food consumed, home-grown items have fallen from 70 to 36 percent in the past twenty years. It makes no allowances for the higher education of the children, unless one presumes they will receive full scholarship aid, which is highly unlikely. Finally, it assumes no major medical expenses in the family, although over half of the poor are not covered by medical insurance.

The actual meals upon which the entire budget is based inspire greater disbelief. The words of the Census that "assuming the homemaker is a good manager and has the time and skill to shop wisely, she may prepare nutritious, palatable meals ... for herself, a husband, and two young children" on a budget of $.70 per day per person inspired one pundit to comment that "Betty Crocker herself would starve." A statistician for HEW described how a housewife must spend her money:

> For a meal all four of them ate together, she could spend on the average only ninety-five cents, and to stay within her budget she must allow no more a day than a pound of meat, poultry, or fish altogether, barely enough for one small serving for each family member at one of the three meals. Eggs could fill out her family fare only to a limited degree because the plan allows less than two dozen a week for all uses in cooking and at the table, not even one to a person a day. And any food extras, such as milk at school for the children or the coffee her husband might buy to supplement the lunch he carries to work, have to come out of the same food money or compete with the limited funds

available for rent, clothing, medical care, and all other expenses. Studies indicate that, on the average, family members eating a meal away from home spend twice as much as the homemaker would spend for preparing one for them at home. The twenty-five cents allowed for a meal at home in the economy plan would not buy much even in the way of supplementation.

Despite the obvious subminimal character of this "minimum budget," some optimism has been generated by the war on poverty and a booming economy, inducing people to believe that the poor are "disappearing." But this optimism needs closer scrutiny. First of all, a $3,000 limit is a ridiculously low level separating the poor from the nonpoor. Second, the government has continued to play games with its own figures ever since the war on poverty began. For example, the cutoff limit of poverty is measured by pre-tax income figures, although the poverty budget was constructed on an after-tax basis. Third, politics has taken a heavy toll on the poor. According to the McGovern committee: "In 1968, government statisticians estimated there were between twenty-two and twenty-seven million Americans living in poverty." But at the beginning of 1969 "the higher of these two figures was dropped without explanation" and the 22 million used as the official estimate. Finally, government economists have consistently underestimated the effect of taxes and inflation on the poor, or so say a group of nongovernment economists (writing in *Life*, August 15, 1969). Since fixture of the $3,000 figure in 1960-61 dollars, inflation and taxes have required a gain of 41 percent in actual income to maintain a real income equivalent. This would require a present definition of the poverty level at $4,240, or $540 more than the government now allows. Such an adjustment would add several million more families to the rolls of the poor.

For the extremely poor, times are now even harder. As the Southern Rural Research Project reported:

The poor and the hungry had their brief moment in the sun: America may lionize its victims, but the vogue of compassion passes quickly on; the hungry have now become somewhat passé. Americans seem to take it for granted that once such alarming conditions are publicly known, the appropriate authorities will automatically step in and clear the matter up."

Dr. Arnold Schaefer, who headed the Public Health Service's National Nutrition Survey, had been among the first to document malnutrition in sample counties in Texas and Louisiana; now the survey has been discontinued, and Dr. Schaefer has passed quietly from the scene. One wonders if the 15 million malnourished have disappeared as quietly.

The Nixon Administration's response to the crisis of poverty remains to be seen, since its proposed revamping of the welfare system has yet to pass Congress. The central feature of minimum income is an advance over existing programs, since it recognizes working as well as nonworking poor; but its own ceilings of aid are so low as to offset the extension in coverage. His proposals to tie Social Security to cost-of-living indices also seem designed to benefit one segment of the poor, but this was rejected in favor of a one-shot 15 percent bonus.

The central fallacy, or perhaps the central design, in the government's designation of the poor is its narrowness. Given the present definition of the poor, we avoid the larger contours of our social reality. Compared with the wealthy or near-wealthy, the gains of the poor have been almost immaterial. In 1946, the bottom 20 percent of all families (the government estimate of the "poor" hovers around 16 percent) received 5 percent of the income; by 1967, the same fifth—now 40 million people—received 5.4 percent. In other words, the intonations of "trickle down" by economists of the fifties now sound hollow indeed.

Crucial to the isolation of the poor is not only the government's action, but the basic American myth. We are people of the *middle* class, bourgeois, home folks, people who still like Norman Rockwell and live decent, unextravagant lives. De Tocqueville did not instigate the myth, but *Democracy in America* certainly strengthened it. His comments on the "tendencies toward the equalization of the conditions of life" set the pattern for all later social scientists and historians who sought to capture the fundamental character of the country. Louis Hartz, as recently as the middle 1950s, still wrote of "irrational Lockeanism" as the controlling factor in American political life, and saw this as a reflection of the dominant "middle class."

The belief in progress has always caused Americans to see their past in an ambivalent light. They have viewed the past romantically, choosing to see our problems as smaller and our victories larger than life. What is imperialism to some has been Manifest Destiny in America. What for some was genocide directed toward the Indian was only "resettlement" of the natives. Even when we made mistakes, there was seldom an accusation of guile or willfulness on our part. The Spanish-American War was "misguided," but it was fought with the best of intentions.

By this kind of logic, our poor today are still better off than 90 percent of the world, and certainly in a better state than they were 50 years ago. The discomfort that greeted disclosures by the muckrakers and writers of the naturalist school at the turn of the century has been replaced today by a comfortable agreement that "things were bad then, but just look at them now." After all, the middle class has always been America's strength and salvation. If we do have poor, well, either they are lazy and inefficient (the conservative view) or they are victimized minorities—blacks, the old, unwed welfare mothers (the liberal view). In any case, nobody opposes welfare anymore—Nixon is pushing the guaranteed income—and besides, as liberal economist Alan Batchelder has assured us, "the poor will continue to disappear as the economy expands."

The fundamental misdirection of all this is away from analysis of the "middle class" to a blind invocation of the myth itself. As recently as October 1969, *Newsweek*, for example, ran an otherwise perceptive article entitled simplistically: *The Troubled American—A Special Report on the White Majority*. Studded with references to "America's vast white middle-class majority," it intoned the familiar lauds: "America has always been the most middle class of nations, the most generous and the most optimistic." But what in fact the article showed most clearly is that for an enormous proportion of the "middle class," embourgeoisement has been a half-filled dream, a set of unsatisfied hopes. These are the people Leon Keyserling has called not the poor but "the deprived Americans"—"above poverty but short of the minimum requirements for a modestly comfortable level of living." In 1964, Keyserling estimated their number at 77 million men, women and children.

Keyserling's distinction between a family income of $3,500 ("poverty") and $4,500 ("deprivation") should be clear to an economist: the "deprived" all work. Unlike the poor, whose ranks are swelled by the elderly, the infirm and the blacks, the "deprived" cannot be dismissed as victims of "nonmarket forces." The "deprived" are functioning, productive members of our economic system: the manual laborers, the clerks, the launderers, the hospital workers of our society. They may have their own home, but it is heavily mortgaged; they may have a late-model car, but it has been financed at steep rates. Their savings, which form a family's cushion against disaster, are marginal: 40 percent are either in debt or have savings of less than $100. Liquid assets show even less room for error: 20 percent of all families own no assets, and 48 percent own less than $500 worth. Yet, as Kolko rightly points out: "Liquid assets—such as checking and savings accounts, shares in savings-and-loan associations and credit unions, and government savings bonds—are of decisive importance to low- and even middle-income families exposed to layoffs, unemployment, or medical and other emergencies. Often they represent the entire margin between security and the relief rolls."

The myth of the middle class serves as a permanent leash on the deprived. Lacking the income, they are still expected to provide their families with the amenities that advertising, television and the academic mythmakers have told them the "middle class" enjoys. Constantly under pressure, they retain all the old American virtues as a desperate bulwark against the encroachment of the "shiftless poor." They, like the poor, bear a heavy burden of the taxation because of regressive tax structures. They aspire to better education for their children, their own home and more leisure. Yet, in a great many cases, both father and mother must work simply to maintain their present condition.

The disparities within the "middle class" and the number of the "deprived" are brought out most clearly when one examines the data of income growth over the past half-century. The

accompanying table shows control of the income shares by
population tenths since 1910. Omitting the top tenth as "upper
class" and the bottom two-tenths as "poor," analysis of the
remaining "middle class" yields striking results.

Table 5.
PERCENTAGE OF NATIONAL PERSONAL INCOME, BEFORE
TAXES, RECEIVED BY EACH INCOME-TENTH*

Year	Highest Tenth	2nd	3rd	4th	5th	6th	7th	8th	9th	Lowest Tenth
1910	33.9	12.3	10.2	8.8	8.0	7.0	6.0	5.5	4.9	3.4
1918	34.5	12.9	9.6	8.7	7.7	7.2	6.9	5.7	4.4	2.4
1921	38.2	12.8	10.5	8.9	7.4	6.5	5.9	4.6	3.2	2.0
1929	39.0	12.3	9.8	9.0	7.9	6.5	5.5	4.6	3.6	1.8
1934	33.6	13.1	11.0	9.4	8.2	7.3	6.2	5.3	3.8	2.1
1937	34.4	14.1	11.7	10.1	8.5	7.2	6.0	4.4	2.6	1.0
1941	34.0	16.0	12.0	10.0	9.0	7.0	5.0	4.0	2.0	1.0
1945	29.0	16.0	13.0	11.0	9.0	7.0	6.0	5.0	3.0	1.0
1946	32.0	15.0	12.0	10.0	9.0	7.0	6.0	5.0	3.0	1.0
1947	33.5	14.8	11.7	9.9	8.5	7.1	5.8	4.4	3.1	1.2
1948	30.9	14.7	11.9	10.1	8.8	7.5	6.3	5.0	3.3	1.4
1949	29.8	15.5	12.5	10.6	9.1	7.7	6.2	4.7	3.1	0.8
1950	28.7	15.4	12.7	10.8	9.3	7.8	6.3	4.9	3.2	0.9
1951	30.9	15.0	12.3	10.6	8.9	7.6	6.3	4.7	2.9	0.8
1952	29.5	15.3	12.4	10.6	9.1	7.7	6.4	4.9	3.1	1.0
1953	31.4	14.8	11.9	10.3	8.9	7.6	6.2	4.7	3.0	1.2
1954	29.3	15.3	12.4	10.7	9.1	7.7	6.4	4.8	3.1	1.2
1955	29.7	15.7	12.7	10.8	9.1	7.7	6.1	4.5	2.7	1.0
1956	30.6	15.3	12.3	10.5	9.0	7.6	6.1	4.5	2.8	1.3
1957	29.4	15.5	12.7	10.8	9.2	7.7	6.1	4.5	2.9	1.3
1958	27.1	16.3	13.2	11.0	9.4	7.8	6.2	4.6	3.1	1.3
1959	28.9	15.8	12.7	10.7	9.2	7.8	6.3	4.6	2.9	1.1

*In terms of "recipients" for 1910-37 and "spending units" for 1941-59.

Source: Data for 1910-37 are from National Industrial Conference Board.
Studies in Enterprise and Social Progress (New York: National Industrial
Conference Board, 1939), p. 125. Data for 1941-59 were calculated by the
Survey Research Center. Figures for 1941-46 are available in rounded form
only.

The most interesting observation is that there are two distinct
strata in the "middle class," the upper of the two having gained
markedly greater control of income. Between 1910 and 1959, the
second, third and fourth deciles increased their percentage of the
total income more than one-quarter, while the fifth, sixth,
seventh and eighth deciles were able to advance only from 26.5
percent to 27.9 percent in the same period.

This information sheds light on much of the writing over the past two decades on the Affluent Society. The "middle class," as a homogeneous group, has done well; but closer examination reveals that success becomes smaller and smaller as one moves down the income scale within that class. The astigmatic concern of the social scientists for suburbia, executive anomie, and the crises of "the abundant society" has proceeded from myths that now seem badly worn—from the myth of the New Affluence, from the myth of "trickle-down" income and wealth redistribution and the omnipotence of Keynes, and from the capstone myth of them all—the myth of the American middle class.

As a matter of fact, the "middle class" may have escaped the grasp of more than the poor and the deprived. If by "middle class" one means a decent, modest standard of living, it seems that perhaps 60 to 70 percent of the country have difficulty in reaching it. In 1966, the Bureau of Labor Statistics announced that the average urban family required $9,191 per year to live comfortably; yet the median income that same year was $1,400 less than that figure.

At this point, it seems wise to stop and make two observations: the first an estimation of some present and possibly future realities; the second, a historical speculation.

The first observation is about the "unmentioned middle class," the professional, technical elite and its immediate support structure. These people are the true beneficiaries of the Affluent Society, and are the class which has sought to reshape the American myths in its image. College-educated, employed as lawyers, engineers, advertisers and real-estate dealers, these people are the upper strata of the middle class that experienced the greatest gains in postwar years. The suburban crises of the fifties were *their* crises, the suburban malaise was drowned in *their* martini glasses. If one were to seek a paradigm for their group, one would find it during the Kennedy era, in the bright young men around the seat of power; but one could also find it in the older and younger men, in corporations and universities. They are those whom Daniel Bell described as the "technocratic elite."

An attack on this group is not immediately relevant. The Vietnam war has already prompted a number of incisive critiques of them, particularly on the university level. However, critique and solution are not synonymous. It seems likely that the import of young people's radicalism will be diffused and co-opted back into electoral party politics, and the thrust of radical restructuring lost, as it was in the New Deal. Already the "beautiful people" seem to be emerging as the new archetype of this social caste—human beings who span Establishment and anti-Establishment factionalism, who work for corporations by day, yet smoke dope by night.

The problem is that their amorality is more difficult to detect because it so often hides behind a veil of rhetorical concern. Unlike the industrial captains of the last century, their contemporary lieutenants feign not indifference but impotence. After all, they *are* concerned, God knows, but they are only vice-presidents or mere managers. They may give occasionally to the political *outré* or talk of "repressive tolerance" at cocktail parties, but those gestures mark the boundaries of their social concern.

One index of that social indifference emerges in an ironic place: Michael Harrington in January had an article in the *Atlantic* entitled "The Betrayal of the Poor." The irony is that the *Atlantic*, for all its enlightenment, is still an organ of that upper-middle class who have not so much resisted, as they have ignored, social change.

The article begins: "For all the rhetoric of recent years about the war on poverty, the poor in America are almost as numerous as ever. . . . Unless the government makes immensely greater commitments of resources and planning, the country is doomed to a social explosion in the seventies that will make the turbulent sixties seem tranquil by comparison." The article, like articles on the malnourished, on housing conditions, on the quality of education in the ghetto, will be read and then lost in the comfortable notion that once federal programs are established, everything will be taken care of. Enter the New Deal, Phase II.

The error in this remains the presumption of the liberal upper-middle class since the first decade of this century: that social legislation by the federal government will cure what ails us. Jane Addams suggested it; Ralph Hunter, one of the nation's first social welfare workers, endorsed it; the New Deal itself put the seal of approval on it; and now even Republicans have begun to see merit in the idea. Unfortunately, the theory has never worked.

The assumption behind liberal optimism about a coalition between the federal government and corporate capitalism has been that things keep getting better all the time. There are more cars, more homes, better schools, etc., than ever before and, in the midst of this prosperity, the distribution of all this largesse has been getting better as well.

Taking the first half of this claim—that the total quantity of goods has increased—there is no dispute. But one *can* make some comparisons between the United States and other industrialized nations. Fifteen nations have higher literacy rates. Ten nations have lower infant mortality rates. To my knowledge, the United States is the only industrialized nation that does not offer comprehensive medical insurance for all its people. It offers perhaps the worst unemployment protection and the worst welfare system among the developed countries. It has 15 million malnourished. It has 30 million poor. It has 77 million deprived. Few other nations can claim such tawdry conditions amid such phenomenal growth.

On the second half of the comfortable liberal optimism—that distribution has been getting better and better—there is a fundamental error in the assumption. Since the Second World War, the only significant redistribution of income in the United States has been between the upper and the upper-middle classes. Overall, distribution has remained essentially stable not only over the past 20 years but over the entire twentieth century.

There are three sources for this statement. The first is the chart on income distribution (see p. 42) that shows the limits of change. The second is from Joseph Pechman, a conventionally liberal economist, writing in *The Public Interest*, who states: "The year 1929 must have been the high point of inequality during the 1920s, so that distribution of income in the more recent period may not have been very different from what it was in the early twenties if account is taken of undistributed profits." The third is a much earlier source. Published in 1904, Robert

Hunter's *Poverty* is probably the first attempt made to estimate the number of poor in America. Highly sympathetic to the poor, it uses the data of state and private welfare agencies (since federal data were nonexistent). While emphasizing the wretched conditions of the poor, Hunter limits their number to only 12 percent of the population. Today economic historians agree that Hunter's estimate was off the mark by 6 percent, thus leaving at the turn of the century a minority poor of 18 percent. Yet 18 percent was the government's estimate of the poor 60 years later!

None of these three estimates is perfect (none ever can be, because crucial data are lacking); but they can give a newer and perhaps more accurate contour of poverty and affluence in America. We are, as de Tocqueville said, and as American social scientists have reaffirmed ever since, "a people of the middle class." But to be middle class is both a social-psychological and economic problem. Among those who call themselves "middle class," perhaps a majority have always lacked the money to be in fact what they believe they are. Not only are the poor still with us, but they have been there for years. Michael Harrington's announcement that our poor are the "first minority poor in history" has been misunderstood; the poor have always been a minority in America, but a stubborn minority that refuses to decrease and disappear. The rich in America just keep getting richer. All the talk of income distribution, of flattening pyramids, and of peaceful economic revolutions has been nonsense, fabricated in part out of optimism, in part out of a myopia in the professional classes who themselves gained so rapidly after the Second World War.

At the end of an account such as this, it is usually expected that the author will offer remedies, specific reforms such as tax legislation or welfare payments—or at least see reason for hope on the horizon. I cannot. First, because "reform" has become the province of politicians and electoral platforms, and deals with our needs about as realistically as someone using a band-aid on a compound fracture. Yet, even liberals accept reformism, as they did when they quietly applauded the Nixon proposal of a guaranteed annual income for the poor, despite the dire (and probably accurate) warning of Michael Harrington that "a guaranteed annual income could be a way to institutionalize poverty at the subsistence level in the United States."

Second, and more important, I do not seek "reform" because, at age 23, I have lost faith in the willingness of America to "reform." I have lived with the poor, eaten their food, slept in their beds and taught their children, in Alabama, in Vermont, in Watts. I know their bitterness, and I share it. John Kenneth Galbraith observed recently that "liberalism has been excessively tender toward the rich." A surprise to liberals, but a fact of life for the poor. Attempts at reform have delivered to the poor nothing but promises. They have watched the war on poverty beaten into ineffectual irrelevance. They have listened to America's liberal politicians promise food as they stare at empty plates. They know the sham of reform.

3

INDIGENOUS ACTION

Self-Help Among the Poor:
New Styles of Social Action

FRANK RIESSMAN

Social action has become fashionable in America. Suddenly, it seems, social science and social work circles are paying as much attention to social action as are the press and the public. Through the impetus and example of the Negro revolt and the civil rights movement, there is widespread interest in such community projects as New York's Mobilization for Youth and HARYOU (Harlem Youth Opportunity Unlimited). But most attention is being focused on the much-publicized social action approach of Saul Alinsky and his Industrial Areas Foundation which began securing national attention as a result of its work in Chicago in 1962 and this year (1965) is concentrating on Rochester, New York.

Although most social work has been alienated from Alinsky's approach to community change, he has received widespread prominence through articles in *Commentary*, the *Saturday Evening Post*, the *Reporter*, and *Harper's*, which in a two-part article this spring labeled Alinsky "the professional radical."

To present any meaningful evaluation of Alinsky's work, it is important to examine the general terms and purposes of social action and to relate the Alinsky approach to other forms of social action and other methods of social change. In this way we can begin to build a theory of institutional change which includes, in an appropriate context, the role of different kinds of social and community action.

It is always interesting to observe just when trends such as this appear. We know that social action is taking place—in a context of Negro and youth revolt—quite independent of government-sponsored projects such as Mobilization for Youth and HARYOU and also independent of social workers and Saul Alinsky. In the past two years rent strikes spread to more than 25 cities in the United States. They were not led by social workers, government-sponsored projects, or Alinsky's self-organized communities. Alinsky has organized more than two million people in 44 communities over the last 30 years but it is striking that so few people knew about it. Until very recently neither the public at large nor most social scientists had even heard of Alinsky and the communities he has helped to build. It had been a most quiet revolution until he moved into the Woodlawn area in Chicago. But everyone seems to have heard very quickly of the Negro movement, of the rent strikes, of the University of California sit-downs, the school boycotts, etc. Unquestionably, this has something to do with the press attention given to Negro might and the youth movement. But we suspect also, that the millions of people organized by Alinsky have not wielded much influence outside of narrowly confined local areas.

One of the most important questions to examine in evaluating any social action program is its relationship to social change. Specifically, how is the social action related to other variables in the change process?

Our thesis is that there are many elements involved in social change—that social action is one very important element, perhaps one that provides the motor force or power under a variety of conditions—but that there are other elements that groups dedicated to various kinds of institutional changes might do well to consider. This is not intended to gainsay in any way the value of a social action approach as a major lever of social change. What is being suggested, rather, is that it is not the only element in institutional change, albeit an important one, particularly in producing a changed equilibrium, a crisis, an opening around which other elements in the change process may operate. The issue then is what kind of social action is most appropriate as a significant element in major social change.

STRATEGIES OF CHANGE

To produce major institutional changes (such as development of the community mental health movement, changes in the educational system directed toward better education for the disadvantaged, or changes aimed at reducing poverty) several different strategic forces have been advocated. The strategies put forth include:

1. Demonstration projects, such as Mobilization for Youth and HARYOU;
2. New methods of in-service and pre-service training;
3. Consultation and the development of improved communication;
4. Use of nonprofessional personnel in new capacities, as advocated by Arthur Pearl, Robert Reiff and Leonard Duhl, to change the character of service provided by the helping professions;
5. Use of "neighborhood law firms" to take cases directed toward changing laws and rulings unfavorable to the poor;
6. Negotiation, particularly with reference to the integration problem.

Literature and the public expression of ideas (ideology) can be potent change forces, as evidenced by Michael Harrington and the poverty issue. And the contributions of John Maynard Keynes, Erich Fromm, David Riesman and other ideologists, including Freud and Marx, must also be considered in the broader historical context.

Currently, the most popular strategy of change is concerned with pressure from below, social action and mass movement as decisive variables in producing change. This was emphasized by Mobilization for Youth and is built into the design of HARYOU.

Social action seems to be a decisive force for producing changes
with regard to integration as well as producing new trends in
education of the disadvantaged. Many school administrators
freely report their concern about the "demand from below," the
demand for changes coming from mass action of "the people."

There can be little question that social action is an important
ingredient in certain kinds of changes. The relevant question is:
For what kinds of change is social action decisive, and how does
social action relate to other aspects of the problem? In some cases
it appears that mass pressure for change has not been decisive, at
least not directly. Thus, with regard to the community mental
health movement emanating from the Kennedy act and the report
of the Joint Commission on Mental Health, there is not much
evidence that pressure from below was a determining element in
providing the impetus for this type of change. In this respect it
seems quite different from the education situation and the
integration area.

It may well prove true that mass pressure, social action by the
poor themselves, is a crucial force in many other forms of change.
Still it is important to understand the range of possibilities within
which changes occur. For example, the demand of minority
groups for improved education for the disadvantaged has led to a
variety of proposals. The Ford Foundation through its demonstration preschool projects (particularly the project of Martin
Deutsch) is having a wide influence on the type of institutional
change being considered by school systems throughout the
country in educational programming for the disadvantaged. The
poor themselves never demanded this preschool emphasis and
might not even be especially attracted to it. Nevertheless, it is a
major response of the educational system to the need for
improved education for the disadvantaged and to the demand for
this improved education by the educationally deprived. Thus,
there appears to be considerable latitude in the types of changes
that can occur in response to demands from below.

In this context we now turn to an analysis of the Alinsky
model. (It should be noted that there does not exist any
systematic presentation of Alinsky's approach, other than the

dated *Reveille for Radicals* [1946]. Most of the discussion of this work appears in popular magazines.) Alinsky's Industrial Areas Foundation, functioning on a low budget without government support, has two major objectives in the communities it helps to organize: eradication of local grievances such as consumer fraud, and the development of independence and dignity on the part of the presumably apathetic, dependent peoples.

To achieve these goals, Alinsky stresses conflict. He looks for some enemy who is weak enough to be defeated or he unites an opposition composed of diverse elements in the community, serving as the "big" outsider, such as the University of Chicago.

Alinsky will not help a community unless he is called in by a group representing at least some of its different interests. While strongly supported by Catholic groups, Alinsky has been able to bring together many religious denominations as well as local merchants, workers and a wide range of local groups. He has been very successful in developing local "united fronts."

His announced aim is to surrender his power, to leave within three years, and to develop sources of power, particularly funding, in the local organization itself (although he and the IAF may continue to advise from a distance).

Alinsky contends that he has no values or political goals to impose on the communities—they are supposed to decide for themselves what they are going to do. But, most of his community groups seem to be fairly progressive, with the notable exception of the Chicago Back-of-the-Yards group which ultimately became anti-Negro.

Alinsky has a great flair for colorful tactics ("truth squads," "death watches") and Alinsky himself has frequently provided tactical advice to civil rights groups; however, in Chicago, his home base, he and his methods appear to be disliked by civil rights forces. It is not at all true, as pro-Alinskyites would have us believe, that only reactionaries and social workers attack Alinsky.

Alinsky employs a staff of organizers with varied backgrounds and skills, and this staff provides tactical advice and technical consultation where the local groups require it—for example, a critique of an urban redevelopment plan. These organizers are typically very dedicated, frequently quite colorful, and willing to meet and talk about tactics until four in the morning on a fairly regular basis.

Alinsky's model deserves careful attention for a number of factors it demonstrates:

1. Social action and community organization can be accomplished in low-income communities. (The poor, apparently, are not as apathetic as they are said to be when given appropriate alternatives to be unapathetic about.)
2. Social action can be quite inexpensive and does not require a huge outlay of government funds.
3. Representatives of all religions and classes can be united in community action groups.
4. Social action organizations can withstand witch hunt tactics.
5. It is relatively easy to find indigenous leadership in poor communities.

Furthermore, Alinsky has developed some interesting approaches to organization and tactics of which any social action movement should be aware (although he has borrowed more heavily than is realized from traditional trade union and leftist practices). Alinsky is a tactician *par excellence* and has a great feeling for action.

But the model has a number of fairly obvious limitations, the most important being its extremely localistic character. As S.M. Miller and Martin Rein observe:

> . . . only some of the problems of the poor can be solved through neighborhood, or even city, changes. Increasingly, national action is needed. Consequently, the poor have to be organized on a continuing and wide basis in order to gain the political clout that will produce sweeping reforms.

A more severe critic states in the Newsletter of the National Committee for Full Employment:

> Alinsky eschews ideology and program, seeking only to develop lower class protest movements which will, he has faith, evolve their own programs—as if in some mystical way lower class people will gain the technical and ideological means to fathom the larger economic and political forces that affect them. Alinsky's strategy is block-by-

block, low level organization and "no holds barred" techniques. He is true to the American pragmatic tradition which exalts action and denies the practical value of theory.

ACTION AS THERAPY

Alinsky does not appear to have a long-range plan or theory, and he is quite anti-intellectual. With the possible exception of some of the IAF groups in California, the communities he has organized remain essentially isolated from each other, and Alinsky rejects the notion of bringing them together. They may change the local situation, but they have no influence on national issues of unemployment, housing and the like. Sometimes they appear to function more as sociotherapy than social action. They are sociotherapeutic in the sense that the people who participate in them profit from this involvement psychologically and feel more independent, and this is all to the good. However, the question must arise, how long can sociotherapy continue if thoroughgoing changes in the social structure are not produced? Perhaps disillusionment sets in, and all kinds of secondary problems involved in organizational survival develop. Perhaps communities become very narrow and (as in the case of the Back-of-the-Yards project in Chicago) turn against minority groups.

It is striking that Alinsky's most publicized project, The Woodlawn Organization in Chicago clearly reflects the Negro trend. Thus social action takes on real meaning when connected to significant social forces and movements in the larger society and is not dependent on the local area alone. Appraisals of the Alinsky model have overemphasized The Woodlawn Organization project as though it were typical of all of the communities that Alinsky has helped to organize. Actually, a case could easily be made that it is quite an exception. But, regardless of whether it is exceptional or not, attention should be called to other communities that Alinsky has organized such as the Chelsea Community in New York which was a complete fiasco, the Back-of-the-Yards community in Chicago which was successful in many respects but ultimately developed a strong anti-Negro orientation, and many other Alinsky-organized middle-class communities which have nothing special to recommend them. All these communities should be included in any overall evaluation of Alinsky.

SOCIAL ACTION AND SOCIAL MOVEMENTS

What, then, are the implications for social action in the present period in the United States and where does Alinsky fit in? What must we know about the relationship of social action to other variables in the change process in order to develop meaningful strategies of change?

The task is to delineate carefully the different factors involved in social change: the role of negotiation at certain points, the role of ideas and ideology, and particularly the roles of different types of social action (and how they interpenetrate with other forces producing change).

In America, this would include an examination of some of the larger social movements in our history. The suffragette and the populist movements could be reexamined. In the modern period, the peace movement of the sixties, the labor movement of the thirties, the Progressive party in 1948, all provide potentially illuminating illustrations. It is noteworthy that most of these movements were relatively short-lived, and for the most part their demands were absorbed into the mainstream of American life.

No enduring social movement, no broad, well-developed ideology has emerged in the United States. It is particularly interesting that the "establishment" in the United States has shown remarkable resiliency in being able to absorb and even occasionally anticipate some of these social demands. Thus, the New Deal absorbed the labor movement, and it is quite possible that many of the demands of the present civil rights movement will also be adopted by the power forces of this society as in the civil rights law. In certain cases the establishment can anticipate the demands of various social movements. Thus, the present war on poverty reflects, in part, some anticipation of a potential demand by segments of the poor for a basic involvement in the economic life of the nation. This demand is likely to find most advanced expression in the Negro movement, as it becomes increasingly responsive to the Negro poor. Sometimes these anticipations function as diversions, distracting the main energy and force of the potential social movement. But things are not necessarily so simple, and sometimes plans go astray. Thus it is possible that the war on poverty might open the doors to a social movement of the poor. But this is in no way a present actuality or immediate potentiality.

What is important to see, however, in evaluating social movements and social action, is that no matter how influential such movements have been in America, they have not developed long-term properties.

With regard to the civil rights movement, we can see the role of objective conditions in producing possible openings or opportunities for social change. This movement arose at a time when the cold war was lagging, and the African nations' freedom demands were on the rise. The civil rights movement also coincides with increasing awareness of the automation trend in the economy, with its prospect for the decline in need for unskilled labor. Also in evidence in this period is the continued migration of the poor to the cities, the declining power of the rural areas (particularly the South), and long-term structural unemployment.

These various factors reflect themselves in many different trends, including the Supreme Court decision regarding reapportionment in the states. This decision, we believe, reflects the change in the rural-urban power distribution. Hence, the civil rights movement could respond to these larger changes in the society with a vastly increased organized demand for the rights of the Negro people. The fact of a relatively friendly Kennedy administration, and an establishment which had far less need for Negro segregation, lent further support to the possibility of a social movement arising in the 1960s. The widespread support for this movement came from many diverse sources; most outstanding perhaps were the communications media. The society was, so to speak, ripe for such a movement and Negro leadership was correct in assessing this and taking advantage of it.

What then are some of the possibilities for social action of different types in the present period?

The Alinsky model. Despite the limitations we have discussed, there is one extremely important possibility: namely that the various Alinsky-organized communities could, in fact, be brought together. They could be united around larger issues of relevance to the poor, thus increasing their political clout and removing them from their overemphasis on local concerns. This could provide the potential for a larger social movement. Such an undertaking obviously presents many difficulties, as social movements have rarely been built in this way. The question arises immediately as to what larger issues would unite these diverse local groups.

The labor movement. The labor movement's potential unity with community organization groups and with the war on poverty creates a possibility for social action. Walter Reuther has spearheaded the Citizen's Crusade against Poverty (CCAP) which could play a powerful role in developing community action, and conceivably at a certain point, could articulate with the civil rights movement and the Alinsky community groups.

The civil rights movement. There are numerous possibilities for the movement's expansion in the present period. It could develop neighborhood-based community action programs (CORE is planning such a project) and could unite further with the growing youth movement. It could unite with the Alinsky forces, and it could unite with the intellectuals, who are searching for new forms of citizen involvement. What we are suggesting is that the civil rights movement could use its clout best in support of well-developed, well-thought-out, economic, political and social programs related to housing, education, integration, employment, antipoverty measures. Intellectuals, because of their isolation from the power forces in the society, could benefit enormously by being stimulated to develop programs in these areas. Through the demand of civil rights forces, intellectuals would recognize that they had an audience and a power force behind them to implement these programs—a new and exciting unity might emerge. Similarly, intellectuals might work together with the Alinsky groups and with community action organizations led by the labor movement. Both the intellectuals and the groups they work with, might profit enormously from this form of involvement—the movements could achieve far greater breadth and theoretic focus from such a coalition.

To utilize social action most effectively it would seem necessary to view it in relation to other strategies of change (ideology) and in relation to the history of relatively effective social movements in America that were not rooted in neighborhood-based social action (the labor movement, peace movement, civil rights movement, youth movement).

In the present period, characterized as it is by great interest and experiment in social action, it may be helpful not to idealize any one system such as Alinsky's, but to critically appraise a great variety of approaches.

The Alinsky model appears to be somewhat narrow, essentially localistic, not sufficiently concerned with large-scale institutional changes (hardly "radical" in program) and fails to bring together the various communities that are developed. It is also perhaps unnecessarily manipulative and "gimmick-oriented" in contrast to the civil rights movement which is far less manipulative. It may be unappealing to large ranges of people and thus far seems lacking in the social movement properties that characterize the civil rights movement today or the peace movement of three years ago. Alinsky appeals, in the main, to one level of social action interest, namely, the activist militant type. People who prefer milder, more subtle forms, do not respond, for the most part, to the Alinsky model. Alinsky's failure to present his approach in a systematic comprehensive published form is a serious shortcoming that limits meaningful exchange and development.

But Alinsky has made an enormous contribution by leading the way in working with church groups, in developing local all-class "united fronts," in originating highly imaginative tactics, and in giving the poor a voice. All of us concerned with the development of community action have much to learn from the Alinsky model and we can probably utilize this learning best by careful critical evaluation and serious exchange of ideas.

Rent Strikes: Poor Man's Weapon

MICHAEL LIPSKY

The poor lack not only money, but power. Low-income political groups may be thought of as politically impoverished. In the bargaining arena of city politics the poor have little to trade.

Protest has come to be an important part of the politics of low-income minorities. By attempting to enlarge the conflict, and bring outside pressures to bear on their concerns, protest has developed as one tactic the poor can use to exert power and gain greater control over their lives. Since the sit-in movement of 1960, Negro civil-rights strategists have used protest to bring about political change, and so have groups associated with the war on poverty. Saul Alinsky's Industrial Areas Foundation continues to receive invitations to help organize low-income communities because it has demonstrated that it can mobilize poor people around the tactics of protest.

The Harlem rent strikes of 1963 and 1964, organized by Jesse Gray, a dynamic black leader who has been agitating about slum housing for more than 15 years, affected some tenants in approximately 150 Harlem tenements. Following the March on Washington in August 1963, the rent strikes played on the liberal sympathies of New Yorkers who were just beginning to re-examine the conditions of New York City slums. Through a combination of appeal and threat, Jesse Gray mounted a movement that succeeded in changing the orientation of some city services, obtained greater *legal* rights for organized tenants, and resulted in obtaining repairs in a minority of the buildings in which tenants struck. Along with rent strikes conducted by Mobilization for Youth, a pre-war poverty program, the rent strikes managed to project images of thousands of aroused tenants to a concerned public, and to somewhat anxious reform-oriented city officials.

The rent strikes did not succeed in obtaining fundamental goals. Most buildings in which tenants struck remained in disrepair, or deteriorated even further. City housing officials became more responsive to housing problems, but general programs to repair slum housing remained as remote as ever. Perhaps most significant, the rent strike movement, after a hectic initial winter, quickly petered out when cold weather again swept the Harlem streets. Focusing upon the rent strikes may help explain why this protest failed, and why protest in general is not a reliable political weapon.

PROTEST HAS LONG-RANGE LIMITS

Protest as a political tactic is limited because protest leaders must appeal to four constituencies at the same time. A protest leader must: 1) nurture and sustain an organization composed of people who may not always agree with his program or style; 2) adapt to the mass media—choose strategies and voice goals that will give him as much favorable exposure as possible; 3) try to develop and sustain the protest's impact on third parties—the general public, sympathetic liberals, or anyone who can put pressure on those with power; and 4) try to influence directly the targets of the protest—those who have the power to give him what he wants.

The tensions that result from the leader's need to manipulate four constituencies at once are the basic reason why protest is an unreliable political tactic, unlikely to prove successful in the long run.

Protest activity may be defined as a political activity designed to dramatize an objection to some policies or conditions, using unconventional showmanship or display and aimed at obtaining rewards from the political system while working within that system. The problem of the powerless is that they have little to bargain with, and must acquire resources. Fifteen people sitting in the mayor's office cannot, of themselves, hope to move City Hall. But through the publicity they get, or the reaction they evoke, they may politically activate a wider public to which the city administration is sensitive.

The tactic of activating third parties to enter the political process is most important to relatively powerless groups, although it is available to all. Obviously any organization which can call upon a large membership to engage in political activity—a trade union on strike, for example—has some degree of power. But the poor in individual neighborhoods frequently cannot exert such power. Neighborhood political groups may not have mass followings, or may not be able to rely on membership participation in political struggles. In such cases they may be able to activate other political forces in the city to enter the conflict on their behalf. However, the contradictions of the protest process suggest that even this tactic—now widely employed by various low-income groups—cannot be relied upon.

Take, for example, the problem of protest leaders and their constituents. If poor people are to be organized for protest activities, their involvement must be sustained by the symbolic and intangible rewards of participation in protest action, and by the promises of material rewards that protest leaders extend. Yet a leadership style suited to providing protesters with the intangible rewards of participating in rebellious political movements is sometimes incompatible with a style designed to secure tangible benefits for protest group members.

Furthermore, the need of protest leaders to develop a distinctive style in order to overcome the lack of involvement of potential group members diffuses as well as consolidates support. People who want psychological gratification (such as revenge or

public notice and acknowledgment), but have little hope of
material rewards, will be attracted to a militant leader. They want
angry rhetoric and denunciation. On the other hand, those people
who depend on the political system for tangible benefits, and
therefore believe in it and cooperate with it to some extent, are
likely to want moderate leadership. Groups that materially profit
from participation in the system will not accept men who
question the whole system. Yet the cohesion of relatively powerless groups may be strengthened by militant, ideological leadership that questions the rules of the game, that challenges their
morality and legitimacy.

On the other hand, the fact that the sympathies and support
of third parties are essential to the success of protesters may
make the protesters' fear of retribution, where justified, an asset.
For when people put themselves in danger by complaining, they
are more likely to gain widespread sympathy. The cattle-prod and
police-dog tactics of Alabama police in breaking up demonstrations a few years ago brought immediate response and support
from around the country.

In short, the nature of protesters curtails the flexibility of
protest leadership. Leaders must limit their public actions to
preserve their basis of support. They must also limit protest in
line with what they can reasonably expect of their followers. The
poor cannot be expected to engage in activities that require much
money. The anxieties developed throughout their lives—such as
loss of job, fear of police or danger of eviction—also limit the
scope of protest. Negro protest in the South was limited by such
retributions or anxieties about facing reprisals.

Jesse Gray was able to gain sympathy for the rent strikers
because he was able to project an image of people willing to risk
eviction in order to protest against the (rarely identified) slumlords, who exploited them, or the city, whose iceberg pace aided
landlords rather than forced them to make repairs. In fact, Gray
used an underutilized provision of the law which protected
tenants against eviction if they paid their rent to court. It was one
of the great strengths of the rent strikes that the image of danger
to tenants was projected, while the tenants remained somewhat
secure and within the legal process. This fortunate combination is

not readily transferable to other cases in which protest activity is contemplated.

Apart from problems relating to manipulation of protest group members, protest leaders must command at least some resources. For instance, skilled professionals must be made available to protest organizations. Lawyers are needed to help protesters use the judicial process, and to handle court cases. The effectiveness of a protest organization may depend upon a combination of an ability to threaten the political system and an ability to exercise legal rights. The organization may either pay lawyers or depend on volunteers. In the case of the rent strikes, dependence on volunteer lawyers was finally abandoned—there were not enough available, and those who were willing could not survive long without payment.

Other professionals may be needed in other protest circumstances. A group trying to protest against an urban-renewal project, for example, will need architects and city planners to present a viable alternative to the city's plan.

Financial resources not only pay lawyers, but allow a minimum program of political activity. In the Harlem rent strikes, dues assessed against the protesters were low and were not collected systematically. Lawyers often complained that tenants were unwilling to pay incidental and minor fees, such as the $2 charge to subpoena departmental records. Obtaining money for mimeo flyers, supplies, rent, telephones and a small payroll became major problems. The fact that Jesse Gray spent a great deal of time trying to organize new groups and speaking all over the city prevented him from paying attention to organizational details. Furthermore, he did not or could not develop assistants who could assume the organizational burden.

Lack of money can sometimes be made up for by passionate support. Lawyers, office help and block organizers did come forth to work voluntarily for the rent strike. But such help is unreliable and usually transient. When spring came, volunteers vanished rapidly and did not return the following winter. Volunteer assistance usually comes from the more educated and skilled who can get other jobs, at good salaries. The diehards of *ad hoc* political groups are usually those who have no place else to go, nothing else to do.

Lack of money also can be overcome with skilled nonprofessionals; but usually they are scarce. The college students, Negro and white, who staffed the rent-strike offices, handled paper work and press releases, and served as neighborhood organizers, were vital to the strike's success. Not only could they communicate with tenants, but they were relatively sophisticated about the operations of the city government and the communications media. They could help tenants with city agencies, and tell reporters what they wanted to hear. They also maintained contacts with other civil rights and liberal organizations. Other workers might have eventually acquired these skills and contacts, but these student organizers allowed the movement to go into action quickly, on a citywide scale, and with a large volume of cases. One of the casualties of "black power" has been the exclusion of skilled white college students from potentially useful roles of this kind.

Like the proverbial tree that falls unheard in the forest, protest, politically speaking, does not exist unless it is projected and perceived. To the extent that a successful protest depends on appealing to, or perhaps also threatening, other groups in the community, publicity through the public media will set the limits of how far that protest activity will go toward success. (A number of writers, in fact, have noticed that the success of a protest seems directly related to publicity outside the immediate protest area.) If the communications media either ignore the protest or play it down, it will not succeed.

When the protest *is* covered, the way it is given publicity will influence all participants including the protesters themselves. Therefore, it is vital that a leader know what the media consider newsworthy, and be familiar with the prejudices and desires of those who determine what is to be covered and how much.

MEDIA'S DEMANDS MAY BE DESTRUCTIVE

But media requirements are often contradictory and hard to meet. TV wants spot news, perhaps 30 seconds' worth; newspapers want somewhat more than that, and long stories may appear only in weekly neighborhood or ethnic papers. Reporters want topical newsworthiness in the short run—the more exciting the better. They will even stretch to get it. But after that they want evidence, accuracy and reliability. The leader who was too accommodating in the beginning may come to be portrayed as an irresponsible liar.

This conflict was well illustrated in the rent strike. Jesse Gray and the reporters developed an almost symbiotic relationship. They wanted fresh, dramatic news on the growth of the strike— and Gray was happy to give them progress reports he did not, and could not, substantiate.

Actually, just keeping the strikes going in a limited number of buildings would have been a considerable feat. Yet reporters wanted more than that—they wanted growth. Gray, of course, had other reasons for reporting that the strike was spreading—he knew that such reports, if believed, would help pressure city officials. In misrepresenting the facts, Gray was encouraged by sympathetic reporters—in the long run actually undermining his case. As a *New York Times* reporter explained, "We had an interest in keeping it going."

Having encouraged Gray to go out on a limb and overstate the support he had, the reporters later were just as eager for documentation. It was not forthcoming. Gray consistently failed to produce a reliable list of rent-strike buildings that could withstand independent verification. He took the reporters only to those buildings he considered "safe." And the newspapers that had themselves strongly contributed to the inflation of Gray's claims then helped deflate them and denied him press coverage.

The clash between the needs of these two constituencies—the media and the protesters—often puts great strain on leaders. The old-line leader who appeals to his followers because of his apparent responsibility, integrity and restraint will not capture the necessary headlines. On the other hand, the leader who finds militant rhetoric a useful weapon for organizing some people will find the media only too eager to carry his more inflammatory statements. But this portrayal of him as an uncompromising firebrand (often meant for a limited audience and as a limited tactic) will alienate him from people he may need for broad support, and may work toward excluding him from bargaining with city officials.

If a leader takes strong or extreme positions, he may win followers and newspaper space, but alienate the protest's target. Exclusion from the councils of bargaining or decision-making can have serious consequences for protest leaders, since the targets can then concentrate on satisfying the aroused public and civic groups, while ignoring the demands of the protesters.

What a protest leader must do to get support from third parties will also often conflict with what he must do to retain the interest and support of his followers. For instance, when Negro leaders actually engage in direct bargaining with politicians, they may find their supporters outraged or discouraged, and slipping away. They need militancy to arouse support; they need support to bargain; but if they bargain, they may seem to betray that militancy, and lose support. Yet bargaining at some point may be necessary to obtain objectives from city politicians. These tensions can be minimized to some extent by a protest organization's having divided leadership. One leader may bargain with city officials, while another continues rhetorical guerilla warfare.

Divided leadership may also prove useful in solving the problem that James Q. Wilson has noted: "The militant displays an unwillingness to perform those administrative tasks which are necessary to operate an organization." The nuts and bolts of administrative detail are vital. If protest depends primarily on a leader's charisma, as the rent strikes did to some extent, allocating responsibility (already difficult because of lack of skilled personnel) can become a major problem. In the rent strike, somebody had to coordinate court appearances for tenants and lawyers; somebody had to subpoena building and health department records and collect money to pay for them; and somebody had to be alert to the fact that, through landlord duplicity or tenant neglect, tenants might face immediate eviction and require emergency legal assistance. Jesse Gray was often unable or unwilling to concentrate on these details. In part, failures of these kinds are forced on the protest leader, who must give higher priority to publicity and arousing support than to administrative detail. However, divided leadership can help separate responsibility for administration from responsibility for mobilization.

Strain between militancy to gain and maintain support and reasonableness to obtain concessions can also be diminished by successful "public relations." Protest groups may understand the same words differently than city officials. Imperatives to march or burn are usually not the commands frightened whites sometimes think they are.

BARGAINING IS FOR INSIDERS

Protest success depends partly upon enlarging the number of groups and individuals who are concerned about the issues. It also depends upon ability to influence the shape of the decision, not merely whether or not there will be a decision. This is one reason that protest is more likely to succeed when groups are trying to veto a decision (say, to stop construction of an expressway), than when they try to initiate projects (say, to establish low-cost transportation systems for a neighborhood).

Protest groups are often excluded from the bargaining arena because the civic groups and city officials who make decisions in various policy areas have developed relationships over long periods of time, for mutual benefit. Interlopers are not admitted to these councils easily. Men in power do not like to sit down with people they consider rogues. They do not seek the dubious pleasure of being denounced, and are uneasy in the presence of people whose class, race or manners are unfamiliar. They may make opportunities available for "consultation," or even "confrontation," but decisions will be made behind closed doors where the nature of the decision is not open to discussion by "outsiders."

As noted before, relatively powerless protest groups seldom have enough people of high status to work for their proposals. Good causes sometimes attract such people, but seldom for long. Therefore protest groups hardly ever have the expertise and experience they need, including professionals in such fields as law, architecture, accounting, education, and how to get government money. This is one area in which the "political impoverishment" of low-income groups is most clearly observed. Protest groups may learn how to dramatize issues, but they cannot present data or proposals that public officials consider "objective" or "reasonable." Few men can be both passionate advocate and persuasive arbiter at the same time.

Ultimately the success of a protest depends on the targets.

Many of the forces that inhibit protest leaders from influencing target groups have already been mentioned: the protesters' lack of status, experience and resources in bargaining; the conflict between the rhetoric that will inspire and hold supporters, and what will open the door to meaningful bargaining; conflicting press demands, and so on.

But there is an additional factor that constrains protest organizations that deal with public agencies. As many students of organizations have pointed out, public agencies and the men who run them are concerned with maintaining and enhancing the agency's position. This means protecting the agency from criticism and budget cuts, and attempting to increase the agency's status and scope. This piece of conventional wisdom has great importance for a protest group which can only succeed by getting others to apply pressure on public policy. Public agencies are most responsive to their regular critics and immediate organizational allies. Thus if they can deflect pressure from these, their reference groups, they can ease the pressure brought by protest *without meeting any of the protest demands*.

At least six tactics are available to targets that are inclined to respond in some way to protests.

1. They may respond with symbolic satisfactions. Typical, in city politics, is the ribbon-cutting, street-corner ceremony, or the mayor's walking press conference. When tension builds up in Harlem, Mayor Lindsay walks the streets and talks to the people. Such occasions are not only used to build support, but to persuade the residents that attention is being directed to their problems.

   City agencies establish special machinery and procedures to prepare symbolic means for handling protest crises. For instance, in those New York departments having to do with housing, top officials, a press secretary, and one or two others will devote whatever time is necessary to collecting information and responding quickly to reporters' inquiries about a developing crisis. This is useful for tenants: it means that if they can create enough concern, they can cut through red tape. It is also useful for officials who want to appear ready to take action.

During the New York rent strikes, city officials responded by: initiating an anti-rat campaign; proposing ways to "legalize" rent strikes (already legal under certain conditions); starting a program to permit the city to make repairs; and contracting for a costly university study to review housing code enforcement procedures. Some of these steps were of distinct advantage to tenants, although none was directed at the overall slum problem. It is important to note, however, that the announcement of these programs served to deflect pressure by reassuring civic groups and a liberal public that something was being done. Regardless of how well-meaning public officials are, real changes in conditions are secondary to the general agency need to develop a response to protest that will "take the heat off."

2. Another tactic available to public officials is to give token satisfactions. When city officials respond, with much publicity, to a few cases brought to them, they can appear to be meeting protest demands, while actually meeting only those few cases. If a child is bitten by a rat, and enough hue and cry is raised, the rats in that apartment or building may be exterminated, with much fanfare. The building next door remains infested.

Such tokenism may give the appearance of great improvement, while actually impeding real overall progress by alleviating public concern. Tokenism is particularly attractive to reporters and television news directors, who are able to dramatize individual cases convincingly. General situations are notoriously hard to dramatize.

3. To blunt protest drives, protest targets may also work to change their internal procedures and organization. This tactic is similar to the preceding one. By developing means to concentrate on those cases that are most dramatic, or seem to pose the greatest threats, city officials can effectively wear down the cutting-edges of protest.

As noted, all New York City agencies have informal arrangements to deal with such crisis cases. During the rent strikes two new programs were developed by the city whereby officials could enter buildings to make repairs and exterminate rats on an emergency basis. Previously, officials had been confined to trying to find the landlords and to taking them to court (a time-consuming, ineffective process that has been almost universally criticized by knowledgeable observers). These new programs were highly significant developments because they expanded the scope of governmental responsibility. They acknowledged, in a sense, that slum conditions are a social disease requiring public intervention.

At the same time, these innovations served the purposes of administrators who needed the power to make repairs in the worst housing cases. If public officials can act quickly in the most desperate situations that come to their attention, pressure for more general attacks on housing problems can be deflected.

The new programs could never significantly affect the 800,000 deteriorating apartments in New York City. The new programs can operate only so long as the number of crises are relatively limited. Crisis treatment for everyone would mean shifting resources from routine services. If all cases receive priority, then none can.

The new programs, however welcomed by some individual tenants, help agencies to "cool off" crises quicker. This also may be the function of police review boards and internal complaint bureaus. Problems can be handled more expeditiously with such mechanisms while agency personnel behavior remains unaffected.

4. Target groups may plead that their hands are tied—because of laws or stubborn superiors, or lack of resources or authority. They may be sympathetic, but what can they do? Besides, "If-I-give-it-to-you-I-have-to-give-it-to-everyone."

Illustratively, at various times during the rent strike, city officials claimed they did not have funds for emergency repairs (although they found funds later), and lacked authority to enter buildings to make emergency repairs (although the city later acted to make emergency repairs under provisions of a law available for over 60 years). This tactic is persuasive; everyone knows that cities are broke, and limited by state law. But if pressure rises, funds for specific, relatively inexpensive programs, or expansion of existing programs, can often be found.

5. Targets may use their extensive resources and contacts to discredit protest leaders and organizations: "They don't really have the people behind them"; they are acting "criminally"; they are "left-wing." These allegations can cool the sympathies of the vital third parties, whether or not there is any truth behind them. City officials, especially, can use this device in their contacts with civic groups and communication media, with which they are mutually dependent for support and assistance. Some city officials can downgrade protesters while others appear sympathetic to the protesters' demands.

6. Finally, target groups may postpone action—time is on their side. Public sympathy cools quickly, and issues are soon forgotten. Moreover, because low-income protest groups have difficulty sustaining organization (for reasons suggested above), they are particularly affected by delays. The threat represented by protest dissipates with time, the difficulty of managing four constituencies increases as more and more information circulates, and the inherent instability of protest groups makes it unlikely that they will be able to take effective action when decisions are finally announced.

SURVEY RESEARCH AS PROCRASTINATION

The best way to procrastinate is to commit the subject to "study." By the time the study is ready, if ever, the protest group will probably not be around to criticize or press for implementation of proposals. The higher the status of the study group, the less capable low-status protest groups will be able to effectively challenge the final product. Furthermore, officials retain the option of rejecting or failing to accept the reports of study groups, a practice developed to an art by the Johnson administration.

This is not to say that surveys, research and study groups are to be identified solely as delaying tactics. They are often desirable, even necessary, to document need and mobilize public and pressure group support. But postponement, for whatever reason, will always change the pressures on policy-makers, usually in directions unfavorable to protest results.

Groups without power can attempt to gain influence through protest. I have argued that protest will be successful to the extent that the protesters can get third parties to put pressure on the targets. But protest leaders have severe problems in trying to meet the needs and desires of four separate and often conflicting constituencies—their supporters, the mass media, the interested and vital third parties, and the targets of the protest.

By definition, relatively powerless groups have few resources, and therefore little probability of success. But to survive at all and to arouse the third parties, they need at least some resources. Even to get these minimal resources, conflicting demands limit the leader's effectiveness. And when, finally, public officials are forced to recognize protest activity, it is not to meet the demands, but to satisfy other groups that have influence.

Edelman has written that, in practice, regulatory policy consists of reassuring mass publics symbolically while at the same time dispensing tangible concessions only to narrow interest groups. Complementing Edelman, I have suggested that public officials give symbolic reassurances to protest groups, rather than real concessions, because those on whom they most depend will be satisfied with appearances of action. Rent strikers wanted to see repairs in their apartments and dramatic improvements in slum housing; but the wider publics that most influence city officials could be satisfied simply by the appearance of reform. And when city officials had satisfied the publics this way, they could then resist or ignore the protesters' demands for other or more profound changes.

Kenneth Clark, in *Dark Ghetto*, has observed that the illusion of having power, when unaccompanied by material rewards, leads to feelings of helplessness and reinforces political apathy in the ghetto. If the poor and politically weak protest to acquire influence that will help change their lives and conditions, only to find that little comes from all that risk and trouble, then apathy or hostility toward conventional political methods may result.

If the arguments presented in this article are convincing, then those militant civil-rights leaders who insist that protest is a shallow foundation on which to build long-term, concrete gains are essentially correct. But their accompanying arguments—the fickleness of the white liberal, the difficulty of changing discriminatory institutions as opposed to discriminatory laws—are only part of the explanation for the essential failure of protest. An analysis of the politics involved strongly suggests that protest is best understood by concentrating on problems of managing diverse protest constituencies.

It may be, therefore, that Saul Alinsky is on soundest ground when he recommends protest as a tactic to build an organization, which can then command its own power. Protest also may be recommended to increase or change the political consciousness of people, or to gain short-run goals in a potentially sympathetic political environment. This may be the most significant contribution of the black power movement—the development of group consciousness which provides a more cohesive political base. But, ultimately, relatively powerless groups cannot rely on the protest process alone to help them obtain long-run goals, or general improvements in conditions. What they need for long-run success are stable political resources—in a word, power. The American political system is theoretically open; but it is closed, for many reasons suggested here, to politically impoverished groups. While politicians continue to affirm the right to dissent or protest within reason, the political process in which protest takes place remains highly restricted.

FURTHER READINGS

Dark Ghetto: Dilemmas of Social Power by Kenneth B. Clark (New York: Harper and Row, 1965), explores the implications of powerlessness in the ghetto on the psychology of individuals and on the viability of political movements.

Neighborhood Groups and Urban Renewal by J. Clarence Davies, III (New York: Columbia University Press, 1966). One of the few systematic studies of the interaction of political organizations and city agencies at the neighborhood level.

The Symbolic Uses of Politics by Murray Edelman (Urbana, Illinois: University of Illinois Press, 1964) is a highly suggestive study of the symbolic meaning of government activity and the ways such activity affects political consciousness and activism.

In the Valley of the Shadows: Kentucky

BRUCE JACKSON

Along the roadsides and in backyards are the cannibalized cadavers of old cars: there is no other place to dump them; there are no junkyards that have any reason to haul them away. Streambeds are littered with old tires, cans, pieces of metal and plastic. On a sunny day the streams and creeks glisten with pretty blue spots from the Maxwell House coffee tins and Royal Crown cola cans. For some reason the paint used by Maxwell House and Royal Crown doesn't wear off very quickly, and while the paint and paper on other cans are peeling to reveal an undistinctive aluminum color, the accumulating blues of those two brands make for a most peculiar local feature.

Winter in eastern Kentucky is not very pretty. In some places you see the gouged hillsides where the strip and auger mines have ripped away tons of dirt and rock to get at the mineral seams underneath; below the gouges you see the littered valleys where the overburden, the earth they have ripped and scooped away, has been dumped in spoil banks. The streams stink from the augerholes' sulfurous exudations; the hillsides no longer hold water back because the few trees and bushes are small and thin, so there is continual erosion varying the ugliness in color only.

Most of the people around here live outside the town in hollers and along the creeks. Things are narrow: the hills rise up closely and flatland is at a premium. A residential area will stretch out for several miles, one or two houses and a road thick, with hills starting up just behind the outhouse. Sometimes, driving along the highway following the Big Sandy river, there is so little flat space that the highway is on one side of the river and the line of houses is on the other, with plank suspension bridges every few miles connecting the two. Everything is crushed together. You may ride five miles without passing a building, then come upon a half-dozen houses, each within ten feet of its neighbor. And churches: the Old Regular Baptist church, the Freewill Baptist church, the Meta Baptist church. On the slopes of the hills are cemeteries, all neatly tended; some are large and old, some have only one or two recent graves in them.

In winter, when the sun never rises very far above the horizon, the valley floors get only about four hours of direct sunlight a day; most of the days are cloudy anyhow. One always moves in shadow, in greyness. Children grow up without ever seeing the sun rise or set.

The day of the company store and company house is gone. So are most of the big companies around here. This is small truck mine country now, and operators of the small mines don't find stores and houses worth their time. The old company houses worth living in have been bought up, either as rental property or for the new owner's personal use; the company houses still standing but not worth living in comprise the county's only public housing for the very poor.

At the end of one of the hollows running off Marrowbone Creek, three miles up a road you couldn't make, even in dry weather, without four-wheel drive, stands an old cabin. It is a log cabin, but there is about it nothing romantic or frontiersy, only grim. Scratched in the kitchen window, by some unknown adult or child, are the crude letters of the word *victory*. Over what or whom we don't know. It is unlikely anyway. There are no victories here, only occasional survivors, and if survival is a victory it is a mean and brutal one.

Inside the cabin a Barbie doll stands over a nearly opaque mirror in a room lighted by a single bare 60-watt bulb. In the middle of the room a coal stove spews outrageous amounts of heat. When the stove is empty the room is cold and damp. There is no middle area of comfort. The corrugated cardboard lining the walls doesn't stop drafts very well and most of the outside chinking is gone. On one side of the room with the stove is the entrance to the other bedroom, on the other side is the kitchen. There are no doors inside the house. A woman lives here with her nine children.

If all the nine children were given perfectly balanced full meals three times a day from now on, still some of them would never be well. A 15-year-old daughter loses patches of skin because of an irreversible vitamin deficiency, and sometimes, because of the suppurations and congealing, they have to soak her clothing off when she comes home from school. Last month the baby was spitting up blood for a while but that seems to have stopped.

It might be possible to do something for the younger ones, but it is not likely anyone will. The husband went somewhere and didn't come back; that was over a year ago. The welfare inspector came a few months ago and found out that someone had given the family a box of clothes for the winter; the welfare check was cut by $20 a month after that. When the woman has $82 she can get $120 worth of food stamps; if she doesn't have the $82, she gets no food stamps at all. For a year, the entire family had nothing for dinner but one quart of green beans each night. Breakfast was fried flour and coffee. A friend told me the boy said he had had meat at a neighbor's house once.

BONY HILLS

This is Pike County, Kentucky. It juts like a chipped arrowhead into the bony hill country of neighboring West Virginia. Pike County has about 70,000 residents and, the Chamber of Commerce advertises, it produces more coal than any other county in the world. The county seat, Pikeville, has about 6,000 residents; it is the only real town for about 30 miles.

The biggest and bitterest event in Pike County's past was sometime in the 1880s when Tolbert McCoy killed Big Ellison Hatfield: it started a feud that resulted in 65 killed, settled nothing and wasn't won by either side. The biggest and bitterest thing in recent years has been the war on poverty: it doesn't seem to have killed anyone, but it hasn't settled anything or won any major battles either.

About 7,500 men are employed by Pike County's mines: 1,000 drive trucks, 500 work at the tipples (the docks where coal is loaded into railway cars) and mine offices, and 6,000 work inside. Most of the mines are small and it doesn't take very many men to work them: an automated truck mine can be handled by about eight men. Some people work at service activities: they pump gas, sell shoes, negotiate contracts (there are about *40* lawyers in this little town), dispense drugs, direct traffic, embalm—all those things that make an American town go. There are six industrial firms in the area; two of them are beverage companies, one is a lumber company; the total employment of the six firms is 122 men and women.

A union mine pays $28 to $38 per day, with various benefits, but few of the mines in Pike County are unionized. The truck mines, where almost all the men work, pay $14 per day, with almost no benefits. The United Mine Workers of America were strong here once, but when times got hard the union let a lot of people down and left a lot of bitterness behind. Not only did the union make deals with the larger companies that resulted in many of its own men being thrown out of work (one of those deals recently resulted in a $7.3 million conspiracy judgment against the UMWA and Consolidation Coal Company), but it made the abandonment complete by lifting the unemployed workers' medical cards and shutting down the union hospitals in the area. For most of the area, those cards and hospitals were the only source of medical treatment. There has been talk of organizing the truck mines and someone told me the UMW local was importing an old-time firebreathing organizer to get things going, but it doesn't seem likely the men will put their lives on the line another time.

With Frederic J. Fleron, Jr., an old friend then on the faculty of the University of Kentucky in Lexington, I went to visit Robert Holcomb, president of the Independent Coal Operator's Association, president of the Chamber of Commerce and one of the people in the county most vocally at war with the poverty program. His office door was decorated with several titles: Dixie Mining Co., Roberts Engineering Co., Robert Holcomb and Co., Chloe Gas Co., Big Sandy Coal Co. and Martha Colleries, Inc.

One of the secretaries stared at my beard as if it were a second nose; she soon got control of herself and took us in to see Holcomb. (Someone had said to me the day before, "Man, when Holcomb sees you with that beard on he's gonna be sure you're a communist." "What if I tell him I'm playing Henry the Fifth in a play at the university?" "Then he'll be sure Henry the Fifth is a communist too.") Holcomb took the beard better than the girl had: his expression remained nicely neutral. He offered us coffee and introduced us to his partner, a Mr. Roberts, who sat in a desk directly opposite him. On the wall behind Roberts' head was a large white flying map of the United States with a brownish smear running over Louisiana, Mississippi and most of Texas; the darkest splotch was directly over New Orleans. The phone rang and Roberts took the call; he tilted back in his chair, his head against New Orleans and Lake Pontchartrain.

Holcomb was happy to talk about his objections to the poverty program. "I'm a firm believer that you don't help a man by giving him bread unless you give him hope for the future, and poverty programs have given them bread only." The problem with the Appalachian Volunteers (an antipoverty organization partially funded by OEO, now pretty much defunct) was "they got no supervision. They brought a bunch of young people in, turned 'em loose and said, 'Do your thing.' . . . I think they have created a disservice rather than a service by creating a lot of disillusionment by making people expect things that just can't happen."

EXPANDING AND WRECKING

He told us something about what was happening. The coal

industry had been expanding rapidly. "Over the last eight years the truck mining industry has created an average of 500 new jobs a year." He sat back. "We're working to bring the things in here that will relieve the poverty permanently." He talked of bringing other kinds of industry to the area and told us about the incentives they were offering companies that were willing to relocate. "We know a lot of our people are not fitted for mining," he said.

(It is not just a matter of being "fitted" of course. There is the problem of those who are wrecked by silicosis and black lung who can do nothing but hope their doctor bills won't go up so much they'll have to pull one of the teenage kids out of school and send him to work, or be so screwed by welfare or social security or the UMW pension managers or the mine operators' disability insurance company that the meager payments that do come into some homes will be stopped.)

The truck mines play an ironic role in the local economy: half the men working in them, according to Holcomb, cannot work in the large mines because of physical disability. The small mines, in effect, not only get the leftover coal seams that aren't fat enough to interest Consol or U.S. Steel or the other big companies in the area, but they also get the men those firms have used up and discarded.

From Holcomb's point of view things are going pretty well in Pike County. In 1960 there were $18 million in deposits in Pikeville's three banks; that has risen to $65 million. There are 700 small mines in the county, many of them operated by former miners. "This is free enterprise at its finest," he said.

The next morning he took us on a trip through the Johns Creek area. As we passed new houses and large trailers he pointed to them as evidence of progress, which they in fact are. In the hollers behind, Fred and I could see the shacks and boxes in which people also live, and those Holcomb passed without a word. I suppose one must select from all the data presenting itself in this world; otherwise living gets awfully complex.

We drove up the hill to a small mine. Holcomb told us that the eight men working there produce 175 tons daily, all of which goes to the DuPont nylon plant in South Carolina.

A man in a shed just outside the mine mouth was switching the heavy industrial batteries on a coal tractor. The miner was coated with coal dust and oil smears. He wore a plastic helmet with a light on it; around his waist was the light's battery pack, like a squashed holster. He moved very fast, whipping the chains off and on and winding the batteries out, pumping the pulley chains up and down. Another mine tractor crashed out of the entrance, its driver inclined at 45 degrees. The tractor is about 24 inches high and the mine roof is only 38 inches high, so the drivers have to tilt all the time or get their heads crushed. Inside, the men work on their knees. The tractor backed the buggy connected to it to the edge of a platform, dumped its load, then clanked back inside.

I went into the mine, lying on my side in the buggy towed by the tractor with the newly charged batteries.

Inside is utter blackness, broken only by the slicing beams of light from the helmets. The beams are neat and pretty, almost like a lucite tube poking here and there; the prettiness goes away when you realize the reason the beam is so brilliant is because of the coal and rock dust in the air, dust a worker is continually inhaling into his lungs. One sees no bodies, just occasional hands interrupting the moving lightbeams playing on the timbers and working face. Clattering noises and shouts are strangely disembodied and directionless.

Outside, I dust off and we head back towards town in Holcomb's truck.

"The temperature in there is 68 degrees all the time," he says. "You work in air-conditioned comfort all year 'round. Most of these men, after they've been in the mine for awhile, wouldn't work above ground." (I find myself thinking of Senator Murphy of California who in his campaign explained the need for bracero labor: they stoop over better than Anglos do.) The miners, as I said, make $14 a day.

"When you see what's been accomplished here in the last ten years it makes the doings of the AVs and the others seem completely insignificant. And we didn't have outside money." The pitted and gouged road is one-lane and we find ourselves creeping behind a heavily loaded coal truck heading toward one of the tipples up the road. "We think welfare is fine, but it should be a temporary measure, not a permanent one. And any organization that encourages people to get on welfare is a detriment to the community." The truck up front gets out of our way, Holcomb shifts back to two-wheel drive, we pick up speed. "These poverty program people, what they tried to do is latch on to some mountain customs and try to convince people they have come up with something new."

He believes business will help everybody; he believes the poverty program has been bad business. He is enormously sincere. Everyone is enormously sincere down here, or so it seems.

So we drove and looked at the new mines and tipples and Robert Holcomb told us how long each had been there and what its tonnage was and how many people each mine employed and how many mines fed into each tipple. One of his companies, he told us, produced 350,000 tons of coal last year and operated at a profit of 15.7 cents per ton.

Hospital death certificates cite things like pneumonia and heart disease. There is no way of knowing how many of those result from black lung and silicosis. The mine owners say very few; the miners and their families say a great many indeed. A lot of men with coated lungs don't die for a long time, but they may not be good for much else meanwhile. Their lungs won't absorb much oxygen, so they cannot move well or fast or long.

"This is a one-industry area," Holcomb had said, "and if you can't work at that industry you can't work at anything." Right. And most of the residents—men wrinkled or contaminated, widows, children—do not work at anything. Over 50 percent of the families in Pike County have incomes below $3,000 per year. Like land torn by the strip-mining operations, those people simply stay back in the hollers out of sight and slowly erode.

We talked with an old man who had worked in the mines for 28 years. He told us how he had consumed his life savings and two years' time getting his disabled social security benefits.

"See, I got third-stage silicosis and I've got prostate and gland trouble, stomach troubles, a ruptured disc. Now they say that at the end of this month they're gonna take the state aid medical card away. And that's all I've got; I've got so much wrong with me I can't get no insurance. I've had the card two years and now they say I draw too much social security because of last year's increase in social security benefits and they're gonna have to take my medical card away from me after this month. I don't know what in the hell I'm gonna do. Die, I reckon."

"Yeah, yeah," his wife said from the sink.

"It don't seem right," he said. "I worked like hell, I made good money and I doublebacked. Because I worked a lot and draw more social security than lots of people in the mines where they don't make no money, I don't see where it's right for them not to allow me no medical card."

He opened the refrigerator and showed us some of the various chemicals he takes every day. In a neat stack on the table were the month's medical receipts. He said something about his youth, and I was suddenly stunned to realize he was only 51.

"You know," he said, "sand's worse than black lung. Silicosis. It hardens on the lung and there's no way to get it off. In West Virginia I worked on one of those roof-bolting machines. It's about eight, nine-foot high, sandstone top. Burn the bits up drillin' holes in it. And I'd be there. Dust'd be that thick on your lips. But it's fine stuff in the air, you don't see the stuff that you get in your lungs. It's fine stuff. Then I didn't get no pay for it."

"You got a thousand dollars," his wife said.

"A thousand dollars for the first stage. They paid me first stage and I just didn't want to give up. I kept on workin', and now I got third stage. . . . I just hated to give up, but I wished I had of. One doctor said to me, 'If you keep on you might as well get your shotgun and shoot your brains out, you'd be better off.' I still kept on after he told me that. Then I got so I just couldn't hardly go on. My clothes wouldn't stay on me."

The woman brought coffee to the table. "He draws his disabled social security now," she says, "but if he was to draw for his black lung disease they would cut his social security way down, so he's better off just drawing his social security. There's guys around here they cut below what they was drawing for social security. I don't think that's right."

It is all very neat: the black lung, when a miner can force the company doctors to diagnose it honestly, is paid for by company

insurance, but payments are set at a level such that a disabled
miner loses most of his social security benefits if he takes the
compensation; since the compensation pays less than social
security, many miners don't put in their legitimate claims, and
the net effect is a government subsidy of the insurance companies
and mine owners.

Mary Walton, an Appalachian Volunteer, invited Fred and me
to dinner at her place in Pikeville one night during our stay. It
turned out Mary and I had been at Harvard at the same time and
we talked about that place for a while, which was very strange
there between those darkening hills. Three other people were at
Mary's apartment: a girl named Barbara, in tight jeans and a white
shirt with two buttons open and zippered boots, and two men,
both of them connected with the local college. One was working
with the Model Cities project, the other worked in the college
president's office; one was astoundingly tall, the other was built
like a wrestler; they all looked aggressively healthy. Barbara's
husband worked for the Council of the Southern Mountains in
Berea.

The fellow who looked like a wrestler told me at great length
that what was going on in Pikeville wasn't a social or economic
attack on the community structure, but rather an attack on the
structure of ideas and only now was everyone learning that. I
asked him what he meant. He said that the poverty workers had
once seen their jobs as enlightening the masses about how messed
up things were. "We were ugly Americans, that's all we were.
That's why we weren't effective. But now we've learned that you
don't change anything that way, you have to get inside the local
community and understand it first and work there."

I thought that was indeed true, but I didn't see what it had to
do with the structure of the community's ideas; it had to do only
with the arrogance or naivete of the poverty workers, and that
was awfully solipsistic. He hadn't said anything about his
clients—just himself, just the way his ideas were challenged, not
theirs.

The apartment was curiously out of that world. On the walls
were posters and lithos and prints and pictures of healthy human
bodies looking delicious. The record racks contained the Stones

and *Tim Hardin No. 3* and a lot of Bach. Many of the recent books we'd all read and others one had and the others meant to, and Mary and I talked about them, but there was something relative, even in the pleasantness, as if it were an appositive in the bracketing nastiness out there.

When we got back to the car I took from my jacket pocket the heavy and uncomfortable shiny chromeplated .380 automatic pistol someone had once given me in San Antonio. I put it on the seat next to Fred's .357 revolver. They looked silly there; real guns always do. But people kept telling us how someone else was going to shoot us, or they recounted the story of how Hugh O'Connor, a Canadian film producer down in the next county the year before to make a movie, was shot in the heart by a man with no liking for outsiders and less for outsiders with cameras, and it did seem awfully easy to be an outsider here.

We went to see Edith Easterling, a lifelong Marrowbone Creek resident, working at that time for the Appalachian Volunteers as director of the Marrowbone Folk School. "The people in the mountains really lives hard," Edith said. "You can come into Pikeville and go to the Chamber of Commerce and they'll say, 'Well, there's really no poor people left there. People are faring good.' Then you can come out here and go to homes and you'd just be surprised how poor these people live, how hard that they live. Kids that's grown to 15 or 16 years old that's never had a mess of fresh milk or meats, things that kids really need. They live on canned cream until they get big enough to go to the table and eat beans and potatoes."

She told us about harassment and redbaiting of the AVs by Robert Holcomb, Harry Eastburn (the Big Sandy Community Action Program director, also funded by OEO, a bitter antagonist of any poverty program not under his political control), and Thomas Ratliff, the commonwealth's attorney (the equivalent of a county prosecutor).

Some of the AVs came from out of state, especially the higher paid office staff and technical specialists, but most of the 14 field workers were local people, like Edith. Since becoming involved with the poverty program Edith has received telephone threats and had some windows shot out. The sheriff refused to send a deputy to investigate. Occasionally she gets anonymous calls; some are threats, some call her "dirty communist." She shrugs those away: "I'm a Republican and who ever seen a communist Republican?"

CHANGING A WAY OF LIFE

The Appalachian Volunteers began in the early 1960s as a group of students from Berea College who busied themselves with needed community band-aid work: they made trips to the mountains to patch up dilapidated schoolhouses, they ran tutorial programs, they collected books for needy schools. The ultimate futility of such work soon became apparent and there was a drift in the AV staff toward projects that might affect the life style of some of the mountain communities. In 1966 the AVs decided to break away from their parent organization, the conservative Council of the Southern Mountains. The new, independent Appalachian Volunteers had no difficulty finding federal funding. During the summers of 1966 and 1967 the organization received large OEO grants to host hundreds of temporary volunteer workers, many of them VISTA and Peace Corps trainees. According to David Walls, who was acting director of the AVs when I talked with him, the organization's mission was to "create effective, economically self-sufficient poor people's organizations that would concern themselves with local issues, such as welfare rights, bridges and roads, water systems and strip mining."

It didn't work, of course it didn't work; the only reason it lasted as long as it did was because so much of the AV staff was composed of outsiders, people who had worked in San Francisco and Boston and New York and Washington, and it took a long time before the naivete cracked enough for the failure to show through.

The first consequence of creating an organization of the impoverished and unempowered is not the generation of any new source of residence of power, but rather the gathering in one place a lot of poverty and powerlessness that previously was spread out. In an urban situation, the poor or a minority group may develop or exercise veto power: they can manage an economic boycott, they can refuse to work for certain firms and encourage others to join with them, they can physically block a store entrance. It is only when such efforts create a kind of negative monopoly (a strike line no one will cross or a boycott others will respect) that power is generated. When that negative monopoly cannot be created, there is no power—this is why workers can successfully strike for higher wages but the poor in cities cannot get the police to respect their civil liberties enough to stop beating them up; if everyone refuses to work at a factory, the owner must cooperate or close down, but there is nothing anyone can refuse a policeman that will remove the immediate incentive for illegal police behavior. The poor in the mountains cannot strike—they are unemployable anyway, or at least enough of them are to make specious that kind of action. Even if they were to get something going the UMW would not support them. The poor cannot start an economic boycott: they don't spend enough to hold back enough to threaten any aspect of the mountain coal economy. (There have been a few instances of industrial sabotage—I'll mention them later on—that have been dramatic, but pitifully ineffective.) One of the saddest things about the poor in the mountains is they have nothing to deny anyone. And they don't even have the wild hope some city poor entertain that something may turn up; in the mountains there is nothing to hope for.

Another problem with organizations of the very poor is they do not have much staying power: the individual participants are just too vulnerable. So long as the members can be scared or bought off easily, one cannot hope for such groups to develop solidarity. In Kentucky, where welfare, medical aid, disability pensions and union benefits all have a remarkable quality of coming and going with political whims, that is a real problem. Edith Easterling described the resulting condition: "These people are scared people, they are scared to death. I can talk to them and I can say, 'You shouldn't be scared, there's nothing to be scared about.' But they're still scared."

"What are they scared of," Fred asked her, "losing their jobs?"

"No. Some of 'em don't even have a job. Most of the people

don't have jobs. They live on some kind of pension. They're scared of losing their pension. If it's not that, they're scared someone will take them to court for something. 'If I say something, they're going to take me to court and I don't have a lawyer's fee. I don't have a lawyer, so I'd rather not say nothing.' When you get the people to really start opening up and talking, that's when the county officials attack us every time with something."

PUBLICITY AND REVENGE

For someone who brings troublesome publicity to the community, there are forms of retaliation far crueler than the mere cutting off of welfare or unemployment benefits. One poverty worker told of an event following a site visit by Robert Kennedy a few years ago: "When Kennedy was down for his hearings one of his advance men got in contact with a friend of ours who had a community organization going. They were very anxious to get some exposure, to get Kennedy involved in it. They took the advance men around to visit some families that were on welfare. He made statements about the terrible conditions the children there in two particular homes had to live under. He wasn't indicting the families, he was just talking about conditions in general. These were picked up by the local press and given quite a bit of notoriety—Kennedy Aide Makes the Scene, that sort of thing. After he left, about three days later, the welfare agency came and took away the children from both of those families and put them in homes . . . . This is the control that is over people's lives."

The group with the potential staying power in the mountains is the middle class, the small landowners. They have concrete things to lose while the poor (save in anomalous atrocities such as the one with the children mentioned above) have nothing to lose, they only have possible access to benefits that someone outside their group may or may not let them get. There is a big difference in the way one fights in the two situations. Something else: it is harder to scare the middle class off, for it has not been conditioned by all those years of humiliating control and dependency.

One Appalachian Volunteer, Joe Mulloy, a 24-year-old Kentuckian, realized this. He and his wife decided to join a fight being waged by a Pike County landowner, Jink Ray, and his neighbors, against a strip-mine operator who was about to remove the surface of Ray's land.

RIGHTS FOR PENNIES

The focus of the fight was the legitimacy of the *broadform* deed, a nineteenth century instrument with which landowners assigned mineral rights to mining companies, usually for small sums of money (50 cents per acre was common). When these deeds were originally signed no landowner had any thought of signing away all rights to his property—just the underground minerals and whatever few holes the mining company might have to make in the hillside to get at the seams. In the twentieth century the coal companies developed the idea of lifting off all the earth and rock above the coal, rather than digging for it, and since the broadform deed said the miner could use whatever means he saw fit to get the coal out, the Kentucky courts held that the miners' land rights had precedence over the surface owners'—even though that meant complete destruction of a man's land by a mining process the original signer of the deed could not have imagined. The strip miners are legally entitled, on the basis of a contract that might be 90 years old, to come to a man's home and completely bury it in rubble, leaving the owner nothing but the regular real estate tax bill with which he is stuck even though the "real estate" has since been dumped in the next creekbed. First come the bulldozers to do the initial clearing (a song I heard in West Virginia, to the tune of "Swing Low, Sweet Chariot," went: "Roll on, big D-9 dozer, comin' for to bury my home/I'm getting madder as you're gettin' closer, comin' for to bury my home."), then they roll in the massive shovels, some of which grow as large as 18.5 million pounds and can gobble 200 tons of earth and rock a minute and dump it all a city block away. Such a machine is operated by one man riding five stories above the ground.

On June 29, 1967, Jink Ray and some neighbors in Island Creek, a Pike County community, blocked with their bodies bulldozers that were about to start stripping Ray's land. With them were Joe and Karen Mulloy. The people themselves had organized the resistance; the Mulloys were simply helping.

With the strip-mining fight on the mountain, the AVs were for the first time involved in something significant. It was also dangerous: the members of the Island Creek group were challenging not only the basis of the local economy, but the federal government as well: the big mines' biggest customer is the Tennessee Valley Authority, and the Small Business Administration supports many of the smaller mine operators. The poverty program and other federal agencies were moving toward open conflict.

What happened was that the poverty program backed down and the local power structure moved in. Eleven days after Governor Edward Breathitt's August 1 suspension of the strip-mine company's Island Creek permit (the first and only such suspension), Pike County officials arrested the Mulloys for sedition (plotting or advocating the violent overthrow of the government). Arrested with them on the same charge were Alan and Margaret McSurely, field workers for the Southern Conference Educational Fund (SCEF), a Louisville-based civil rights organization. McSurely had been hired as training consultant by the AVs during the Spring of 1967, but the real reason he had been hired was to restructure the cumbersome organization. One of the first things he did was get the AVs to allow local people on the board of directors, he was fired in a month and went to work for SCEF; they even arrested Carl Braden (SCEF's executive director) and his wife, Anne. Anne Braden had never been in Pike County in her life; the first time Carl Braden had been there was the day he went to Pikeville to post bail for McSurely on the sedition charge.

In Washington, the response to the arrests was immediate;

Sargent Shriver's office announced that AV funds would be cut off; no funds previously granted were taken away, but no new money was appropriated after that.

The Pike County grand jury concluded that "a well-organized and well-financed effort is being made to promote and spread the communistic theory of violent and forceful overthrow of the government of Pike County." The grand jury said also that "communist organizers have attempted, without success thus far, to promote their beliefs among our school children by infiltrating our local schools with teachers who believe in the violent overthrow of the local government." Organizers were "planning to infiltrate local churches and labor unions in order to cause dissension and to promote their purposes." And, finally, "communist organizers are attempting to form community unions with the eventual purpose of organizing armed groups to be known as 'Red Guards' and through which the forceful overthrow of the local government would be accomplished."

UNTOUCHABLE VOLUNTEERS

The AVs came unglued. The Mulloys became pariahs within the organization. "We spent that whole summer and no AV came to see us at all in Pike County," Joe Mulloy said. "Once they came up to shit on us, but that was the only time. Then the thing of our getting arrested for sedition was what just really flipped everybody. This was a real situation that you had to deal with, it wasn't something in your mind or some ideological thing. It was real. Another person was under arrest. I think that the feeling of a number of people on the staff was it was my fault that I had been arrested because I had been reckless in my organizing, that I had been on the mountain with the fellas and had risked as much as they were risking and I deserved what I got, and that I should be fired so the program would go on; that was now a detriment."

That fall, a special three-judge federal court ruled the Kentucky sedition law unconstitutional so all charges against the Mulloys, the Bradens and the McSurelys were wiped out. But the

AVs were still nervous. "After the arrests were cleared away," Mulloy said, "things started to happen to me on the staff. I was given another assignment. I was told that I couldn't be a field man any more because I was a public figure identified with sedition and hence people would feel uneasy talking to me, and that I should do research. My truck was taken away and I was given an old car, and I was given a title of researcher rather than field man. It took away considerable voice that I had in the staff until then."

Karen Mulloy said she and Joe really had no choice. "If we had organized those people up there, with possible death as the end result for some of them—fortunately it was kept nonviolent —and if we weren't with them they wouldn't have spoken to us. We took as much risk as they did. We said to them, 'We're not going to organize something for you that we won't risk our necks for either.' An organizer can't do that."

"These people have gone through the whole union experience and that has sold them out," Joe said. "And a great number of people have gone through the poverty war experience and that hasn't answered anybody's problems, anybody's questions. Getting together on the strip-mining issue—if there was ever one issue that the poverty war got on that was good, that was it. It all fell through because when we started getting counterattacked by the operators the poverty war backed up because their funds were being jeopardized. The whole strip-mining issue as an organized effort has collapsed right now and the only thing that's going on is individual sabotage. There's a lot of mining equipment being blown up every month or so, about a million dollars at a time. These are individual or small group acts or retaliation, but the organized effort has ceased."

(Later, I talked with Rick Diehl, the AV research director, about the sabotage. He described two recent operations, both of them very sophisticated, involving groups of multiple charges set off simultaneously. The sheriff didn't even look for the dynamiters: he probably wouldn't have caught them and even if he had he wouldn't have gotten a jury to convict. "And that kind of stuff goes on to some degree all the time," Diehl said. "There's a growing feeling that destroying property is going to shut down the system in Appalachia. The people don't benefit from the coal companies at all, 'cause even the deep mines don't have enough employees. The average number of employees in a deep mine is 16 people. So, you can see, there is nothing to lose. It's that same desperation kind of thing that grips people in Detroit and Watts.")

ORGANIZING OUTRAGE

Even though the sedition charges were dropped, the Mulloys and McSurelys weren't to escape punishment for their organizing outrages.

One Friday the 13th Al McSurely came home late from a two- or three-day trip out of town, talked with his wife a little while, then went to bed. Margaret went to bed a short time later. "I wasn't asleep at all," she said, "but he was so tired he went right to sleep. I heard this car speed up. Well, I had got into the habit of listening to cars at night, just because we always expected something like this to happen. And sure enough, it did. There was this blast. The car took off and there was this huge blast, and glass and dirt and grit were in my mouth and eyes and hair, and the baby was screaming. So I put on my bathrobe and ran across the street with the baby."

"The state trooper was pretty good," Alan said. "He gave me a lecture: 'The next time this happens call the city police first so they can seal off the holler. They can get here much faster than I can.' I said, 'I'll try and remember that.' "

Joe Mulloy was the only AV with a Kentucky draft board; he was also the only AV to lose his occupational deferment and have his 2-A changed to 1-A. Mulloy asked the board (in Louisville, the same as Muhammed Ali's) for a rehearing on the grounds of conscientious objection, and he presented as part of his evidence a letter from Thomas Merton saying he was Mulloy's spiritual adviser (the two used to meet for talks in Merton's cabin in the woods) and could testify to the truthfulness of Mulloy's CO claim. The board refused to reopen the case because, they said, there was no new evidence of any relevance or value. In April

1968 Mulloy was sentenced to five years in prison and a $10,000 fine for refusing induction.

He was fired immediately by the Appalachian Volunteers. Some wanted him out because they honestly thought his draft case would be a major obstacle to his effectiveness with the oddly patriotic mountain people. (In the mountains you can be against the war, many people are, but if your country calls you, you go. It would be unpatriotic not to go. The government and the country are two quite independent entities. The government might screw up the poverty program, run that bad war, work in conjunction with the mine owners and politicians, but it isn't the government that is calling you—it is the country. Only a weirdo would refuse that call. But once you're in you are working for the government, and then it is all right to desert.) Others on the AV staff objected to Mulloy's getting involved in issues that riled up the authorities. The staff vote to get rid of him was 20 to 19.

What the AVs failed to admit was that the changing of Mulloy's draft status was an attack on them as well: the only reason for the change was the strip-mine fight. The draft board had joined the OEO, the TVA, the mine owners, the political structure of the state and the UMW in opposition to effective organization of the poor in the mountains.

I asked Joe how he felt about it all now. "I don't know if I can really talk about this objectively," he said. "I feel in my guts as a Kentuckian a great deal of resentment against a lot of these people. And some of them are my friends that have come in and stirred things up and then have left. The going is really tough right now. I'm still here, all the people that have to make a living out in those counties are still there with their black lung. I don't think anything was accomplished. It's one of those things that's going to go down in history as a cruel joke: the poverty war in the mountains."

The two bad guys of the story, I suppose, should be Robert Holcomb, spokesman for the mine owners in the county, and commonwealth's attorney Thomas Ratliff, the man who handled the prosecution in the sedition and who was (coincidentally, he insists) Republican candidate for lieutenant governor at the time; Ratliff got rich in the mine business, but is now into a lot of other things. Like most bad guy labels, I suspect these are too easy. I'll come back to that.

I rather liked Ratliff even though there were things I knew about him I didn't like at all. It is quite possible he really does believe, as he said he does, that the McSurelys and the Bradens are communist provocateurs; there are people in America who believe such menaces exist, though not very many of them are as intelligent as Ratliff.

He claims the defendants in the sedition case had "a new angle on revolution—to do it locally and then bring all the local revolutions together and then you got a big revolution. Now whether it would have succeeded or not I don't know. I think it possibly could have, had they been able to continue to get money from the Jolly Green Giant, as they call Uncle Sam. I certainly think with enough money, and knowing the history of this area, it was not impossible."

What seems to have bothered him most was not the politics involved but the bad sportsmanship: "The thing that rankled me in this case, and it still does, this is really what disturbed me more about this thing than anything else, was the fact that . . . they were able to use federal money . . . to promote this thing. Frankly, I would be almost as opposed to either the Republican party or the Democratic party being financed by the federal money to prevail, much less a group who were avowed communists, made no bones about it that I could tell, whose objective was revolution, the forceful and violent overthrow of the local government and hopefully to overthrow the federal government, and it was being financed by federal tax money!"

Once Ratliff got off his communist menace line, I found myself agreeing with him as much as I had with some of the remarks Joe Mulloy had made. Ratliff spoke eloquently on the need for a negative income tax, for massive increases on the taxes on the mine operators, things like that. (Whether he meant the things he said is impossible to tell; one never knows with politicians, or anyone else for that matter.)

"It's the reaction to this sort of situation that really bothers me," he said, "because—there is no question about it—there is some containment of free speech, free expression, when you get a situation like this. People become overexcited and overdisturbed. And the laws of physics play in these things: for every action there's a reaction, and the reaction, unfortunately, is often too much in this kind of situation. You begin seeing a communist behind every tree. That's bad. Because there isn't a communist behind every tree, or anything like that."

"But I think they've accomplished one thing, not what they thought they would. . . . That's the tragic part of it, I don't think they've uplifted anybody. I think they have left a lot of people disappointed, frustrated. . . . But I think they have scared the so-called affluent society into doing something about it. Maybe. I think there are people more conscious of it because of that."

It is so easy to write off Holcomb or Ratliff as evil men, grasping and groping for whatever they can get and destroying whatever gets in the way; for a poverty worker it is probably necessary to think such thoughts, that may be the mental bracing one needs to deal as an opponent.

But I think it is wrong.

Holcomb is an ex-miner who made it; uneducated and not particularly smart, he somehow grooved on the leavings in that weird economy and got rich. He thinks what he did is something anyone ought to be able to do: it is the American dream, after all. His failure is mainly one of vision, a social myopia hardly rare in this country. From Holcomb's point of view, those people stirring up the poor probably are communist agitators—why else would anyone interfere with the "free enterprise system at its best?" If you tried to tell him that a system that leads to great big rich houses on one side of town and squalid leaky shacks on the other might not be the best thing in this world he'd think you were crazy or a communist (both, actually) too. And Thomas Ratliff is hardly the simple Machiavelli the usual scenario would demand.

Picking out individuals and saying the evil rests with them is like patching schoolhouses and expecting the cycle of poverty to be broken. Even when you're right you're irrelevant. What is evil in the mountains is the complex of systems, a complex that has no use or place or tolerance for the old, the wrecked, the incompetent, the extra, and consigns them to the same gullies and hollers and ditches as the useless cars and empty Maxwell House

coffee tins and Royal Crown cola cans, with the same lack of hate
or love.

The enemies of the poverty program, malicious or natural,
individual or collective, turn out to be far more successful than
they could have hoped or expected. One reason for that success is
the cooperation of the victims: groups like the AVs become, as
one of their long-time members said, "top-heavy and bureaucratic, a bit central office bound. We are . . . worried about
maintaining the AV structure, and responding to pressures from
foundations and OEO, rather than from community people." The
federal government, presumably the opponent of poverty here,
plays both sides of the fence: it supports activities like the AVs
(so long as they are undisturbing), but it also supports the local
Community Action Program, which is middle-class dominated
and politically controlled; it created a generation of hustlers
among the poor who find out that only by lying and finagling can
they get the welfare and social security benefits they legitimately
deserve; it strengthens the local courthouse power structures by
putting federal job programs in control of the county machines
and by putting the Small Business Administration at its disposal;
it commissions studies to document the ill effects of strip mining
and simultaneously acts, through TVA, as the largest consumer of
the product.

The mood is much like the McCarthy days of the early 1950s:
actual legal sanctions are applied to very few people, but so many
others are smeared that other people are afraid of
contagion, of contamination, even though they know there is
nothing to catch. They avoid issues that might threaten some
agency or person of power, they stop making trouble, stop
looking for trouble, they keep busy or they stay home—and no
one ever really says, when faced by the complex, "I'm scared."

Everyone has something to do: busy, busy, busy. I remember a
visit to the AV office in Prestonsburg; they had there what must
have been one of the largest Xerox machines in the state of
Kentucky; it was used for copying newspaper articles; someone
on the staff ran it. There was an AV magazine assembled by a
staff member who, if some of the foundations grants had come

through, would have gotten a full-time assistant. The mining went on, the acting director of the AVs, Dave Walls, went about hustling private foundations grants and being sociable and vague and disarming to visitors, and not much of anything really happened.

I visited eastern Kentucky again a short time ago. There were some changes. The weather was softer and some leaves were on the trees, so you couldn't see the shacks back in the hollers unless you drove up close; you couldn't see the hillside cemeteries and junkyards at all.

I found out that Governor Louis Nunn had blocked any new AV funds and most of the other money had gone, so there were ugly battles over the leavings, mixed with uglier battles over old political differences within the organization itself.

Edith Easterling was fired; she now has a Ford grant to travel about the country and look at organizing projects. Rick Diehl has gone somewhere else. Mary Walton is now a staff reporter for the Charleston (W. Va.) *Gazette.* The Prestonsburg AV office is still open—with a small group of lawyers working on welfare rights problems; that is the only AV activity still alive and no one knows how much longer there will be any money for that.

I ran into Dave Walls in a movie house in Charleston. The show was *Wild River* with Montgomery Clift and Lee Remick, and it was about how good TVA is and what a swell guy Montgomery Clift is and how homey and true mountain girl Lee Remick is. Anyway, I saw Dave there and we talked a moment during intermission. He still draws a subsistence salary from the AVs, still lives in Berea, over in the Bluegrass country far and nicely away from it all. He is going to school at the University of Kentucky in Lexington, doing graduate work in something. He looked just the same, no more or less mild. Someone asked him, "What's going on in the mountains now? What happened to everything?" He shrugged and smiled, "I don't know," he said, "I haven't gone to the mountains in a long time."

Well, for the other people, the ones who were there before, things are pretty much the same. That woman and her nine children still live in that shack in Poorbottom. The man who

worked the mines for 28 years is still kept marginally alive by the
chemical array in his refrigerator he still somehow manages to
afford.

A DISTRUST OF STRANGERS

Jink Ray, the man who faced down the bulldozers, I met on
that recent trip. When we drove up he had just put out some bad
honey and the bees were a thick swarm in the front of the house.
We went into a sitting room-bedroom where his wife sat before an
open coal fire and each wall had one or two Christs upon it. We
talked about the strip-mine fight. On one wall was a photo of him
with Governor Breathitt the day the governor came up to stop
the strippers. We went outside and talked some more, standing by
the overripe browning corn standing next to a patch of corn just
about ripe, the hills thickly coated and overlapping to form a lush
box canyon behind him. He pointed to the hillside the other side
of the road and told us they'd been augering up there. "You can't
see it from down here this time of year, but it's bad up there."
The seepage killed the small streams down below: nothing lives in
those streams anymore. "We used to get bait in them streams,
nothing now, and fish used to grow there before they went to the
river. Not now." Suddenly his face hardened, "Why you fellas
asking me these questions?" We told him again that we were
writing about what had happened in Pike County. "No," he said,
"that ain't what you are. I believe you fellas are here because you
want to get stripping going again, you want to know if I'll back
off this time." He talked from a place far behind the cold blue
eyes that were just so awful. We protested, saying we really were
writers, but it didn't work—it's like denying you're an undercover
agent or homosexual, there's no way in the world to do it once
the assumption gets made, however wrong. He talked in postured
and rhetorical bursts awhile and it seemed a long time until we
could leave without seeming to have been run off. Leaving him
standing there looking at the yellow Hertz car backing out his
driveway, his face still cold and hard, polite to the end, but . . .
But what? Not hating, but knowing: he knows about strangers

now, he knows they are there to take something away, to betray, to hustle, he knows even the friendly strangers will eventually go back whereever strangers go when they are through doing whatever they have come down to do, and he will be just where he is, trying with whatever meager resources he's got to hold on to the small parcel of land he scuffled so hard to be able to own. He'll not trust anyone again, and for me that was perhaps the most painful symptom of the failure and defeat of the poverty program in the mountains.

The others: Joe Mulloy, after about two years in the courts, finally won the draft appeal he should never have had to make in the first place; Al and Margaret McSurely were sentenced to prison terms for contempt of Congress after they refused to turn over their personal papers to a Senate committee investigating subversion in the rural South. Tom Ratliff is still commonwealth's attorney, there in the county of Pike, in the state of Kentucky. And Robert Holcomb still has his mines, his colleries, his offices and his fine and unshaken belief in the American Way.

FURTHER READING

Night Comes to the Cumberlands by Harry Caudill (Boston: Atlantic-Little Brown, 1963) is the best book for any outsider who wants a sense of the space and anguish of Appalachia.

Let Us Now Praise Famous Men by James Agee and Walker Evans (Boston: Houghton Mifflin, 1960) is the most poetic document for an outsider who wants a sense of rural poverty in America; it isn't dated yet.

4

PROFESSIONAL
AND
PARAPROFESSIONAL
SERVICES

The Revolution in Social Work: The New Nonprofessional

FRANK RIESSMAN

A new army of people has moved into recently created jobs in social work and education.

Schools throughout the country are employing an increasing number of "team mothers" and parent education coordinators "for such purposes as vision and hearing screening, escorting pupils on field trips, and operating projectors and other equipment. . . ." In some Puerto Rican neighborhoods in New York there is a "Puerto Rican community coordinator" whose special function is to interpret the school and the Puerto Rican community to each other. Typically, these coordinators are not highly trained people, but rather "informal leaders" who have close ties to the neighborhood and its traditions.

Arthur Pearl has used former juvenile offenders at New York State Division for Youth and at Howard University for interviewing and for helping conduct research on delinquency. Homemakers with little education and less professional training have been hired to help welfare recipients at home. Mobilization for Youth in New York used many "indigenous leaders," case aides, parent education aides, homemakers, adventure corps youth leaders and tutors. These are only a smattering of the new kinds of nonprofessional jobs proliferating daily in numbers and variety.

I am especially interested in the "indigenous" nonprofessionals—those who come originally from the disadvantaged communities they serve, and who have special personal knowledge and understanding of the kinds of people and problems with which they deal.

It is easy to be uncritically enthusiastic about them (and many have been) especially in view of the strong chorus of criticism of the professionals who serve the poor. I believe that the achievements of these indigenous nonprofessionals are impressive, their talents unique, and their future in social service and education very bright. However, I think it much more important to consider their best use, their proper training and the problems they bring, rather than merely to sing their praises. If we can successfully capitalize on their special skills—combining them with those of well-trained and dedicated professionals—I believe we may be on our way toward producing a revolution in social work.

Why the rapid rise of the indigenous nonprofessional?

1. Expanded servicing of the poor produces many new jobs.
2. Many middle-class professionals, social workers and teachers are reluctant to work with the poor—so the supply of professionals shrinks at precisely the time the demand increases.
3. The nonprofessional jobs themselves function as opportunities for a large number of people from lower socioeconomic background, and thus directly serve to reduce poverty by transforming dependent welfare cases into homemakers, delinquents into researchers, students into tutors.
4. The new nonprofessional provides an excellent model for the low-income community.

Examination reveals quickly that the great majority of these new jobs are in low-income areas—"gray area" schools and "lower-class" high-delinquency neighborhoods. In part, they merely reflect the increased concern for the poor and unemployed, as expressed through the new poverty programs.

Probably their most important function is to serve as a bridge between the poor and the larger community, especially the schools and the agencies. Most professionals have emphasized one-way communication—they wanted to get the possible recipients of services (the parents of the children they worked with, for instance) into places and frames of mind in which they were receptive to doing what was considered good for them. But a real bridge means two-way traffic. Increasingly, if at first only in a minor key, messages have been coming back, explaining the poor to the school and the city—and bringing such results as a change in the character of PTA meetings to make them more attractive and meaningful to poor parents. Traffic is picking up—and not just communication but influence and action. Across that bridge the social service network is learning who the disadvantaged are and what they need; and the poor are learning that help is available, and by what means and efforts that help can be made most effective.

Merely coming from the same class as the client is not, of course, enough to make a good worker. The native nonprofessional must be carefully chosen and trained. Herbert J. Gans in *The Urban Villagers* has described the problem well:

> These nonprofessionals should be people who have themselves come out of lower-class culture, and have successfully moved into a more stable way of life ... but have not rejected their past. Many mobile people tend to turn their backs on the culture from which they have come, and become more hostile toward it than anyone else. Yet ... some people, in making the change, have developed a considerable amount of empathy toward both old and new culture. ... While these empathetic people exist in large numbers, they are hard to find. ... Most of them never use their talent—for it is a talent—to mediate between the classes.

They must be sought out. They seldom know the value of what they have. They often still carry the psychological marks of the lower class on them and are very conscious of the great gap in training between themselves and professionals.

Many come from a group Gans calls "internal caretakers." These include the proverbial "friendly bartender" (neighborhood counselor, sage and confidant), and storekeeper and neighbors who, in the continually crisis-laden atmosphere of low-income life, informally offer care and understanding otherwise seldom available.

However, internal caretakers tend to be "market-oriented." They aim to please. They value the regard of their neighbors and frequently share the same biases. A woman in need of medical care but who doesn't trust doctors or clinics might well find her resistance reinforced by the neighbor who doesn't trust them either. The personal approach of the internal caretaker can be a handicap as well as an advantage. If advice is rejected he can feel personally rejected and withdraw further help. As Gans says, "Most important, since they have no more knowledge than their clients, the care they give is not always what is needed."

In recruiting indigenous workers it may be advisable therefore not to select former internal caretakers—or if they are selected, those excessively concerned with pleasing their client at any cost should be avoided. In training them, the narrow focus and identification with the client should be kept within "reasonable" bounds—while full use is made of precisely these same qualities for communication and understanding. How can this apparent conflict be resolved? This is the dilemma—and the art—of finding and using the indigenous nonprofessional.

WHAT QUALITIES ARE MOST DESIRABLE?

In accepting applicants for "parent-educator coordinators" who would try to involve reluctant low-income parents with the schools their children attend, Mobilization for Youth stressed:

1. *Maturity*. Applicants had to be at least 25, responsive to ethnic and personal differences, able to tolerate frustration, friendly, sensitive to the feelings of others, and otherwise showing evidence of emotional and physical maturity.
2. *Certain basic objective standards*. These included good health, high school education or better, demonstrated ability to handle the job, and completion of an in-service training program.

But, while these requirements are fundamental, they are still less than minimal. Mary Dowery, coordinator of the program, also looked for certain latent requirements. She wanted "doers," not just "listeners." She did not want gossipers or the overemotional. The pay was very attractive for former slum dwellers, but she wanted more than the talents that could just be bought for pay. She wanted active discontent with the neighborhood and desire for change in it. She wanted strong motivation and willingness to work hard. She wanted her workers independent, curious and even critical—not merely "receptive to training." Most of all, she wanted those who had a "feel" for the work and the people.

The contributions of the indigenous nonprofessional might well be illustrated by enumerating the activities and accomplishments of the parent education aides during the first eight months of the program:

1. Thirty-one informal meetings, each involving ten to 25 parents normally resistant to cooperation, were held. Complaints and problems from and about school, delinquency, drug addiction, housing, work, camping and understanding children were all discussed.

2. The aides worked up an auxiliary recruiting corps of parents who visited other parents and tried to get them to come to meetings.

3. Each aide "cared for" about 35 families—escorted parents to school, welfare agencies, clinics, legal aid, consumer bureau, meetings—and even mediated family quarrels and located apartments.

4. Once a week for six weeks during the summer of 1963, information centers, staffed by aides, were set up on various street corners to listen to complaints and tell the people what rights and resources were available to them. They encouraged—and got—comments and suggestions. Two-way communication became an emphatic reality.

5. Some aides served as consultants with the parent association—acted as mediators between the "old regime" and the new recruits.

6. They organized many group activities: sewing circles, doughnut parties, visits to the UN and the zoo.

7. Working in five junior high and three grade schools, they

won the respect and cooperation of guidance officers, teachers and principals. On the other hand, sometimes the more militant and vocal aides were resented by existing power figures.

8. One aide, a Chinese lady, gave a great deal of help to school personnel who needed to understand cultural factors in the Chinese family that were important to the school performance of Chinese children.

9. The indigenous nonprofessionals of Mobilization for Youth were more effective than any other group, professional or not, in organizing community people for the March on Washington and the voter registration campaign.

Again, the intangibles were even more important than the measurable results: the seriousness and dedication of the aides; the increasing respect for them—and for the agency—among the people in the neighborhood and the professionals; the camaraderie and confidence they developed; and the vitality and spirit they left wherever they went. Their rate of turnover was extremely low. They thought their work important and loved it.

Many writers seem to regard the nonprofessional merely as an extension of the arm of the professional. However true this may be for the middle-class volunteer brought in from outside, it is not true of the indigenous nonprofessional. His contributions are unique and distinct. He brings enthusiasm, lower-class know-how, and personal relationship to low-income people.

The indigenous nonprofessional demands action, motion. He is less tolerant of delay and talk. "Change the Welfare Department rules." "Make the housing manager listen to the people." "Let's make sure everyone gets a chance to talk at PTA meetings."

> I have been trying very hard to make them understand that I am working to help them help themselves. . . . Even when her statements are, "White teachers don't like Negro children" or "White teachers think Negro children can't learn," I realize my client has begun to think about her children's education and future.

From Supervisors:

> One (aide) voluntarily cut her vacation short to be available for shopping when a client's welfare check came. . . . Their

enthusiasm and missionary spirit are almost infectious, often compelling the supervisors to work overtime to keep up with them. They have called us on weekends and in the evenings to report successes that couldn't possibly keep until Monday. . . . These women had walked by deprivation, disaster and depravity all their lives, but now that they were helping, every problem was an emergency that couldn't even wait for the next work day.

They have transformed depressed people into alive and hopeful ones; prodded angry people into becoming more active and organized; and made aloof professionals into involved, concerned citizens.

Low-income living requires special skills and experiences. Gertrude Goldberg in a Mobilization for Youth report portrays this vividly:

The kind of know-how the homemakers have makes it possible to get by on a little, to negotiate life in a slum. You use every opportunity to the hilt; the barber school for free haircuts, the thrift shop, the remnant pile, free recreation, free public clinics, surplus foods if you qualify or if your neighbors do and don't use them.

Social workers simply cannot so easily attend weddings, family gatherings and funerals as can neighborhood people.

Even when indigenous workers make mistakes—and they make many of them—the over-riding relationship apparently carries them through. Gertrude Goldberg says:

The relationship between client and homemaker doesn't suffer from the "mistakes" a homemaker makes. She may show favoritism to one child over another, bawl out a client who's already been beaten down, do for instead of with, "over-identify," scorn, even curse, but she's never thrown out and seldom resisted.

Perhaps most significant is the fact that nonprofessionals view problems very differently from professional social workers and the view of the indigenous worker has a much greater probability of fitting in with "lower-class" expectations.

Although homemakers are in some respects less accepting than professional workers, they are perhaps more tolerant

in another. *They don't perceive people as problems—or
they at least disagree with professionals about what
constitutes a problem. They react more strongly to bad
housing, illness or lack of money perhaps because they
know what it feels like to do without the necessities. . . .*
Mrs. Casey was a "fine person who cared for her children."
And that was the main thing even if she had four
illegitimate offspring. To the social worker, she was
depressed, practically ego-less, "so self-destructive. . . ."

Leaders are essential to the rise and well-being of any
community, and especially of the poor, who need to rise more
than anybody. But potential community leaders go unheralded,
unsung and undiscovered. Some are burdened with family and
financial problems; some are simply unawakened, or have little
chance or reason to want to exercise their talents. Indigenous
personnel have a unique opportunity to bring this leadership out
and make it effective. As parent aides or homemakers, for
instance, they can relieve pressures; through informal personal
contact they can discover leadership, encourage it and give it
direction.

Leadership may turn up in unlikely places—in an overweight
housewife, for instance, heavily burdened with child care, who
"gave the manager holy hell" in tenant meetings until she got
what she wanted for her children and her neighbors. Nonprofessional workers can even provide a kind of "leadership training"
for such persons by deliberately involving them in meetings and
activities, and discussing and evaluating tactics for weeks after-
ward.

The indigenous worker must, of course, be himself set or
primed toward community organization for social action—that is,
he must be able to see the possibility for converting the problems,
needs and interests of neighborhood people into group action.
Homemakers, being "service-oriented," seldom have such inclina-
tions. But other indigenous personnel have proven very useful in
developing leaders who went on to organize house committees
and voter registration drives.

Some leaders, once aroused, have trouble keeping themselves
in problems; when one is solved, they go around looking for

others, or exaggerating minor complaints into "federal cases." One group of leaders, who had successfully organized action in their own building, went on to organize similar activities in other buildings. After a while the original difficulty in their building recurred. We asked them why they didn't do something about it. "Oh, it's not important compared to what's happening in these other buildings."

If indigenous workers have special abilities rising from common experience and common feeling with their charges they also have special problems.

Confidentiality. The poor look upon confiding information. and keeping it confidential, differently from middle-class people. Indigenous workers often think like their cases. An understanding of the need for confidentiality cannot therefore be assumed; it must be carefully explained, and the rules laid out. An even greater trouble comes from the fact that the poor often mistrust outside authority, including that of the agencies and the schools—and the workers share this distrust and are reluctant to pass on information given in confidence. Fundamental, of course, is the necessity for establishing trust of the agency, of its sincerity and good will. The accumulated resentments of decades are not overcome in days, however—and they must be combatted by deeds, not merely pronouncements.

Overidentification with the agency. The nonprofessional has taken a step up in the world—he is pleased with his new status, income and influence. Like the upwardly mobile anywhere, it is often too easy for him to take over what he believes to be the viewpoint of his employer; to be, in effect, "holier than the Pope." This may be expressed in words: "Too many people around here are lazy—won't help themselves." It may take the form of the worker simply considering himself an agent to carry out the "will" of the agency, rather than a bridge to carry communication both ways and help establish understanding and common effort. This is especially true when the agency itself is only interested in one-way communication. Again, the main responsibility falls on the agency, on its attitudes and on the way it trains its nonprofessionals. It must make forcefully clear its disapproval of negative attitudes toward the poor—and that it is not there to alibi for the status quo but to help change the institutions not providing service.

Acceptance of authority. The poor, and the indigenous personnel who come from them, have usually had little experience dispensing or respecting authority except within the family and the church. Formal authority came from the alien "outside"— they received, they did not dispense it—and they usually resisted, resented or were at least apathetic toward it. It is not authority itself which is alien to them, merely its identification with an outside, bureaucratic, unsympathetic source. Trust in the good will and intentions of the agency is primary. Once the indigenous personnel really trust the intentions and techniques of their professional superiors, they will accept and exercise authority.

To the extent that they come to feel that the agency is genuinely concerned with "their people," to that extent will they begin to feel differently regarding the acceptance of authority. (This point is nicely illustrated in trade unions where large numbers of low-income people have accepted authority positions as shop stewards.) As a matter of fact, when they do accept an authority role, they often carry it out very well because of their positive traditionalistic and religious association with authority, and because they do not find it inconsistent with informality and closeness to people. They do not have the ambivalence toward authority *per se* that characterizes many middle-class people, who find it very difficult to execute authority without being authoritarian and cannot easily combine authority with warmth. The low-income individual, while he resents the bureaucratic authority of the power structure, does not resist authority or power as such. Consequently, if he gets past the initial block concerning his use of formal authority, he may dispense it very rationally and smoothly.

Another deterrent, however, to his comfortable use of authority lies in his limited know-how and lack of actual practice in the use of authority. Hence, it is extremely important to provide practice in a permissive setting (such as role-playing typical authority situations; for example, leading a meeting), and to make sure that the nonprofessional acquires detailed knowledge and know-how regarding every phase of the assignment he is to carry out.

Overoptimism turning into defeatism. At the beginning the nonprofessional is often enthusiastic, hopeful, eager to effect change. Tempered by the realities of the situation, these are very useful qualities; but after encountering frustration, inefficiency, apparently insurmountable apathy and delay, it is very easy for him to swing to the opposite extreme and become despondent, impatient or bitter. A middle ground is difficult to find. The fact is that professionals tend to be too cautious, and they need the enthusiasm of the nonprofessional, which should therefore not be dampened too much. The best approach, probably, is to set up a plan of operation, including a timetable which includes setbacks, and against which a worker may realistically measure his progress. He should be warned of difficulties—but realistically, as obstacles which should be planned for and overcome rather than as terrible hazards.

The nonprofessional must not only relate to his clients—he must also somehow work out a satisfactory relationship with his professional colleagues and supervisors. It is no secret that friction exists. Many professionals have difficulty accepting the idea of the worker who does not have the appropriate initials after his name. ("Is he a social worker?" "Is he a college graduate?") Or they have trouble accepting the idea that such "amateurs" should be more than hewers of wood and drawers of water for them.

Nonprofessionals, of course, are often unsure of themselves and sensitive to slights. They may see in the professionals those old enemies of the poor—middle-class bureaucracy, self-righteousness and hypocrisy.

Sometimes small, apparently incidental things lead to estrangement: frequent changes, or the lack of proper working quarters; uncertainty by the nonprofessional as to his status and position; his frequent nonacceptance at the beginning of a program by professionals in other agencies.

All this points to at least three recommendations:

1. Institutions employing nonprofessionals have to carefully define their roles, tasks, competencies to all professional groups with whom these nonprofessionals will be in contact—both within and without the agency.
2. Careful training and preparation of the nonprofessional

before much contact with professionals anywhere. The nonprofessionals should know their roles, rights, responsibilities, the regulations and directives that are relevant to them; their skills and confidence should be developed before they have much professional contact. Working with their "cases" may be the easier role; working with professional colleagues may take more training.

3. Perhaps some indigenous nonprofessionals, who because of style, skill or experience are more acceptable to professionals from other agencies, might serve as trail blazers, making ready a path for the less acceptable to follow.

Since much of the value of the indigenous nonprofessional arises from his spontaneity, pragmatism and generally "lower-class" approach, it is necessary that his training include and reflect these values. Rules the teacher might profitably follow:

1. *Play down the academic.* It is not understood, it interferes with the spontaneous, it tends to fossilize feeling, it creates anxiety and frustration, and it is generally contrary to the tone and facts of low-income life.

2. *Learn as far as possible by doing.* Field work should begin at the same time as orientation, so that the worker can make the connection between the two—and in practical terms.

3. *Use plenty of "role-playing."* This is an excellent teaching device for stimulating verbalization around what can be seen and experienced concretely. While the feeling tone or mood can and often should be informal, warm, humorous —the content should be well structured and definite. It is often assumed that role-playing is highly unstructured, open, and free. In part this is true, particularly in the early phase of setting the problem and mood. But in the middle and later phases (especially the role-training stage), where the effort is made to teach very specific behaviors, role-playing can be highly structured, reviewing in minute detail the various operations to be learned (such as how to run a meeting or organize a conference).

4. *Be explicit.* When training nonprofessionals or anyone else from a low-income background it is terribly important that

the teaching be extremely concrete. Use many illustrations; spell out details; make assumptions explicit. Repeat everything, do not take for granted that the students know anything you know, explain and summarize over and over again. Each time a concept is discussed the group leader must ask himself and the group, "What are the practical implications of the idea?" "How did we get the idea—on what concrete experience is it based?" Illustrations of the principle or concept should be sought from the group and/or given by the group leader in terms of the experience of these particular indigenous workers.

5. *Use the intensive team approach* to build strong group solidarity.

It should be remembered that the nonprofessional is moving toward a whole new pattern of life, both on and off the job. Much of the new is ambiguous and, to varying degrees, threatening. A parent aide who relates well to people and socializes well might still find it quite threatening to organize people in a neighborhood for a parents' meeting. A group of youngsters who were formerly delinquent might find it difficult to imagine themselves as recreation aides, child-care aides, research aides or whatever. The group that is developed in the training process can provide powerful reinforcement and encouragement in the building of the new skills, values and behavior. Arthur Pearl's work in the Community Apprentice Program at Howard University vividly illustrates the importance of the group in providing this support and reinforcement. (Arthur Pearl, "Youth in Lower Class Settings," presented at Fifth Symposium on Social Psychology, 1964, Norman, Oklahoma.) Moreover, in the terms of the helper principle each member of the group in assisting the other actually helps himself a great deal, and this contributes to the rehabilitative function involved in many of the nonprofessional positions. Some of the new jobs may not have a significant rehabilitative function but simply serve as job patterns. But where the nonprofessional person has previously been an unemployed youngster, a delinquent, an ADC mother, a public assistance client, a mental patient—the rehabilitative function is extremely important.

The increasing use of the indigenous nonprofessional is changing the face and pace of social work among the disadvantaged. In the next decade the ratio of professionals to nonprofessionals will change significantly. Perhaps the future will find each professional supervising and teaching five to eight nonprofessionals. The widespread employment of nonprofessionals in the helping professions can achieve the following objectives:

1. It can markedly reduce the manpower shortage in the social service fields;
2. It can help to derigidify the professions, allowing professionals to play their professional roles more fully;
3. It can provide more, better and nearer service for the poor;
4. It can rehabilitate many of the poor themselves through meaningful employment;
5. It can potentially provide millions of new jobs for the unemployed in social service jobs which are not likely to be automated out of existence.

The nonprofessionals are providing a long-sought key which is opening a wide door to more effective social work. Revolution may not be too extreme a term for these changes. But revolutions result in the most good only when their dynamics and limitations, their strengths and weaknesses, are properly understood.

Advocacy in the Ghetto

RICHARD A. CLOWARD and RICHARD M. ELMAN

There are 500,000 people in New York City living on welfare payments, but until November 1965 no delegation of public dependents had been received in the office of a commissioner of welfare for more than 30 years. (The last time was in the days of the Worker's Alliance, a union of recipients and public welfare workers.) Three decades had gone by since welfare recipients had presented their needs and their grievances directly to the man in charge. This is the story of events that led up to that meeting—a story of how social workers turned into advocates in order to secure their clients' rights from the welfare bureaucracy and of how recipients themselves began to organize for action. It suggests a pattern that can be used elsewhere in the country to deal with the daily problems of living under the welfare state.

In November 1962 a social worker from Mobilization for Youth and one assistant moved into an unoccupied storefront at 199 Stanton Street on New York's Lower East Side. It was located in an apartment building which did not then rent to Negroes, Puerto Ricans or persons on welfare.

Across the street was a *bodega*. Another grocery, down the

block, was the principal numbers racket drop for the area. MFY put some chairs and couches in the brightly painted waiting room in the front of the store. Then a sign was painted on the front windows: CENTRO DE SERVICO AL VECENDARIO... NEIGHBORHOOD SERVICE CENTER. On the door was lettered: WALK IN! Many Stanton Street residents, 14 percent of whom are on public assistance, accepted the invitation. They were invited to describe their problems. The MFY workers soon found that the lengthy verbal charge sheet made by people against the hostile environment in which they were forced to live, could be distilled into a grievance against "welfare."

It soon became clear to branch director Joseph Kreisler that unresolved problems with public welfare were a crucial factor in the instability of life along Stanton Street. If people didn't have enough welfare they weren't able to pay their bills at the grocer. If they didn't get their welfare checks on time, they would be in trouble with their landlords. If welfare didn't provide money for school clothing, they would have to keep their children home from school and would have difficulties with the authorities. This day-to-day relationship with the welfare bureaucracy was making people bitter and angry and punitive toward one another.

But, if the pattern seemed clear to Kreisler and his supervisor, Sherman Barr, those who complained most bitterly were not able to pinpoint the sources of their misery quite so precisely. As one man put it, "I feel that the City of New York has abandoned me." Others told of harrowing experiences with welfare officials as if such dealings were the way things should be. Since they had never been led to expect any better treatment from such an agency, they had no awareness of their rights under the law.

It became necessary, therefore, for the MFY workers to assure people that they did have rights, and to demonstrate that their rights could be upheld and defended without recriminations. Such a determination by the workers often required a dogmatic conviction about injustice. One of them put it this way:

> When I think that Mrs. Cortez hasn't gotten any money for her rat allowance I sometimes want to throw up my hands and say: What difference does it make? Why should people in this day and age have rat allowances? (A New York City

welfare policy allows slum families extra allowances toward their utility bills to offset the cost of keeping their lights burning all night as a deterrence against rats.) But when I realize that it isn't just the rat allowance ... that it's a total system of oppressiveness and disrespect for people, why then I've got to get her that rat allowance. I've got to help her get as many things as possible.

Few of the workers were at first so dogmatic. Kreisler, for example, was a veteran of the public welfare systems of New York and Maine, familiar with the savagery of some welfare policies and the Pecksniffian quality of others (such as a New York City regulation which makes it mandatory to mail clients' checks out late before a weekend so that they will not have the money to spend on drink). But even he had his eyes opened by the volume of abuses that were recorded by workers through the testimony of their clients.

BUCKING THE BUREAUCRACY

In its first six months of operation, 199 Stanton Street received more than 200 families from an immediate three-or-four block radius who attested to their antagonistic relationship with the Department of Welfare. Through the neighborhood grapevine many soon learned to come directly to Stanton Street after an affront at one of the local welfare centers. In addition, of the nonwelfare families who came during those first six months, nearly two-thirds listed "insufficient income" as their principal problem, which meant, in many cases, that they were not getting welfare benefits even though they were eligible. At 199 Stanton Street the social workers discovered that the problems of their clients were so tied to the bureaucratic workings of the city that they could keep their storefront open profitably only from 9 to 5 on weekdays, the normal working hours of public agencies.

This came as a distinct surprise to supervisory personnel at MFY. They had originally hoped to bring their workers more intimately in touch with the day-to-day affairs of their clients departing from traditional psychotherapeutic methods and offering instead specific and practical advice on problems of health, housing, welfare, education and employment. But even here they saw their chief function as liaisons between clients and agencies; they did not yet realize that even these concrete activities would fail to resolve issues between the poor and the welfare state. Many workers soon found, however, that they had to do something more than refer, advise and counsel if they were to get results. They were being called upon to take sides in a pervasive dispute between their clients and an agency of the welfare state. When they refused to do so, their clients abandoned them. A new practice soon evolved which came to be known as *advocacy*.

An advocate in this context is one who intervenes between an agency of government and his client to secure an entitlement or right which has thus far been obscured or denied. To act effectively, the advocate must have sufficient knowledge of the law and of the public agency's administrative procedures to recognize injustice when it occurs and then seek a solution in harmony with his client's interests. In practice, the Stanton Street advocates often found that they had to instruct the representatives of welfare agencies in the law and how it should be interpreted. One of the advocate's most demanding tasks was to serve notice on his opposite number within the welfare bureaucracy that he was prepared to move a notch further up the hierarchy if justice was not tendered on the present level.

Thus the advocates listened to endless tales of woe. They counted up scores of welfare budgets to detect possible under-budgeting. They placed telephone calls to a great number of functionaries and sometimes accompanied clients when they went to see these people in person. They argued and they cajoled. They framed rebuttals to cases put forward by welfare, but they also charged negligence.

They attacked as well as defended. When, for example, a Stanton Street woman was charged with child neglect, the alert worker was able to show that she had been consistently under-budgeted for more than a year, making her efforts at successful child-rearing virtually impossible. When another client was evicted for nonpayment of rent, the worker attempted to force welfare to make the payment—because he could show that it had failed repeatedly in its legal obligation to do so.

But, whether their threats were applied with politeness or out of anger, out of careful manipulation or a blustering disregard for the sensibilities of their opposite numbers, the primary force of such advocacy was in serving notice upon the low-level employee that he would be held responsible for his actions to his supervisor and on up the line. Thus advocacy was the bludgeon by which this city agency was made responsive to a portion of its Lower East Side constituency. At 199 Stanton Street the workers came to serve as surrogates for their clients with the bureaucratically arranged world outside the welfare ghetto.

This often-militant advocacy was always carried on with a calculated informality. Young people were not discouraged from idling about the place, any client was free to come and go as he pleased; parties were held on holidays; neighborhood people were employed as janitors, clerks and translators. Many of the professional workers and case aides were either Negro or Puerto Rican, and there was little attention given to any differentiation of duties according to professional status. Moreover, the center managed to keep up an active and informative interviewing referral practice when clients came in with requests for other kinds of service. When a client came for help with welfare it was always possible for him to receive a loan or even a small outright gift of cash to tide him over while his case was being adjudicated. An effort was also made to keep a supply of clean used clothing on hand for those whose requests from welfare might take more than a few hours to resolve.

However, even though as much as $600 was given out in some months in small grants, the major reason that people were drawn to the center was that the workers took sides. They were willing to put themselves out to uphold their clients' rights under the welfare state. One Puerto Rican mother put it this way: "When you go alone to welfare they treat you like dirt. When you go with a social worker it's different."

LITIGATION—NOT INDIGNATION

After a year it became clear to the administration of MFY that the indignation of the social worker was not sufficient protection against the injustices of the social welfare state. So the agency established a free legal service to take referrals from neighborhood centers such as the storefront on Stanton Street. These attorneys applied themselves to eviction proceedings in public and private housing; they dealt with consumer frauds and other specialized areas of practice among the poor. But they also began to challenge decisions concerning welfare clients where the facts were at issue, or where actions had been taken in seeming violation of the intent of the law.

As a case in point, one might cite the New York State Welfare Abuses Act, passed in 1962 as a compromise measure to satisfy demands that New York bar public assistance to applicants from out of state. It was clearly stipulated by the legislators that only persons who could be shown to have come to New York for the express purpose of collecting relief could be lawfully denied such a benefit. In actual practice, however, the new resident's mere appearance at a welfare center to apply for relief was often taken as sufficient justification to deny him benefits.

By 1964 four attorneys were employed full time at MFY on cases brought to their attention by the social workers. It was because these lawyers threatened litigation that the local Department of Welfare center no longer invoked the Welfare Abuses Act as a matter of course. It was fear of litigation which prompted the department to abandon its policy of after-midnight intrusions on the residences of AFDC mothers to detect the presence of males—a policy which seemed a clear-cut violation of the normal guarantees of privacy. The workers at Stanton Street were encouraged to bring those cases to the attention of MFY attorneys through which the legality of administrative acts could be contested in open hearings, so that precedents could be established.

Nevertheless, the lawyers also spent a good deal of their time advising workers and clients about how to adopt lawful and proper strategies to exploit those rights which did seem vested. Working closely with the social workers, the lawyers contested capricious eligibility rulings and attempted to reinstate eligibles whose benefits had been arbitrarily terminated. At times they argued the merits of the case. At other times they argued that the law had been perverted by bad administrative policies. The lawyers were prepared to represent the clients at the formal appeals tribunals of the state Department of Social Welfare, but they found that a majority of client grievances did not need to come before such "fair hearings." Often, just a telephone call from an MFY attorney expressing interest in a particular case served to persuade a functionary that he was acting without respect to a person's rights.

Because of the Department of Welfare's desire to avoid establishing precedents and hence to settle out of court, the MFY legal service was able to litigate only a small percentage of the cases it was called in on, but its impact upon the legal vacuum within the welfare ghetto was impressive. Even after the addition of this free legal service, the workers at Stanton Street continued to be confronted with the bulk of cases requiring immediate advocacy; but they could now defend their clients' rights reinforced by the legal expertise of Edward Sparer (the first MFY legal director) and his associates. Moreover, they were able to increase their sophistication about welfare law through their continuing association with the attorneys, and they passed on some of this education to their opposite numbers in the welfare bureaucracy.

Even the clients benefited educationally from the program. Many had never before had any contacts with attorneys, except, perhaps, as their adversaries. Now these attorneys were representing them in adversary proceedings against the Department of Welfare, and they became aware of the power which proper representation bestows upon the private citizen. As one AFDC mother stated: "I trust the lawyers more than anybody because they would make a living if there were no poor people." When a bitter and prolonged strike afflicted the Department of Welfare in the winter of 1964-1965, some MFY workers and clients from Stanton Street demonstrated in support of the welfare workers to signify that their complaints were against laws and policies, not individuals.

By the summer of 1963 MFY had established three other neighborhood centers along the Lower East Side. The agency's supervisory staff decided to solicit even more clients by publicizing its services through handbills, posters and mass meetings. Some workers had also begun to seek out clients in distress, among other ways by reading newspaper accounts in the Spanish-language press. The strategy of the centers was now fixed. They were given a definite set of priorities for intervention with city agencies, of which Welfare was to be the preeminent target.

This increasing attention to the advocacy tactic meant that the workers had to contend with increasing antagonism from the Welfare Department. The commissioner was angered, for example, by the threats of aggressive court action against Welfare. The lower-echelon functionaries were angered by their harassment by MFY and would often respond with open hostility to calls from Stanton Street employees. "When I go to Welfare," one Stanton Street worker declared, "I don't wait around for the stall. If I don't get treated with respect, I start hollering for the supervisor." Another said: "Any way you cut it they are the enemy." Perhaps this explains what one welfare worker meant when she described MFY's staff as "rude, angry, and nonprofessional." The accusation was also continually being made that some MFY workers lacked information about public-welfare policies in taking on their advocacy positions. But, since many Stanton Street workers were former welfare employees, it seems more reasonable to suppose that they were merely placing more liberal interpretations upon existing welfare regulations. Where, for example, some welfare caseworkers might use improvidence to justify not making an additional grant for a client, the Stanton Street workers would insist upon the person's legal right to such an entitlement beyond his supposed character defect.

One veteran employee with more than 30 years in the Department of Welfare was critical of the MFY policy of giving money to people on some occasions rather than forcing Welfare to make these payments. However, though she found some of MFY's advocacy tactics "a little hard to bear," she was generally appreciative of the effects. "If we were doing our job," she said, "you wouldn't need any neighborhood centers . . . and if there were more neighborhood centers like this in the city of New York," she added, "we might have to begin to do a better job. . . . I learned what my workers were doing with some clients from the neighborhood service center. I might never have known otherwise." When this same person subsequently retired from the Department of Welfare, she was hired as a consultant by MFY to help cut through the knotty complex of rules and regulations by which people on Stanton Street were being governed. "What this proves to me," said one MFY staff member, "is that you have to work 30 years in the department to be able to get people what they are entitled to . . . and they expect our clients to just walk in and apply. . . . "

Such comments reflected the increasing hostility between Welfare and the workers on Stanton Street. The workers also showed a tendency to exhibit hostility toward and impatience with their clients, who by now had transferred some of their previous dependency on Welfare to the storefront on Stanton Street. "Can't these people do anything themselves?" was a phrase frequently heard among the workers.

Many of the workers seemed to be developing a resentment at having to perform rudimentary "nonprofessional" services on behalf of their clients over and over again, and some of the clients were also restless, spurred on, in part, by their activities in various MFY social-action programs. Presently the program heads, Barr and Kreisler, began to wonder whether, if the clients were given staff support and encouragement, they could begin to take over some of these practical efforts to deal with the welfare system. They reasoned, for example, that if 50 clients all needed the same items of clothing it might be more effective to make one request on behalf of 50 rather than 50 individual requests. They reasoned, too, that this strategy might coerce the Department of Welfare into making certain of its grants more automatic, or, rather, less discretionary.

So, after three years, the center on Stanton Street decided to hire a community organizer to bring people together around their most commonly held interest—public welfare.

ORGANIZING ON STANTON STREET

In the hot summer months Stanton Street people rarely go away on vacations. They start worrying about the cold months ahead. They know if they do not begin to bother their welfare workers about clothing for the winter, their requests may never be fulfilled. Thus, in the late summer of 1965, they came to make their usual requests to the advocate at 199 Stanton Street. Would the workers talk to welfare? Would they tell them what they needed? To their surprise they were advised to go next door and speak to the Committee of Welfare Families.

The Committee of Welfare Families was hardly more than a name at the time, although the concept of community action was certainly not novel to people on Stanton Street. Many of the initial membership cadre had already participated in rent strikes and civil rights demonstrations, but, where these were activities of short duration, the committee hoped to be an ongoing organization. Aside from a few of the local women, who had been most active previously, there was an MFY attorney and social-work organizer, Ezra Birnbaum. Birnbaum went to great efforts to make the group appear to be like any other voluntary membership organization, but, in fact, the women continually referred to him as their "social worker."

THE COAT CHECK

When clients went to see Birnbaum and the neighborhood women who were working with him, they were told that the group would bring together Negroes and Puerto Ricans who had common problems with welfare. If they wanted to be part of the group, they were asked to make surveys of their winter clothing needs and then bring them to the committee, which would attempt to act as the bargaining agents for all of them. Within a month over 90 families had agreed to the procedure, and the first tentative strategies were proposed.

"We chose the winter clothing issue," Birnbaum has since pointed out, "because it was something that genuinely concerned people ... because they had so many small children ... and because the injustice was so blatant. Many people hadn't gotten coats in six or seven years. Here was an issue we could exploit which would genuinely benefit our people. ... "

The winter clothing issue also went to the heart of the perennially nagging question of what constituted a welfare entitlement. Every welfare family is budgeted a very small sum semi-monthly with which to augment clothing supplies. Invariably this sum is used for ordinary living expenses because grants for food are so low. In addition, it was department policy to allow special grants of approximately $150 a year per family for winter clothing, but these grants were usually not given out unless requested, and, even then, the family usually got less than the full amount. In October 1965, individual workers at all the welfare centers serving residents of the MFY area began to receive neat, concise letters from their clients. It was clear that they had all been prepared by one agency and mailed out simultaneously, but, since they were written as individual requests, it was not immediately clear to welfare what was behind this sudden flurry of letters which read:

> I would like to request winter clothing for my children and myself. I would appreciate it if you would grant this request as quickly as possible, as the weather is cold at this time. My family is in need of the following items of winter clothing. . . .

There followed individual itemized requests for coats, children's snowsuits, coveralls, boots, scarves, woolen skirts. All these requests had been certified by the committee as being in accord with current welfare schedules. When, after a few weeks, the welfare caseworkers did not reply, a follow-up letter was sent, with copies to supervisory personnel at welfare. When this effort also netted scant results, the committee as a group wrote to Commissioner Louchheim:

> We, as members of the Committee of Welfare Families of the Lower East Side, have written letters to our investigators requesting winter clothing . . . . The first 21 letters were mailed between October 12th and October 15th. Of these, only 9 have received any money at all, and none of these nine have been given enough money to keep their families warm this winter. *More important, the other 12 families have received no money at all!*
>
> We feel that we are being neglected—especially since many of our investigators haven't even been in touch with us to find out about the seriousness of the situation.
>
> Winter is here; our children are cold. Many of us are

unable to keep clinic appointments because we do not have proper clothing. Many of our children have caught colds which can lead to other serious illnesses. Some of our children haven't been to school since the weather turned cold.

In most years, many of us have had to wait until December, January, or even later to buy our winter clothing. This year, we're not willing to wait that long and see our children have to wear thin summer clothing when it gets below freezing. That is why we asked Mobilization for Youth to help us this year.

Commissioner Louchheim—we feel we have waited long enough to receive our winter clothing . . . . We need your help in securing winter clothing for all our members before the weather gets any colder.

We request that our meeting with you be held within the next 3 days.

The committee waited three days. When the commissioner did not respond to their letter, they were prepared to picket at his office but were prevailed upon by MFY to send a telegram instead:

You received letter from us on Monday November 15 requesting meeting with you to discuss our members needs for winter clothing. We received no reply. Our children are cold. Winter is here. Our investigators have not answered our letters or have not given us enough money to keep children warm. We need your help before weather gets colder. We will be at your office to meet with you Tuesday November 23 1:30 p.m.

That same day the commissioner replied by telegram (after attempting to telephone) that he would be able to meet with the committee on Friday, November 26, at 1:30 p.m. In the meantime he would endeavor to get information on each of the cases specified in the documents attached to the committee's original ultimatum.

The meeting which took place between the welfare commissioner and the Committee of Welfare Families was, in the commissioner's own words, the first such meeting between a commissioner and a New York City client group in over 30 years. All of the welfare recipients had been well briefed by Birnbaum on what they would say to the commissioner, but, in fact, protest proved to be unnecessary. The commissioner quickly agreed that all members of the committee who were entitled to winter clothing would receive it, and he further formalized the bargaining status of the committee of Lower East Side families by outlining a formal grievance procedure. Clients were to continue to make their requests either by mail or in person through their workers at the various welfare centers. He would thenceforth instruct all workers to acknowledge the receipt of these requests immediately and in writing. If, within ten days, no reply was received to an individual client's request, the committee was free to contact predesignated liaison personnel at each of the welfare centers serving the neighborhood, who would be empowered to act so that their grievances could be corrected.

FACING NEW ISSUES

The hard-pressed membership of the Committee of Welfare Families was quick to interpret their meeting with the commissioner as a victory. By agreeing to consult with them as a group about their needs, he had implicitly recognized for perhaps the first time in their careers as welfare clients that they had a legitimate corporate interest in helping to determine the rules of their own dependency. In the days that followed many of these families began to receive generous checks from the Department of Welfare to purchase winter clothing.

There were further meetings arranged with the designated liaison personnel at the various welfare centers to arrange bargaining procedures. The women were delighted that they could dictate just who and how many of their number could be in attendance at these formal procedures. Thus, when the department tried to insist that only members of the committee could meet with welfare officials, the women held firm in their insistence that the committee could designate anybody it chose to represent it at these meetings, and the Department of Welfare was forced to give in on this point. And, as most of the Lower East Side families began to have their winter clothing needs satisfied, the women decided to take up other issues such as budgeting. They requested that all members ask for budgets from their caseworkers if they did not already have them and, if they did have them, to bring them to the committee where they could be properly scrutinized.

The committee also began to elect officers. It designated subcommittees to investigate various new problem areas having to do with their welfare dependency. The leadership attended briefing sessions with MFY's attorneys in an effort to acquire a better understanding of their legal rights. Gradually, as the natural leadership potentials of some of the women emerged more clearly, MFY's paid organizer began to function more as an adviser than as a leader. One of the women gave this explanation for the process:

> Some of us know we are going to be on welfare the rest of our lives. They know it and we know it. So it's about time to act like we know it. It's about time we started acting like human beings.

For the unemployed or underemployed men who have still not been organized, Stanton Street's workers have much work to do in beginning to provide them with the entitlements which they have thus far been denied. "It wouldn't be so bad living here," one of these men told us, "if you were rich. We're not rich. All we have is the welfare. That means freezing in the winter and boiling in the summer. It means living on credit when we can't afford it. It means lying. It means doing without . . . . When I come home in the evening my wife has been at Bellevue which is uptown and maybe at Church Street, all the way across town, and I'm wondering where she got the money for the carfare . . . ."

The storefront on Stanton Street has been in existence a little less than four years, and its work has increased tenfold, with two offices added. It is still too early to evaluate its permanent contributions to life in the community. Its powers have been limited. It has not yet been able to change substantially the terms of economic dependency when it still seems to be the consensus among most legislators and their constituents that such dependency is to be discouraged, abhored and punished.

Many more people from Stanton Street are on welfare than before. The storefront's clients are better clothed, better housed and better fed than they were four years ago. Many now have telephones, quite a few have washing machines and television sets.

Are they better people? Are they worse? Such questions seem like the supreme irrelevancy. For if they are not better for their improved economic circumstances, the society is better for their actions against it. Democracy cannot be said to exist where government is allowed to oppress its citizens so blatantly.

Storefront Lawyers
in San Francisco

JEROME E. CARLIN

On April 22, 1968, a United States district court invalidated California's residency requirements for persons seeking public assistance. Previously, applicants had to be residents of the state for at least one year before they could become eligible for benefits. According to the *San Francisco Chronicle* of April 25:

> The Reagan Administration will try to overturn last week's landmark Federal Court decision. . . . Health and Welfare Director Spencer Williams said the decision would add another 24 million dollars to welfare costs, and adds about 6,900 families and 12,000 other individuals to the welfare rolls.

On December 28, 1968 the *New York Times* printed the following story datelined San Francisco:

> POOR WIN VICTORY IN A HOUSING SUIT
> COURT HALTS COAST RENEWAL UNTIL
> RESIDENTS BACK PLAN
> A Federal Court has halted the funding of a $100 million urban renewal project here with a decision that is expected to affect similar projects across the country and aid the

poor in establishing legal rights for themselves. The court order prohibits the Department of Housing and Urban Development from supplying additional funds for the project until an acceptable plan has been approved for relocating uprooted families. . . . In taking the action to court, the Western Addition community group was [represented] by the San Francisco Neighborhood Legal Assistance Foundation. . . .

On August 12, 1969, the following appeared on the front page of the *Chronicle:*

BAY JUDGE ORDERS BOOST IN WELFARE

More money must be paid in rent allotments to people in the biggest welfare program in San Francisco and Alameda Counties, a Superior Court judge ruled here yesterday. Judge Alvin E. Weinberger further ordered the State Department of Social Welfare to take steps that will produce another increase in rent money across the State in a few months time.

He acted in a law suit brought by the San Francisco Neighborhood Legal Assistance Foundation on behalf of all persons receiving Aid to Families with Dependent Children (AFDC) in the two counties. Foundation lawyers charged that most AFDC clients are getting a monthly rent allotment less than the actual rent they are paying. Under State law, the Department's standards for rent must insure "safe, healthful housing." And the Department's own regulations require that its rent standards be based on "current actual costs for housing."

Judge Weinberger said the state and counties must live up to their own laws and regulations. . . .

The total sum required statewide would be $19 million per year. . . . This would pay the actual rent. How much more would be required after the Department hearings, to pay for safe, healthful housing is a matter of dispute. But the total increase could reach $50 million.

These have been some of the more newsworthy activities of a new type of professional organization. The San Francisco Neighborhood Legal Assistance Foundation is a federally financed, community-controlled legal service agency which has been aggressively advocating the rights of the poor since it began operation in October 1966. It is one of about 300 agencies throughout the United States funded by the Office of Economic Opportunity (OEO) to deliver more effective legal services to the nation's poor.

Since the foundation has probably gone farther than almost any of the other legal service agencies in carrying out this mandate and has served as a model for many other programs in the United States, it may be instructive to examine what it set out to accomplish, the extent to which it was able to achieve its objectives, and the problems it encountered. One of the most important issues that emerges from such an inquiry is the apparent incompatibility of the two principal goals of the organization: control by the client community and institutional change.

Having participated in the creation of the foundation, and having served as its head for the first three years of its existence, I will be presenting an insider's view that may well be biased and self-serving. I trust that my training as a sociologist and lawyer will serve to curb any major excesses.

The foundation is a private, nonprofit corporation with a governing board consisting of representatives of the local bar associations, law schools and the poverty community. The bylaws require that a majority of the board members be selected by the five poverty areas in San Francisco and that the board must also have a majority of attorneys. This is accomplished by having each poverty area select at least one lawyer representative. The board hires the coordinator, who is the chief executive officer of the foundation, and the directing attorney (chief counsel) for each of the five neighborhood law offices. The coordinator is responsible for carrying out the overall policies of the organization (which are determined by him and the board), for allocating resources among the various offices and departments and for hiring and supervising administrative and legal staff at the headquarters office (Main Office) of the foundation. Each chief counsel hires and fires his own staff of attorneys, secretaries, law students and aides.

In the fall of 1969 there were more than 120 paid staff persons working at the foundation, including 50 full-time attorneys and about 30 part-time law students. In addition, about 25 law students and ten social work students spent varying amounts of time at the foundation for credit under faculty supervision. Numerous private attorneys, on a volunteer basis, interview clients in the evening at a neighborhood office, make court appearances on default divorces or perform other services.

The staff attorneys are generally young—about one-fourth came to the foundation right out of law school (mostly through the OEO-funded Reginald Heber Smith Fellowship and VISTA programs); only about one-third had at least four years of practice experience before joining the foundation. Most attended top-ranking law schools; approximately one-third graduated from an Ivy League law school (Harvard, Yale or Columbia). One out of four foundation attorneys is from a minority group; there are nine black lawyers.

The yearly budget of the foundation is over a million dollars, practically all of which comes from OEO in the form of an annual grant channeled through the local poverty agency, the Economic Opportunity Council of San Francisco (EOC). Although the foundation must deal both with OEO and EOC, it is essentially the former, and particularly the Legal Services Division within OEO, that has played the principal role in articulating and enforcing general guidelines for the foundation (and other legal service agencies) and evaluating performance.

OEO seeks to shape and control programs and promote certain national objectives, not only through the funding process, but also by means of nationwide training programs, research and back-up centers and fellowship programs that place bright young law school graduates in funded agencies. Many foundation lawyers (particularly those working in the Main Office) maintain close ties with other poverty lawyers throughout the country by taking an active part in these OEO programs as well as meetings of the National Legal Aid and Defender Association (which has become largely dominated by OEO lawyers) and other newly developed associations of poverty lawyers. In the national poverty law movement, OEO's Legal Services (in alliance with the

American Bar Association, if not all or even most state and local bar associations) continues to play a leading role, giving solid support (with only few lapses) to program goals generally more advanced than most funded agencies are willing or able to realize.

Every month over a thousand new clients come into the five neighborhood offices of the foundation. A large majority of the clients are seeing a lawyer for the first time, most are on welfare, and half are in families with an annual income of less than $3,000 a year. About 15 percent of the clients are referred out—mainly to private attorneys or the public defender—because they fall above the foundation's income standard or they have a fee-producing or criminal case. The largest number of clients (about 30 percent) want help with a family problem, and half of these are seeking a divorce. The next biggest group are those having problems with administrative agencies: welfare, unemployment insurance, social security, immigration and naturalization (the bulk of the cases in the Chinatown Office) and the draft. Problems with landlords and merchants (and their collection agents) each constitute about 15 percent of the cases.

A major portion of the family cases, including all divorce matters, are referred to the Domestic Relations Unit, located at the Main Office, for more expeditious handling. This innovation has been adopted by a great many other programs and has contributed significantly to reducing the overall time and resources that need be devoted to this largely routine service.

The Main Office also houses a legal staff handling a limited number of cases that are selected because they raise major poverty issues in public housing, welfare, urban renewal and more recently in the consumer area. The cases are referred to the staff from community organization or neighborhood office lawyers. In time the Main Office attorneys have become specialists in the particular areas in which they work, in contrast with most attorneys in the neighborhood offices who, given the diversity of legal problems they have to deal with and the relatively little time they have to give any particular case, remain essentially general practitioners.

The foundation was largely the creation of Charles Baumbach, a politically astute young lawyer who put together a coalition of

white militant lawyers (primarily Jewish) and minority professionals (mainly black) who held positions in the local poverty
power structure. The founders had a common cause in their
insistence on neighborhood control of legal services.

For the lawyer-founders, community control was in part a
means of negating control by the organized bar which they felt
would be opposed to a more aggressive form of advocacy, one
that would seek to use the law as an instrument of social change.
The lawyers were also committed to altering the conventional
power relation between the poor and the agencies that purport to
serve them. Community control would create new opportunities
for the poor to participate in determining agency policy and
decisions, and this principle should also apply to legal service
programs for the poor, or so it was felt.

For their part, the neighborhood poverty leaders had just
fought and won a battle with the mayor for majority control of
the EOC by representatives from the "target" areas, and they
wanted control of the legal services component as well. Their
reasons were complex: in part they were simply extending the
demand for self-determination; in part they had learned to resent
the paternalism and insensitivity of traditional legal aid. But there
was also a desire to expand a new power base by gaining control
over jobs, services and other rewards for constituents.

Majority control of the board of directors by representatives
of the poor was one expression of the neighborhood leaders'
insistence on community control. Another was the very considerable autonomy given the neighborhood offices. The local leaders
envisioned that each of the poverty areas would in effect have its
own law firm. The chief counsel of the neighborhood office was
to be selected by the board, rather than the coordinator, and it
was assumed that the representatives on the board of a particular
neighborhood would have primary say in choosing the attorney
to head "their" office. Also, limiting the powers of coordinator
would, it was hoped, minimize racial and ethnic jealousies—given
the ethnic mix of San Francisco's poverty areas—and provide a
hedge against a bad director.

Community control was the unifying issue for the lawyers and
neighborhood leaders who established the foundation. It was also

the major issue in the foundation's sometimes bitter struggle with the legal establishment in San Francisco. After a year-long battle, the foundation won a stunning victory when it finally convinced OEO officials to fund it rather than the bar-supported Legal Aid Society of San Francisco. The foundation became the first OEO-funded legal service agency in the United States with majority control by representatives of the poverty community.

Although the neighborhood leaders expressed no particular views regarding the content of the legal program, the lawyer-founders had some very strong ideas about it. These ideas were derived from an analysis of traditional legal aid and some conceptions about law and social change. The lawyers wanted to create an agency that would not only provide remedial assistance to individual clients (albeit in a more sympathetic and aggressive fashion than legal aid), but would also work toward altering conditions that keep the poor powerless and victims of injustice. This aim was based in part upon a recognition of the impossibility, with limited resources, of handling more than a small fraction of the problems urgently calling for legal assistance, and the necessity, therefore, of a more "wholesale" approach. It rested also on the understanding that, as Jan Howard, Sheldon Messinger and I wrote in 1966,

> the legal problems of the poor . . . characteristically arise from systematic abuses embedded in the operation of various public and private agencies, affecting large numbers of similarly situated individuals. Effective solution of the problems may require the lawyer to direct his attention away from a particular claim or grievance to the broader interests and policies at stake, and away from the individual client to a class of clients, in order to challenge more directly and with greater impact certain structural sources of injustice.

Very generally speaking, we came in time to conceive of our mission in this way: to find leverage points in the system to bring about a redistribution of power and income more favorable to the poor. Two general approaches were developed: strategic advocacy and economic development. Under the first, we sought to enter into the variety of forums where the law is made and administered, to facilitate the development of new rights in areas where the law was vague or clearly biased against the poor, or to enforce existing law favorable to the poor which had remained unimplemented (e.g., enforcement of health and safety provisions of the housing code, prohibitions against fraud and misrepresentation in sale of consumer goods).

To a remarkable extent, it appeared that "the system"—be it welfare, urban renewal, private slum housing or the garment industry in Chinatown—could not operate successfully without breaking the law: the cost of compliance is generally greater than the operators of the system are willing to pay, especially since those most likely to be hurt have been least likely to complain. Consequently, we hoped that vigorous law enforcement might serve not only to redistribute income, but also to mount sufficient pressure to change the system.

The test for the efficacy of such activity was whether it would result in increasing the income or political bargaining power of a substantial number of poor persons. Litigation (with an emphasis on class suits) and administrative and legislative advocacy were the principal tools. In time, however, we learned that these measures, particularly court cases, by themselves were frequently ineffective unless combined with the mobilization of political support in the middle class as well as poverty communities.

By means of the second general approach we sought to promote entrepreneurial activity among ghetto residents. This came later and remained a subsidiary strategy.

Whatever else the foundation may have achieved, it gained a reputation in the community of being a tough advocate for the poor, of being willing to take on any and all opponents—police department, Housing Authority, United States Army, welfare department, used-car dealers, Redevelopment Agency, City Hall, board of education. In a skit presented at the Bar Association of San Francisco Annual Ball (December 1968), the following, written by an attorney member, was sung to the tune of "Glowworm":

> *We're from Neighborhood Legal Assistance*
> *We encourage draft resistance*
> *Nasty landlords are our nemesis*

We keep tenants on the premises
We give deadbeats our protection
To frustrate any debt collection
The laws we use are not on your shelf
Cause we make them up ourself

We soon recognized the importance of publicity in building a reputation: it has been said that we won more cases at press conferences than in the courts. We published our own newsletter which reached several thousand persons, mostly private attorneys in San Francisco, with reports of our more important and more interesting cases. We also made it a point to get our cases into the press. Some idea of the coverage, and the developing image, may be seen in the following:

> In one of the most unusual cases handled by the Foundation in recent weeks, 20-year-old Ted Townsend, who had been held for three months in the Presidio stockade as a suspected deserter, was freed after his Neighborhood Legal Assistance attorney pointed out . . . (*San Francisco Progress*, August 24, 1967).

> A poverty program lawyer has filed a complaint with the Public Utilities Commission, seeking to end Pacific Telephone's $25 deposit requirement for certain new customers (*Chronicle*, December 16, 1967).

> The Neighborhood Legal Assistance Foundation filed a suit that seeks to prevent San Francisco policemen from carrying guns while off duty (*Chronicle*, November 9, 1968).

> The San Francisco Neighborhood Legal Assistance Foundation has fired another salvo at the State Department of Social Welfare (*Examiner*, June 27, 1968).

> The unit [the Main Office legal staff] is illustrative both of the length to which the young attorneys in Legal Assistance will go to attempt to help their clients and of the crusading idealism of the men who operate it (*Examiner*, October 9, 1968).

> The Neighborhood Legal Assistance Foundation is seeking a

breakthrough in labor practices to make unions more responsive to the needs of their members, especially minority group members with language and cultural problems (*Argonaut*, October 26, 1968).

The San Francisco Neighborhood Legal Assistance Foundation has joined the legal fight against Rudolph Ford, the Daly City car dealer (*Examiner*, January 14, 1969).

A San Francisco draftee who couldn't get anybody to listen to him finally was heard by a Federal judge who ordered the army to discharge the youth. . . . After a year Bibbs got his story to . . . an attorney with the Neighborhood Legal Assistance Foundation who filed a federal court suit and got Bibbs discharged (*Chronicle*, March 12, 1969).

A quiet little war has been going on between the San Francisco Neighborhood Legal Assistance Foundation and the state over welfare recipients' rights . . . (*Chronicle*, March 17, 1969).

Realtor Walter H. Shorenstein was accused yesterday [in a suit filed by the San Francisco Neighborhood Legal Assistance Foundation] of using his position as president of the Recreation and Park Commission to push the destruction of the International Hotel (*Chronicle*, March 28, 1969).

Our reputation gave us needed leverage in dealing with landlords, merchants, collection agencies, used-car dealers and public agency officials. Often a phone call was all that was necessary; people knew that we meant business and would follow through—indeed we enraged many slumlords' attorneys, who accused us (sometimes in letters to their congressmen) of using taxpayers' money to harass them.

In assessing the clout we developed it must be said that we have primarily benefited particular clients for whom we have been able to get a better deal in bargaining with merchants, landlords, welfare officials and others. Although often gratifying for the lawyer and his client, the benefits are generally remedial and short-lived—very little is basically changed. Housing is a good example. In three years we probably handled at least 4,000 individual cases involving some kind of landlord-tenant dispute. We undoubtedly brought some solace and relief to many individual tenants by delaying an eviction or forcing a landlord to make some repairs. Nevertheless, in those same three years the housing situation for poor people in San Francisco has become a great deal worse. The stock of low-income housing has been further reduced through public and private renewal programs. If plans for the latest renewal project in the Yerba Buena District are not changed, there will be approximately 4,000 fewer units in the city, which means more doubling up or worse, because there are virtually no vacancies among low-income units. The bulk of the housing available to the poor is substandard (at least 60,000 units have been so labeled officially), and is deteriorating further. The waiting list for public housing went up to 5,000, at which point the Housing Authority stopped adding names. Rents have gone up with the decline in the housing stock and increasing taxes—in some areas they have doubled in the past few years. Against this background it might appear as though the foundation had made the process a little more humane without having any effect on the underlying machinery. But that is not quite the case.

There are two areas—redevelopment and welfare—in which we have made at least a small dent in the system, which may well mark the beginning of an even greater impact.

In surveying the general housing situation for the poor in San Francisco, it was clear that top priority had to be placed on preventing any further reduction in the stock of low-income housing. The principal offender in San Francisco, as in other parts of the United States, has been the federal urban renewal program administered through local redevelopment agencies. This program has proceeded on the understanding that there would be no enforcement of those provisions of the Federal Housing Act which require that persons displaced from a project area be relocated into safe, decent and sanitary housing at rents they can afford. If these provisions were to be enforced, then the renewal program would have to go into the business building low-income housing—and this it has never been willing or able to do. As a result, the program has produced a drastic net decline in housing for the poor and has substantially worsened slum conditions.

In 1966 redevelopment was on the move again in San Francisco after nearly a two-year lull caused by the voters' approval of the anti-fair housing Proposition 14. The Redevelopment Agency was eager to proceed with its plans to demolish approximately 4,500 dwelling units of predominantly low-cost housing in the Western Addition, thereby displacing close to 10,000 persons—mostly poor and black. Failure of the agency to comply with the relocation provisions of the Federal Housing Act would provide, we hoped, the necessary leverage to challenge the project. (Not only was the relocation plan patently deficient—given San Francisco's unbelievably tight low-income housing market and the absence of any provisions for constructing new housing for displacees—but it turned out that the Department of Housing and Urban Development [HUD] had been honoring agency requisitions for financing the project without having first given its approval of the agency's relocation plan—a clear and gross violation of federal law.) The major obstacle that we faced was the fact that the courts had, unfortunately, refused to monitor federal urban renewal programs on behalf of project residents, on the theory that persons whose homes were being destroyed did not have sufficient stake in the outcome of litigation to give them standing to sue and that such suits involved technical matters too complex for the courts to get into. Even though public officials might be violating the law to the grievous detriment of thousands of poor residents forced out of their homes into even worse circumstances, the courts refused to open their doors to hear these complaints. The principle hurdle, then, was the court itself. Before anything else could be done we had to establish for our clients a most basic right—the right to be heard before a judicial tribunal.

A year and a day after the suit was filed in conjunction with the NAACP Legal Defense Fund—and 16 months after filing an administrative protest with HUD—the court finally reached a decision on the jurisdictional question: it found that our clients had standing to challenge the legality of the agency's relocation plan and issued a preliminary injunction bringing the renewal project in the Western Addition to a grinding halt. This was clearly a landmark decision; it finally brought the federal renewal program under the scrutiny of judicial review, and for the first time in the United States a renewal project had been stopped in midstream.

The case had been brought on behalf of the Western Addition Community Organization (WACO), a federation of grass roots neighborhood organizations, put together a couple of years earlier by a Student Nonviolent Coordinating Committee organizer to fight the second round of redevelopment in the Western Addition (the first round had been decisively lost—only a handful of families out of the many thousands previously residing in the area ever returned). As a result of the court victory, WACO and the residents of the project area were at last given a voice in the decisions and plans so vitally affecting their lives—both in the sense of having gained entree into the court and also by establishing a viable bargaining position with the Redevelopment Agency. Although the injunction was later dissolved by the court, the Redevelopment Agency had been significantly shaken—and a new and broader-based coalition emerged in the Western Addition which, under agreement with the agency, became an official participant in the renewal process.

Pressure on the Redevelopment Agency has been kept up as projects begin to move in other areas. The Yerba Buena project, which calls for the destruction of 4,000 housing units to make way for a new commercial complex, was also challenged by the foundation in a federal court suit. The clients, who are generally old as well as poor, have literally no place to go. The fight with the Redevelopment Agency, particularly in Yerba Buena, brought the foundation into a head-on confrontation with the San Francisco power structure, and the pressure began to mount, especially from City Hall. Nevertheless, the political alliances that had been forged in support of our clients' interests—including our allies among respectable middle-class groups and civic organizations—held firm. And once again, and far more rapidly than before, a federal court order was issued temporarily halting relocation of residents.

What then have we accomplished? We have at least slowed down the rate of destruction of low-income housing by public and private agencies. (By saving the International Hotel, which houses the remnant of the Filipino community in San Francisco, from demolition by private developers, we were able to extend some of the principles established in the WACO case into the private sector.) We have also helped fashion a legal-political force that the Redevelopment Agency and the city power structure will have to bargain with in determining housing policies for San Francisco. And we have provided hard evidence that in the area of redevelopment the arbitrary exercise of public power by local authorities and the federal government can be checked.

The other area in which the foundation has made some progress in its goal of institutional change is welfare. To begin with, we have enabled many more poor people to obtain public assistance: at least 60,000 people became eligible to receive welfare benefits as a result of our suit that invalidated California's residency requirement. We also prevented the cutoff of close to 2,000 needy persons from general assistance as an economy move by the San Francisco Department of Social Services. The foundation, moreover, has won several court decisions which, if and when they are implemented, will substantially increase dollar benefits to recipients. In the *Ivy* case the Superior Court ordered that rent allotments for AFDC recipients in San Francisco and Alameda counties be raised immediately to cover actual rentals (this will add about $19 million when extended statewide) and that a new list of rent allotments be issued reflecting the cost of safe and sanitary housing as required by state law (and this could add at least $30 million more). In the *Nesbitt* case (which we brought with the Alameda County Legal Aid Society), the court held that the state Department of Social Welfare was violating recent state and federal regulations which, as an encouragement to seek employment, exempt a certain portion of the earnings of working recipients in calculating their welfare grant. As a result, it was estimated that working recipients were getting approximately $30 a month less than they were entitled to. Enforcement of this decision could increase payments to recipients by about $9 million. In the *Kaiser* case, also brought with the Alameda County Legal Aid Society, the federal court declared unconstitutional a California statute placing a ceiling on the amount of money that could be granted to AFDC recipients, a ceiling that was actually lower than the state's own determination of the minimum required for subsistence.

Insofar as we have sought to increase the amount of money going to welfare recipients, we appear to have been successful in adding somewhere between $50 and $100 million—this includes the $25 to $30 million a year estimated increase in welfare costs resulting from the residency decision. Not bad for a $3 million investment in legal services in San Francisco.

These figures, however, may turn out to be something less than firm. The state has many options to limit, delay or in other ways frustrate the carrying out of the courts' decisions. The state Department of Social Welfare can engage us in lengthy appellate proceedings; it can adopt new regulations to reduce the cost of particular decisions; it can simply refuse to comply with court orders (as it is now doing in the rent case); or the legislature may change the state law that was the basis for the court victory.

It became necessary, therefore, for us to attend to these other arenas. This required not only our presence at hearings and meetings of state and county welfare bodies and appearances before legislative committees, but the mobilizing of welfare recipients and others to bring pressure to bear on administrative and legislative decision-makers. Formation of an active citywide welfare rights organization was achieved in part through a series of welfare advocates' classes conducted in various neighborhoods by the foundation's welfare specialists.

Pressure from the poverty community has been fairly effective in San Francisco, much less effective in Sacramento. Effectiveness in Sacramento requires not only statewide organization, but support from other than welfare recipients, and it is certainly questionable whether this support will be forthcoming when most middle-class voters feel that more money for welfare inevitably comes out of their pockets. Nevertheless, an important effect of the residency decision is that states like California, with relatively high benefits, will bring pressure on Congress for some kind of national income maintenance program.

Our aim has been not only to increase dollar benefits, but to enable recipients to gain some control over the welfare system—to render it less arbitrary and oppressive. We have been able to reform procedures within the welfare department to bring them more in line with constitutional, due process requirements. One of the cases, in which we have challenged the failure of the state to give recipients a hearing before their benefits are cut off, is now before the United States Supreme Court. In a sense, however, everything we've done in the welfare area has been calculated to maintain constant pressure on the system to maximize its responsiveness to the poor. We have in part succeeded. We have shaken up the system and even encouraged many on the inside to make changes they felt they could not make before.

The retiring director of the state Department of Social Welfare acknowledged the impact of our efforts, and those of other poverty lawyers in California, in the statement he gave at his final news conference on November 28, 1969:

> Here in California we have been challenged on dozens of issues, all of them coming back to the fact that for the first time, the poor have real and effective advocacy in our courts. This, again, is the significant point transcending all other considerations and consequences. An era of advocacy has begun out of which, I am sure, public assistance is never going to be the same. Not only is this happening through the courts, but also in the meetings and hearings of welfare boards, advisory commissions and administrators at every government level. The poor have come out of their apathy, and our accountability for what we do and why we do it is theirs to know—as it always has been under the law but never before so vocally sought.

As I indicated earlier, one of the strategies for institutional change was promotion of economic development in the poverty community. The foundation was one of the first legal service programs to launch a serious undertaking in this area. The initial project, a laundromat in the Mission District financed with the first Small Business Administration loan in the West to a business owned and operated by poor persons, was highly successful. This venture led to the establishment of the San Francisco Local Development Corporation (LDC), which was designed to serve as a catalyst in the development of other ghetto-owned enterprises, and eventually perhaps serve as a neighborhood development bank. This approach seemed to us to provide a more direct route to the redistributive goal than litigation. Although the LDC continues to function, and has assisted a number of ghetto residents in financing and managing new businesses, we have actually accomplished a great deal less over the past year or two in the economic area than we have in the courts. The slow pace of the LDC may be accounted for in part by staff problems and the time and energy that was consumed in obtaining initial funding. We also underestimated the difficulties in accumulating the capital and expertise necessary to move beyond the small retail or service business.

As we have seen, the foundation was initially conceived as a collection of largely autonomous neighborhood law firms with a central administrative staff to "keep the machinery running" and to provide liaison among the neighborhood offices and between them and the board and various outside agencies. This highly decentralized system was designed to insure maximum responsiveness to the particular needs of the various poverty communities.

I had become convinced from a brief study I had conducted for OEO in the summer of 1966 that a central research and planning staff was essential to implement the broader, strategic goals of the legal services program. Notwithstanding the greater dedication and competence of the attorneys in the OEO-funded agencies, I argued in my report that without structural changes that go beyond simply shifting the location of the office (into the neighborhood) there would be little difference in actual impact and operation between OEO legal programs and conventional legal aid. I suggested, therefore, a division of function between a central office and neighborhood offices. Lawyers in the central office would develop strategies for change and take the necessary steps to implement these strategies through test cases, class actions and the like. I contended that they should also maintain close relations with neighborhood organizations, "for the task of creative advocacy ought to reflect consultation with the slum community as well as feedback from the caseload of the neighborhood offices." The main task of the neighborhood office would be that "of serving a large volume clientele on something like a mass production basis," with some research and other assistance from the specialist attorneys.

Over the years, a strong central legal staff was built up in the Main Office of the foundation. The attorneys became specialists in housing and redevelopment, welfare and other areas, and they were responsible for the major cases of the foundation. The office was started with two attorneys. In the fall of 1969, there were approximately 15 attorneys (including most of the foundation's allotment of Reginald Heber Smith Fellows) and a total staff of about 25, not including the many law students working in the clinic program. The Main Office legal staff was now larger than any of the neighborhood offices. The Main Office attorneys were the "cosmopolitans" in the foundation: they were much more likely than the neighborhood attorneys to have contacts with other poverty lawyers across the United States—in OEO programs, the Legal Defense Fund—to attend regional and national conferences and training sessions, and to keep up with the growing body of legal literature in their field.

From the very beginning, relations between the neighborhood offices and the Main Office were strained. In my report to OEO I had pointed out that one of the problems that might arise in setting up a separate structure for the strategic cases was

> the tension between service to a mass clientele and creative advocacy. At any point the decision to allocate limited resources to a central planning staff may seem arbitrary, even heartless. For the decision will necessitate turning away desperate people who are, after all, entitled to the service. But unless this is done, little will be accomplished for the large majority of slum dwellers, and many of those who are served will receive only temporary relief.

Neighborhood attorneys felt that they were carrying the burden of providing legal services to the poverty community with little or no help from their Main Office colleagues. The latter were viewed as an expensive luxury—their case loads immorally small, the pace of their work annoyingly relaxed and the results highly dubious. Was the WACO case really worth all the time and effort that had gone into it, and what about the welfare cases that put a few more dollars in a recipient's pocket, if that? Is it fair to spend such a large share of the foundation's resources on these highly speculative cases when there are clear, tangible results obtained in eviction cases and divorce cases, where people really hurt? These questions bothered many neighborhood attorneys. Their growing resentment of Main Office attorneys was hardly diminished by the incidental benefits they seemed to enjoy—the many trips to conferences and meetings, the publicity in the newspapers and on television.

From the point of view of the Main Office attorneys, neighborhood lawyers were not only essentially engaged in a band-aid operation, but even on a remedial basis were frequently unable to give effective representation to their clients, given the unwillingness of the neighborhood offices either to limit case-loads or to accept more efficient, routinized procedures. Further-more, several chief counsels were viewed as the prime perpetua-tors of a system in which the client community was often the loser.

Main Office attorneys were also unhappy about what appeared to be the political restrictions on some neighborhood offices. The principal example was the unwillingness of the Western Addition office to represent WACO in its fight with the Redevelopment Agency. This decision, it was felt, was motivated in part by a reluctance to oppose the black establishment in the Western Addition (including the local EOC leaders) which supported redevelopment in exchange for more jobs for blacks in the agency and sponsorship of projects within the renewal area. Similarly, the Chinatown office was extremely reluctant to take an aggressive position against established interests in Chinatown. Thus it was fully two years before any action at all was taken against the sweatshops. It was no accident that these were the two offices in which the local establishment had most to do with the selection of the chief counsel.

Tensions were heightened by racial and ethnic differences. The Main Office legal staff has been predominantly white (it is interesting that a black lawyer who joined the staff has had little sympathy for the goals and methods of the office) and largely Jewish. Criticism of the Main Office has undoubtedly been affected by the feeling that it was inappropriate for white lawyers to be deciding what is best for poor blacks.

Although the neighborhood lawyers continued to be critical of the increase in staff at the Main Office and its failure to operate primarily as a back-up resource for them, an uneasy truce emerged between the neighborhood offices and the Main Office. The chief counsels agreed to leave the Main Office alone if it would not interfere in internal operations of the neighborhood offices. The sovereignty of the neighborhood offices was not to be trifled with. This was not a very happy solution. Indeed, it became increasingly difficult to effect even a modest degree of coordination. At stake was raising the quality of service in the neighborhood offices—and at the very least, preventing a deterioration in quality. This meant being able to do something about recruitment of attorneys, training of new attorneys and increasing office efficiency. Development of a rational recruitment program to take advantage of the foundation's nationwide reputation to attract top legal talent, particularly minority lawyers, simply was not possible with each office refusing to yield on its absolute power to hire and fire staff. A staff training program never really existed—some chief counsels resented the interference, and one refused to permit his attorneys to attend training sessions. Development of standard legal forms and office procedures, sharing of information on cases, research memos and briefs to avoid duplication of effort and to insure the best thinking or approach to a case—all of these seemed unattainable despite repeated campaigns to bring them about. In response to a grant condition from OEO, the director of litigation (who is in effect the chief counsel for the Main Office legal staff) drew up a minimal plan to insure that information on more important or unusual cases would be made available to him and to the chief counsels in advance of filing, but leaving final control over the cases in the hands of the chief counsels. For a long period the chief counsels for one reason or another were unwilling to consider the plan on its merits.

We were caught in a bind. Our efforts to assist neighborhood offices in raising the quality of service to clients were generally opposed as undermining the autonomy of the neighborhood offices. As a result, the neighborhood job got tougher—with increasing resentment against the Main Office and a lowering of the quality of service to the clients in the neighborhoods. The offices continued operating essentially as independent law firms. Within the offices there was no real division of labor or specialization. Attorneys handled as best they could whatever cases and matters came their way on their interview days. Case loads were large and becoming more burdensome as the backlog of unfinished cases slowly but surely built up. Work with neighborhood groups was confined mostly to incorporation of essentially paper organizations. Moreover, the staff became less experienced, given the tendency to fill vacant slots with younger attorneys. And there was little effective supervision, since in most offices the chief counsel was playing primarily a political role in the community, having turned over the day-to-day administration of the office to his senior staff attorney or senior secretary. Consequently, in spite of the dedication and ability of most neighborhood attorneys, the quality of the work product in general declined.

The goal of community control had been institutionalized in the autonomous neighborhood offices, while the aim of institutional change was embodied in the Main Office legal staff. It was obvious that the growing antagonism between these two structures in large measure represented a conflict between the two goals. The lawyer-founders had been wrong in assuming that control by the client community was a necessary condition for, let alone compatible with, a program of institutional change. We were unfortunately burdened with some romantic notions of the poor.

The neighborhood leaders, particularly those identified with the poverty program, were following an old pattern fashioned by other ethnic groups as they fought their way up the power ladder. These leaders were, by and large, not out to change or seriously challenge the system; they simply wanted to be cut in. They were willing to have an understanding with the older, white establishment: in exchange for greater control of public programs aimed at helping the poor, and more control over jobs and other rewards for their constituents, they would keep the peace. The WACO suit was, of course, embarrassing: it was not until the Redevelopment Agency by its arrogance alienated its black allies in the Western Addition that the neighborhood leaders were able to openly support WACO's position.

It may well be the case that, with respect to their conception of legal services, the neighborhood leaders at this point are much closer to the conservative Republicans than to the militant white lawyers.

It is always possible, of course, that the neighborhood leaders may become radicalized—and the violent repression of the Panthers may be doing just that. And it is also possible that the young black lawyers coming out of the Reginald Heber Smith program may press for a more radical approach to legal services. Neither group, so far, however, seems to be prepared to move much beyond the issue of community control. The two principal demands of the black Reginald Heber Smith Fellows in a recent confrontation with OEO officials were higher salaries and control of the program.

By the spring of 1969 I was convinced that there would have to be some basic change in the structure of the foundation: although much of our work, particularly in housing and welfare, was beginning to pay off, the tensions within the foundation were becoming critical. The changes that would have to be brought about would necessarily mean limiting, if not doing away with, the autonomy of the neighborhood offices. In my view, this could only be accomplished by a black coordinator dedicated to institutional change, that is, by a militant black lawyer. I tried unsuccessfully for several months to find such a person. Finally, in October, having held the office for three years, and with a sense that we had accomplished in some ways a great deal more than I had ever expected, I resigned as coordinator of the foundation. It was now up to the board to find my successor, and hopefully a solution to our dilemma.

In December of 1969 my successor was chosen. The new coordinator is a black lawyer who had been a staff attorney in one of the neighborhood offices, and more recently held a top administrative post in the EOC. He is an able attorney, with a strong sense of professionalism and a flair for administrative efficiency. Although not unsympathetic to the aims and approach of the Main Office legal staff, he clearly represents the interests and perspective of the neighborhood offices. The tensions within the foundation should be significantly reduced, the divisions healed. I assume that the commitment to institutional change will gradually become weaker and that the Main Office legal staff will be reduced in size and given a different direction—to serve primarily as back-up resource for the neighborhood offices.

In retrospect, this probably represents the only solution that was realistically open to the foundation. Reorganization in the image of the Main Office legal staff would have brought the foundation into more direct and intolerable confrontations with the establishment and would have seriously jeopardized neighborhood support. Perhaps at this point the main objective should be the survival of the foundation as a major institution serving the ghetto under ghetto control.

If the militant white lawyers move on, this should not be interpreted simply as a reaction to a shift in leadership and possible direction of the foundation. Some have become disillusioned with the capacity of the legal system to respond; others may be following new fashions. In one way or another, however, the old coalition will very likely be dissolved. Looking back, I suppose we have each used the other—the black professionals and neighborhood leaders have gained an organization, and we had the chance to put our theories into practice. Still, it's sad the partnership couldn't last.

FURTHER READING

Civil Justice and the Poor by Jerome Carlin, Jan Howard and Sheldon Messinger (Russell Sage Foundation, 1967).

New Careers:
Issues Beyond Consensus

ALAN HABER

"New careers"—training and employing nonprofessionals as auxiliary personnel in human services—is now widely supported. A favorable image has been built; legislative precedents have been set; demonstration programs are being replaced by operational designs; and the circle of committed advocates has expanded from a few dozen academics and reformers to a few thousand people spanning numerous professional, governmental, foundation, trade union, social welfare, university and political movement groupings.

My purpose in this chapter is to clarify the ideology behind new careers by describing the major components of the new careers model. I will also discuss strategies for improving and expanding the program.

BASIC COMPONENTS OF THE NEW CAREERS MODEL

It is important at the outset to describe a typical "new

This chapter is based on a paper presented at the National Council for New Careers Organizing Conference, June 20-23, 1968, in Detroit.

careers" program. Following are the basic elements in such a program.

1. Creation of entry-level positions which do not require prior education and training, so that workers can be productive to the employer immediately.

2. Provision of training immediately available and integrally connected to the entry-level position.

3. Assurance that entry-level positions have an adequate, nonpoverty salary income ($4,000 is the figure commonly used), provide reasonable pay increments for each advancement up the career ladder, and reward both on-the-job experience and completion of formal training and educational curricula.

4. Existence of a visible, complete career ladder between the entry positions and higher positions within the job hierarchy, up to and including professional levels.

5. Availability of relevant training and education for upgrading to higher positions on the career ladder, including remedial or equivalency education for those without high school diplomas, on-the-job training in job-related skills, and released time with pay for requisite formal education.

6. Giving present employees access to the career ladder and to all training and educational opportunities, including opportunity for lateral entry to the career ladder at all levels.

7. Institutionalization of agency responsibility for career training through the development of a specialized training resource, either within the employing agency or through a subcontract.

8. Development of certified higher education programs specifically keyed to the career advancement needs of nonprofessional workers, including accrediting on-the-job experience for meeting the requirements for level advancement; modifying the traditional intellectual curriculum by tailoring it to draw on the job experience of the student/worker; and providing some course work on the job site.

9. Assurance of long-term security by formally incorporating

the jobs into the regular agency structure and budget projections.

10. Standardization of experience and education certification so that lateral mobility is possible between comparable career levels in different agencies and in different human service areas.*

IMPLICATIONS OF THE MODEL

It should be clear that this new careers model involves substantially more than a job program for unemployed or underemployed workers. The model links new careers to a whole series of significant changes in labor market operation, education and employer use of manpower. It specifically decreases reliance on formal education as the primary basis for job access, credentialing and career mobility. It broadens the employer's responsibility to his employees to provide not simply wages in exchange for productivity, but also training for continual upgrading of productivity. It introduces the state as an active participant in employment, both in setting guidelines for training and education responsibilities and in subsidizing costs of educating employees. Finally, it creates a channel to professional status that ties credentials to performance and job-associated training and education.

These changes involve not simply one segment of new workers but the entire work force. They involve a reclassification of jobs and of promotions, bypassing questions of seniority and of traditional skill certification. By implication, the introduction of a new set of job categories, some involving new tasks and others tasks previously performed by professionals, imposes the need for new types of relationship and teamwork between professionals and nonprofessionals.

---

* In principle, the new careers model is a general one, applicable to any employer organization and any group of workers. In practice, however, it is primarily applied in the human services and primarily employs the poor. My discussion generally assumes this limitation of practice.

What the Model Does Not Do

The new careers model does not require redefining or improving services. An employer may use nonprofessionals to change his mode of functioning and service delivery. But the decision to make that change is independent of the decision to adopt a new careers program. Nor does the model impose any need to change professional practice, although, hopefully, the program will release the innovative and creative energies of professionals by freeing them of the burdens of low-level work, and will serve to educate professionals about some of the intangibles of service delivery through interaction with people whose lives have been primarily in the client population.

The model does not impose the need for institutional change in areas other than manpower. In particular, it does not require either the democratization of the established organizational structure or that it become accountable to the consumers of its services or to the community it serves. Who makes the decisions, designs the jobs or evaluates the performance, are unchanged by the new careers model.

These are important issues. Most advocates of new careers count such institutional changes among their objectives. They are not, however, explicit in the new careers model, and the model could be adopted in full without any change in organizational control or service quality. . . .

IMPROVING AND EXPANDING NEW CAREERS PROGRAMS

The Issue of Professionalism

Rather than emphasizing professionalism, advocates of new careers programs must begin to formulate an explicit critique of professional practice. Such people should not be antiprofessional in the sense of devaluing knowledge, training or competence. Nor should they be romantic in assuming that the poor can solve all their own problems or that nonprofessionals have the intuitive expertise to perform all the tasks previously seen as professional.

But neither should new careers advocates accept the present structure and ideology of professional practice as their model in defining the career objectives of *new* careers.

First of all, few of the human service professions actually have a theory or service technology which works. Usually they rely on a combination of pseudoscientific witchcraft, common sense and traditional morality. It is only very recently that one has had a better chance of regaining his health by seeing a doctor rather than by relying on home remedies. In most other professions (casework, psychotherapy, teaching, etc.) there is little *hard* evidence that professional competence (measured by mastery and utilization of some body of "scientific knowledge") is significant in service effectiveness. Most people who are good in professions are not good because they have special knowledge, or because they have aides and helpers. They are good because they have a compelling authenticity and honesty in their relations with others and because they convey respect and interest in the people they work for. Technique and professional competence may help them, but it cannot substitute for these innate qualities.

Second, much professional education is useless, dull and vacuous, some is pernicious, and a great deal has no relation to the problems of practice. Social work and education schools are the most notorious, but there is substantial testimony that the same can be said of law, urban planning, nursing and even medicine. Training is tolerated for the sake of the "union card" it bestows, not because students believe it is valuable. Its primary purpose is socialization to the values, modes of practice and social philosophy of the profession and to select out of the profession those people who cannot stomach the established code.

And third, professional status does not necessarily ensure expertise or competence. Much "professionalism" is a status defense rather than a quality defense, providing justification for nonidentification, distance and objectification of clients. Credentialing, accreditation and tenure are mixed blessings. While providing some quality control and latitude for experimentation, they also provide a haven for the mediocre and traditional. Many professionals—like other people—are noninnovative and non-creative. Their professional capacity may be underutilized in terms of some ideal norm, but, in fact, they are functioning at their own desired level of routine and nonchallenge. This status consciousness and self rather than service orientation can be seen in those human services which have recently become channels of mobility into the middle class.

While recognizing these charades and facades may help demystify the professions and set us on guard against adopting standards of professional knowledge, education and credentialing uncritically, still they do not get to the heart of the critique of professionalism. The real problem is that the professions, as now practiced, are elitist and authoritarian in their fundamental character, and hence they are both antidemocratic and supportive of the status quo.

New careers is not a gift to ignorant poor people. It is an ideology to help professionals shed certain attitudes which seriously damage their own usefulness—attitudes about knowledge, client relations, human problems and the origin of values.

Attitude toward knowledge. The professional often treats knowledge as a privileged possession, as private property above democratic review. Rather than seeing his responsibility to share and teach his knowledge and skills, he guards them jealousy. Rather than seeing himself and the quality of his service as accountable to the people he serves, he seeks a privileged status—buttressed by credentials, objective detachment, codes of ethics and other such regalia—immune from the criticism, evaluation or even egalitarian discussion with the people affected by his work and dependent upon his performance. The social message is that problems are solved by people with expertise. The people affected by those problems might be consulted for public relations purposes or to increase the effectiveness of social manipulation, but not to define the goals or course of treatment. Their job is to consent and to recognize that considerations beyond their understanding are proper guides.

Reactions with clients. In the professional-client relationship, legitimate power rests solely with the professional, presumably giving him leverage in prescribing the appropriate "helping" strategy. Whatever the outcome of this help, its byproduct is socialization of the client to remain dependent, obedient and deferential to others in regard to the issues of his own life. The person receiving help must acknowledge his incompetence. The integrity of an individual's own perception of reality is undercut by the professional's assertion of a superior and inaccessible body of knowledge which is the real guide to right thinking and behavior. People subject to this kind of professional relationship are not helped to trust and respect themselves as autonomous beings, able to govern their own lives and make decisions about things important to them.

The view of human problems. For the most part, professionals assume that problems reside in individuals, not in systems. The professional is treatment-oriented, seeking to assist people to adapt to what is. Even if he understands the oppressive and causative character of environmental conditions in his orientation to client problems, his objective is still to change people rather than to change systems. He fragments problems according to his specialization, not according to their objective character. Professional responsibility (and, usually, competence) does not include helping people to understand their situation and to act to change that situation. The professional's purpose is to help people stay out of trouble and make the best of bad situations.

Source of values. The professions are for the most part conservative, more like traditional guilds in organization and self-protectiveness than like centers of innovation and progress. They are carriers of mainstream social values and morality, guardians of stability. They seek distance and "detachment" from the people they serve. But the concept of detachment is not as neutral as it seems. The factors beyond the existential situation of the client which guide professional judgment are rarely objective and scientific. Rather, they tend to be social conventions and socially defined objectives to which the client must be reconciled. So the question is: Whom does the professional serve? And the answer usually is: not the client or the particular community of which the client is a part, but the "social good" and the interests of the "community as a whole," as defined by professional associations, governmental decrees and social influentials.

Without quibbling over the details and qualifications, and even acknowledging the presence of a progressive minority, it is difficult to dispute the general accuracy of this characterization of professionalism in practice. Our rhetoric of pro-professionalism clearly needs revision. New careers advocacy should not be linked to the professions as they are; it advances no worthy social purpose to ratify the current definitions of professional competence, education, status and practice; and it does a disservice to nonprofessionals to maintain the mythology of professionalism and to use it as a focus for their career aspiration and emulation.

The professions need a new body of knowledge, a new means of education, a new kind of relationship with the people they serve. These should be the goals of new careers: *new* professionals, not nonprofessionals.

And, in fact, new careers offers a tremendous opportunity to advance these objectives. It creates great numbers of jobs in the human services which are not constrained by prior professional education and socialization. These jobs necessitate the development of wholly new training programs and formulations of requisite knowledge. Insofar as they are not yet integrated into the professional system, they allow experimentation with new forms of practice and service relationship.

If we seize this opportunity, perhaps we can begin to define and advance a "new professionalism": in which professionals function as equals with the people they serve and as educators, attempting to share and diversify those skills which they have; in which problems are connected with their social causes, and helping a person cope with the immediate situation is paralleled by the effort to help him understand and operate on the broader situation as an autonomous, self-determining agent; in which the organization of service is accountable to the people who are served, with community residents selecting their own members to sit on boards of directors rather than having service structured from the top down in accord with the values and interests of professionals and "civic leaders."

The training of people who understand the need for such a system and who could begin to staff it, and the actual creation of a new professionalism in embryo, at the lower levels of present service bureaucracies, should be the objective of new careers programs. Such programs would, of course, be in continual tension with established professionalism. And new careerists trained in these programs would not be welcomed and readily credentialed by the professional associations. But is that really important? If they did, in fact, function as professionals should, they would get the recognition of the people they served—and they would begin to create a manpower alternative to traditional professional practice. It is only when there is such a labor alternative that the power and moral authority of the old guilds can be broken.

Even though it is unlikely that people established in the professions would be enthusiastic associates in the creation of this alternative, many nontraditionalists and radicals in the professions and many students in the professional schools have begun to see through the facade of professionalism. These people would cooperate in a program to transform the professions. They are the ones developing most sharply the critique of professional practice and pointing most accurately to the need for change. If these people were involved in the design of new careers training and education programs—taking not the profession but human needs of the community as the beginning point—perhaps we could make some significant breakthroughs in developing whole new approaches to teaching, social work, family aid, health and so forth.

The Issue of Good Jobs

It is not sufficient to define jobs in the human service systems as good jobs—even if they are economically secure, socially valued and provide opportunity for upward advancement. In theory, the human services are an area of great importance, and employment in such work should be charged with an idealism that encourages self-esteem. In fact, however, the institutions that comprise human services include some of the most deformed and totalitarian institutions in American society. It is not necessary to make a blanket condemnation of all human service agencies. But it is blind to ignore the substance (and truth) of the far-reaching criticisms which have been made of the welfare system, of public housing administration, of the public schools, of hospitals, especially those serving the poor, and of police and "corrections" agencies. Many of the jobs performed in these institutions should not be performed at all. There is nothing progressive or ennobling in employing nonprofessionals as agents to improve the functional efficiency of these bureaucratic systems as presently constituted.

Institutional criticism and a model of institutional change must govern the task of job design. Good jobs cannot exist in bad institutions. And we cannot assume that the involvement of nonprofessionals will lead in a benign, conflictless, inarticulate way to institutional change.

In looking at the specific types of jobs that nonprofessionals are being trained to perform, this point becomes clearer. It is useful to identify several types of jobs and their relevance to the employment of nonprofessionals:

Direct service—helping homemakers, providing child care, tutoring, information-giving, recreation supervision, counseling, consumer aid, etc. These are clearly tasks that need to be performed, and various professional agencies are seeking to take them on, with the aid of nonprofessionals. But should they be done by professional agencies at all? Primarily they represent the traditional type of neighborhood mutual aid and support services and have been important integrating factors in neighborhood community life. Rather than being absorbed in complex institutional structures, they might better be deprofessionalized and decentralized. They could be part of an effort to create a cohesive fabric of community life—rather than increasing encroachments of organizations outside of the community. Professionals employed in these tasks, no less than the nonprofessionals, should be accountable to and directed by the community they serve.

Professional helper—teacher's aide, doctor's aide, case aide, research aide, etc. These are jobs providing complex service. The structure of these jobs should recognize the interdependence of tasks and the organic quality of the service function. The nonprofessional should be part of a service team, rather than an adjunct to a professional who operates as the center of authority. The necessary division of labor and specialized training must be balanced by colleague relations within the service team and general training regarding the total service process. The training of nonprofessionals must be paralleled by the equally intensive retraining of professionals.

Clerical and menial work—the whole range of jobs concerned mainly with paper, people and dirt processing. These jobs are for the most part unproductive. Many of them are unnecessary. They provide little on-the-job learning for career advancement. They are created and multiply with the increasing scale of organization (representing decreasing returns to scale) and they derive in part from the record-keeping mania of bureaucracies and legislatures. They are not good jobs. They are not preprofessional and they should not be included as entry level—or any other level— positions in the new careers program.

Control and pacification jobs—hall monitors, welfare and public housing investigators, community agents of authoritarian institutions, police aides, etc. These jobs, too, should not be performed at all. The need for them reveals the failure of institutions to meet community needs and gain client support. Pacification techniques may work in maintaining order and in masking the institutional failures which create disorder. But advocates of new careers should have nothing to do with providing the manpower for such techniques.

Another way to look at job functions is to ask what skills need to be learned. We have just considered skills that are needed by agencies. But it is also appropriate to ask what skills are needed by the community. The worker's competence should find expression not only on the job; it should have generalized benefit for his friends and neighbors. Indeed the strength of middle-class communities rests in large part on the transferability of the occupational competencies of middle-class workers to non-work-based needs of community participation and mobilization. This is particularly pertinent in new careers programs because the communities from which the new workers are being recruited are very underskilled. New careers jobs should be seen, in part, as a means of upgrading the skill level available to the community in defining and meeting its own needs. Some deficiencies which could be improved are in the areas of: entrepreneurial skills—for which training in business and organizational administration is needed, such as in setting-up, fund-raising, use of consultants, knowledge of resources, etc.; organizing skills—for which training is needed in handling meetings, committee functions, writing, communicating, expediting, maintaining accountability, etc.; organizational analysis and policy evaluation skills—for which knowledge is needed about what is going on, how decisions are made, what constraints and forms of accountability exist, etc.

A new careers job design should be geared not only to perform legitimate agency functions, but also to maximize inclusion of tasks requiring development of these sorts of skills, with the recognition that, in general, these tasks will involve a more central presence of the nonprofessional in agency administrative and political functions than is currently characteristic of new careers jobs.

The Nature of Work

Besides looking at the kinds of job functions that it is desirable to create in the human services (and those which should be opposed), it is important to look at the nature of work itself. New careers advocacy has stressed the value of work, both in terms of social productivity and individual self-realization. But we have not analyzed what makes work good and, conversely, what kind of work is socially nonproductive and personally self-destructive.

Most jobs and careers, new and old, professional and nonprofessional, for the poor or the prosperous, consist of alienating, unhappy labor. They are built on repressive self-discipline, separating task performance from emotional engagement. Personal relation to the work is in terms of external benefits or objectives defined by others. These jobs are embraced not for their intrinsic worth or satisfaction, but as a necessary means to get income, so that the worker can afford greater consumer satisfactions. Material acquisition is the culturally sanctioned surrogate for work satisfaction. Career orientation and mobility aspiration reflect not a desire to participate in increasingly important and productive work activity, but rather a seeking for greater freedom from the more onerous aspects of work. Competitiveness is built into most jobs as part of the struggle for freedom from work and as a part of a need for status symbols to label our drudgery worthwhile.

In the design of new jobs, the effort should be to avoid a repetition of competitive mobility striving and extrinsic measurement of work satisfaction. This is, of course, tremendously difficult. It runs counter to the whole thrust of our culture: consumerism, material measurement of status and value, separation of economic life from personal life, definition of self in terms of position within hierarchical organizations and status structures, etc. It is not clear exactly what the features of good jobs would be. But people who genuinely like their work, *qua* work, tend to identify certain characteristics as being important: individual pleasure in performing intellectually (or physically or esthetically) challenging tasks; relations of cooperation and respect among co-workers in a nonauthoritarian atmosphere; a combination of specificity in expectations, so that workers have feelings of competence, mastery and achievement; and participation in the whole process, so that the specifics have meaning in terms of something larger. In addition, looking at work socially, as well as personally, one would want it to have some human benefit and recognized social worth, being responsive to and jointly controlled by the various groups of people involved in that benefit.

Job socialization is also political socialization. Do we create jobs which separate job holders from the indigenous forces of political reconstruction in their communities or do we attempt to design and define jobs in a way which encourages the job holder to strengthen his identification with those forces and see himself as their agent within the system he and they are seeking to change?

Individual Mobility as Career Definition

Career implies hierarchy: a differentiated, graded set of task and role obligations. Learning one set of functions and the adequate performance of their associated role provides the base for movement to another set of functions and another role. The more steps that are designed, the more jobs are broken down into trainable functions. This process is implicit in the dominant thrust of present new careers training. It emphasizes task functions and behavioral performance—to get people to see themselves in terms of segmented roles and functions, contingent on particular, externally specified organizational objectives—and process—which is central to the destruction of personal autonomy involved in traditional career definitions. Career striving, along with rewards for advancement, are the inducements to transform the integrated self into a fragmented set of roles serving the objectives of external structures, creating dependence on them for definition and attribution of worth.

We should want to see the jobs we create through new careers programs as contributing a counterbalance, rather than a new ingredient to hierarchical bureaucracies. If we are inventive, and willing politically to press our inventions, there is a chance that new careers can have this potential. Nonprofessional people from "deprived" backgrounds have not been socialized from their youth to bureaucratic organizations, in contrast to those from middle-class origins. They still have difficulty performing well in traditional organizational settings. We can take this as our problem and try to remake these people—through diligent application of training regimes and continual reminders of career inducements. Or we can take this as their strength, and try to design jobs and training which build on and protect it.

Besides the personal, there is also a socially relevant consideration. Is individual mobility a desirable social value? A specific answer to that question depends on the social context. It is the urban poor, and the black and brown poor in particular, from whom the new professionals are being recruited; and it is primarily this group that they and their employing agencies are supposed to serve. For this group, the objective of individual mobility is not a desirable social value. It should not be the fundamental thrust of our antipoverty efforts. First of all, it will not work. Secondly, it is not what is needed at this time. The realities are simply too stark for us to ignore this.

The vast majority of the ghetto population will not be benefited by new careers. Most of the now poor will remain unemployed, or in the dead-end manual/menial jobs they now hold, or in the entry levels of the human services. And most of the black poor will continue to live in the ghettos, and even most of our new careerists will find it a hard route out. If we had the power to create *enough* jobs and to break the back of housing segregation and racism, then we would be dealing with an entirely different kind of situation. But we don't have that power and nobody does now. And until that power is built, the future of the black population is in the ghetto. The hope for the black population is the economic and political development of the ghetto.

Either new careers will support that goal—in which case we must focus all energies in that direction—or we are against it—which is the operational meaning of the illusion (or the fact for a few) that there is an integrationist solution for individuals apart from the collective development of the black community.

Defining new careers in terms of collective mobility is no easy job, and it underscores the fact that, if we are serious about the social potential of new careers, we must define it in an increasingly political context. The collective mobility of the black community means building new economic institutions controlled by the community; it means expelling "colonial entrepreneurs" who accumulate capital in the ghetto and then take it out either through personal consumption or external investment. It means building pride and commitment in community—working in it, rather than to get out of it. The objective of economic development is not simply to create jobs, rebuild the housing and raise income levels within the ghetto; it is to provide the institutional and psychological base for political independence and community cohesion. These are the essential conditions for integration: integration on the basis of strength, so that institutions as well as people's locations change. The issue in integration is the relation of people to their community roots. Does new careers try to strengthen this relation, and encourage power and position in white institutions to flow back to the community? Or does it try to weaken that relation by suggesting the possibility of individual mobility, and greasing the tracks of individual careers out of the ghetto?

The Issue of The Public Sector

The new careers program is focused primarily on the public sector, in part because program organizers see the public sector as a location where employment must be expanded, and, in part, because organizers feel that jobs created in the public sector will be stable. This acceptance of the public sector as our frame of reference needs closer scrutiny.

Public sector development has, in the past, assumed the preeminence of the private sector, organized along modern corporate capitalist lines. Its growth has been conditioned *not* by an independent social impulse to provide a just and humane context for individual freedom and self-determination. It has rather been the result of efforts to relieve the problems caused by the unjust and inhumane workings of the private economy; and to provide the manpower resources, infrastructure and socialization which the private economy requires in order to function. The current inadequacies and irrationalities of the public sector can, without significant exception, be traced to its subordination to the private sector.

Is our purpose to strengthen the bulwarks which public spending and public institutions provide from the established political economy? Or is it to redesign the public sector as a means for more basic structural reform in the society, attacking those nonpublic inequities of the political economy that generate the problems which the public sector is called upon to solve or ameliorate? The former choice allows new career advocates to operate in harmony with traditional liberal reform, and it abdicates any effort to actualize the social potential of the new careers idea. The latter requires alliance with the political movements which stand in radical opposition to the American mainstream, but it also gives prominence to the social vision of the new careers idea.

This question also has direct bearing on our notion of new

careers jobs as stable, and hence on the kind of training and future perspective we convey to new careerists. It is clear that the public sector, as an aggregate spending category in the national accounts, will continue to grow. But it does not follow that the jobs which are created in the public sector will be stable. Quite the contrary, these jobs are now, and will continue to be, under constant attack. While some of this attack is reactionary—seeking to deny public responsibility for human needs—the main thrust is progressive—challenging the nonpublic character of the institutions in which these jobs reside and the content of the services they provide.

If we see the issue of the public sector as neutral and accept new careers within the traditional public sector structure, then we work at cross-purposes against the most progressive forces within the human service professions, and communities served by those professions, which are opposing the whole structure of the public sector. These groups will be opposing them as part of a general attack on the hierarchical, centralized, nondemocratic organization of service.

And then where will the new careerists be as a political force: allied with the agency system in terms of which their jobs are defined, or allied with the groups seeking to destabilize these jobs, seeking to subject them to community control, to embroil them in fights which put them at odds with their funding source, to destroy their hope of having a successful "career" by keeping out of trouble? Are new careerists to be another group incorporated into the system and made dependent for their sense of security on its stability—meaning politically that they will resist external forces seeking to disrupt that stability? Or does the ideology, training and organizational expression of new careers advocacy attempt to prepare them for instability? Does the future conveyed to new careerists help them to live with the tension of holding jobs which need to be changed, and identifying with the forces attempting to change these jobs?

How these questions are dealt with will largely determine whether new careerists as a "constituency" function as reactionaries, or whether they aid and contribute to the mobilization of the public power needed to transform the public sector.

The Issue of Service Improvement

The foregoing critique of the consensus values in new careers politics has had as its implicit reference the improvement of service. The point is that we cannot see service improvement as an abstract objective, disconnected from the context of political forces which are defining what needs to be improved. Thus it is not sufficient to consider the creation of a bridge between agency and community as service improvement. The bridge is important only if it allows the progressive forces of the community to assert increasingly decisive control over the services. Likewise, expansion of the range of services, is not, *per se*, an improvement. It is an improvement only if it comes about through a decentralization of agencies and a reversal of the authority system, so that it is at neighborhood centers that needs are defined and services provided, with centralized, professionalized agencies called upon for specific assistance and accountable to the locality for their performance.

Essentially the question is: Service improvement for whom? For the agency—providing additional manpower, rationalizing internal organization and making it better able to carry out the functions it sets for itself, while reducing the pressures on its personnel in the process? Or for the people needing service? The latter means dealing with the real problems these people face: the problems of getting authoritarian service agencies off their backs; of building self-determining, economically viable, normatively integrated communities; and of developing the requisite political and organizational competence to operate as citizens in the struggle against institutions and against other citizens whose actions are oppressive.

Service improvement is inseparable from the struggle to transform the basis of the service system and the position of the people served in the society as a whole.

These reflections are only a beginning in the definition of new careers politics. They point, in almost every aspect of the new careers program, to conflict: conflict with organizational structures, with professional traditionalism and with the work expectations of the new careerists themselves. We have no reason for optimism that this projection of the new careers potential will prevail politically. But without political intervention and leadership in defining the terms of the conflict, it is sure to go the other way and simply recapitulate the model of human services which provide bad jobs, bad service and bad values.

If we take new careers beyond its minimal definition, then it is a radical program. Not radical in the sense that it is a critical catalyst whose introduction will have far-reaching, reinforcing and ramifying consequences, transforming the whole situation far beyond the expectations or desires of its agents. That kind of secret radicalism by the back door is nonsense.

It is radical in that it touches on the issues that are central to the radical political movements now taking shape in America: the attack on the centrality of the private economy, the nature of professions, the nature of work and bureaucracy; the struggle for community; liberation of black people; and popular control of government.

We can acknowledge this by defining the content of "new careers" in the context of these struggles and by allying our efforts with programs and organizations which manifest this radicalism.

May 1968

New Careers
in Mental Health Systems:
Epilogue to a Survey

ALVIN E. GREEN AND EDWARD JOHNSON

Employment of mental health workers who do not hold graduate degrees has grown rapidly during the last decade. Early experimental projects designed to demonstrate the therapeutic effectiveness of nonprofessional personnel in mental health were often initiated in response to critical manpower needs, and these early projects proved so effective that their continued development today has been based increasingly upon choice. But the use of nonprofessional personnel is not new. Rather, it is an expansion and extension of earlier employment and manpower practices, since delivery of mental health services has long depended on nonprofessional staff.

With the development of new careers, a new dimension in the employment of nonprofessional personnel was offered. The new careers movement, while seeking to improve mental health services and relieve manpower shortages by providing capable non-

This essay is the epilogue to a paper resulting from a project supported by Grant MH 17285-01 from the National Institute of Mental Health. ©The Menninger Foundation, 1972.

professional personnel, simultaneously raised other significant issues. It sought to remove many people from the despair and degradation of unemployment by employing them in meaningful human services, while providing a structure that permitted career growth. Regardless of project goals, it is the provision of new opportunities for career growth (vertical and horizontal mobility) that makes new careers "new." An additional and unique aspect of the new careers movement is its valuing of life experiences and its notion that certain aspects of living can qualify people for employment in the human services. Thus, qualifying characteristics and/or credentials previously held as absolute are no longer seen as the sole prerequisites for employment and career advance-ment.

The development of the new careers concept has heartened many people. They see the slow but developing acceptance of new careers, by public and private agencies, as moving towards significant social and economic achievement. Certainly, new careers projects make a contribution when they provide disadvantaged people with useful work, with remedial education, with on-the-job training and with the opportunity for job advancement. The introduction of the new careerist often serves to shake loose rigid ideas about professional practice, and helps generate new service ideas, particularly about community mental health services to unserved and underserved populations. The nature of mental health services and the manner in which they are delivered often changes as people with different types of backgrounds and training join the service delivery team. Collaboration between traditional professional and "new professional" personnel has led to an exciting new base for collective growth. And, with good training and supervision, workers who have not traveled the traditional route to professional competency have demonstrated that they can offer services of high quality.

These advantages of employing workers with different kinds of training in mental health are well established and well documented. New careerists have been acknowledged to provide services which are: 1) congenial to the consumer population, 2) effectively therapeutic and 3) innovative. The projects we visited worked within established institutions in an effort to vitalize them, rather than to replace them. Essentially, the projects argued that necessary change could be fostered from within the service institutions through cooperation and collaboration. These observations and perspectives were shared by agency administrators regardless of setting, degree of appropriation of "new careers" components, or extent to which the projects were able to achieve the complex administrative changes necessary to achieve project objectives.

Yet, with all the reports that speak to the contributions made by new careers, we found that the development and establishment of new careers continues to be treated as experimental, even after years of apparently highly valued contributions. The projects we visited appeared to operate in many respects as though they were embarking on a new and untested venture. It was our impression that project members did not make sufficient use of the available literature nor of knowledgeable consultants. Many programs have been discontinued following termination of grant support; and graduates of programs often have not been employed at a level appropriate to their training and skills.

The question is, how can we account for the slow and tedious adoption of an innovation so widely viewed as effective and important? Certainly, the implementation of a new careers program is complex. Such programs seek to respond to complex issues, and their introduction brings new complexities as well. We have presented a variety of problems which confronted organizations as they established their new careers program. But we do not feel that such problems were very different from many other problems that attend the development of other "new" programs. Yet other novel programs seem to have met with greater acceptance, and appear to have greater structural integrity than new careers programs. In our effort to understand the unique resistance to new careers programs, we offer the following observations and thoughts.

We found (as have many others) that much resistance to new careers came from the professionals. However, most of the initial questions raised by the professionals were satisfied as the projects progressed. Fears of reducing quality of care or replacing professional personnel were unfounded. Yet, one fact stands out clearly. The new careers movement represents a partial challenge to professionalism. It speaks to the need for greater responsiveness on the part of professional practice, professional organizations and the organizations directed by professionals to the needs of the consumer. It calls for greater consumer participation in decision-making, a prerogative previously assumed solely by the professionals themselves. Thus the new careerist may be used by the organization as a representative for and/or as a reflection of the consumers' perspective; he may also enter into organizational positions at levels that carry status and the power to influence and effect organizational decisions. Professionals may feel threatened politically when they realize that consumers share in an organization's policy decisions. Therefore, the new careers movement has implications for professional power and politics. Its acceptance as a program will, in part, be influenced by the process and resolution of this sociopolitical shift in the relationship between consumer and care-givers, user community and resource community. We believe that the resolution of this issue will, in part, necessitate a full reassessment of professional education, for it is in their educational training that our professional disciplines learn their responsibilities to and with their consumer public. At the same time, the political issues between the consumer community and the resource agencies will require resolution in the political arena.

An additional factor in the slow and conflicted development of the new careers movement may also rest within its origins. Although new careers was initiated by professionals, it generated or contributed further to the development of labor organization. When new careerists organize to strengthen their objectives, they are engaging in something akin to unionization, and in some instances new careerists are affiliating with unions. In professional groups not accustomed to such efforts, this type of organization represents a particular political threat that must be reckoned with.

We also believe that the origin of new careers as an antipoverty program contributes to difficulty in making it accepted nationally. As Pearl and Riessman state, "Hiring the poor to serve the poor, we argue, is a fundamental approach to poverty in an automated age."* Although we fully agree with the objectives of the concept, its practical implementation poses several problems. There is little evidence to suggest that new careers is an effective or substantial answer to unemployment or underemployment. We do not believe that sufficient funds have been made available for this purpose. And we see little evidence to suggest that funds will be made available to support extensive training of large numbers of people to fill an equally large number of new jobs. Until secure long-term funding is available, which will support a large number of *permanent* jobs, agency administrators will be reluctant to make more than minimal organizational commitments to new careers programs. This, we found, was often enunciated by agency administrators who said that new careers projects require too much alteration and dislocation of traditional or current operations for organizations to undertake on short-term grants.

Also, if the employment of new careerists is designed to relieve a shortage of professionals in less affluent areas, then it will be seen as an inequitable solution—especially if a simultaneous effort is not being made to redistribute professional talent from the more affluent to the less affluent sectors. Therefore, new careerists may eventually become the primary therapeutic agents for the poor. The possibility then exists that a class system of service, associated with quality of care, will either develop or become completely entrenched (depending on one's current view of the situation).

New careers is unique in another sense; and again, its uniqueness contributes to its being resisted. The new careerists are both the agents of and targets for the program. They are targets of the program in a special sense. New careers has been promulgated on the idea that the new careerists—the unemployed or the underemployed disadvantaged—would themselves benefit from the antipoverty and rehabilitative aspects of the program. This emphasis, often more pronounced than the essential and necessary service contributions they can make, contributes a special problem. As long as the public sees "new careers" as "make-

---

*Arthur Pearl and Frank Riessman, *New Careers for the Poor* (New York: The Free Press, 1965) p. vii.

work" for the poor and the black, it will be highly vulnerable to economic and political forces. It will be looked upon as temporary or conditional as long as the public sees it as a stop-gap measure in the full "professional" staffing of services. A program that emphasizes jobs for the unemployed poor is unlikely to capture continuing interest and support. And, like many programs for the poor, we believe it may generate much ideological support and little substantive support or resources. Therefore, the concept of it as a program solely for the poor may hinder its acceptance and implementation.

Certainly the legislative programs and other efforts that introduced the basic new careers concept are praiseworthy: without them the soundness of the concept would neither have been seen nor tested. In this sense, the programs, to date, have served as landmarks. But we believe a new thrust is necessary. If the new careers notion is to be accepted, emphasis must now be shifted from the benefits new careers provides to its participants—the new careerists—to emphasis on the benefits the program provides to the consumer—the user public. In addition, the "consumers" should not be specifically identified only as the poor and underprivileged. Rather, the service contributions such programs can make to the entire public should be emphasized.

We believe that legislation should emphasize quality care for all, and quality care is, to a great extent, a product of quality care-givers. The fundamental concepts in new careers point to the development of quality care-givers for all communities. Legislative and other means need to be developed whereby the entire health and educational systems adopt new career principles throughout their systems, rather than in parts of them. The soundness of new careers is based on its applicability and functional quality for all, rather than a few. Where subsidization and the development of supportive services for the disadvantaged will facilitate their entree, then these should be provided. But the difference here is not in the type of program or its location. The difference is the facilitation of the means to participate fully in a sound and effective system.

We do not believe that the proven benefits and contributions of "indigenous" qualities would be threatened by making new careers an integral aspect of all programs. In fact, we believe it could be strengthened. When alternative and progressive access routes to career advancement are available and equally recognized (licensed, certified or credentialed) and rewarded, people will be able to maintain their basic values and commitments.

We believe that the development of the associate arts degree program in mental health, with flexible admission requirements, stipend support for those in need of financial assistance, and working in cooperation with employment settings. is one significant route that should be strongly encouraged and supported.

5

SOCIAL POLICY

Will the War on Poverty Change America?

S. M. MILLER AND MARTIN REIN

The war on poverty has been greeted by sharp criticism from friends as well as opponents, liberals as well as conservatives. It has been interpreted as a war *on* the poor: "Under the delusion that we are pressing against poverty (we may) exert pressure against poor people" (Alvin Schorr, *Children*, July-August 1964). It has been thought of as a "hodge-podge of programs . . . designed to achieve the single objective of securing votes" (minority views of the Senate Committee on Labor and Public Welfare). Described as "a mockery," "a deliberate fraud" and "a conservative embracing of the status quo" (David Komatsu, *New Politics*, Spring 1964), it has also been characterized as a gimmick designed to show that poverty can be eliminated without changing the structure of society to reduce inequalities (Richard Titmuss, *The Nation*, Feb. 8, 1965).

Its supporters defend it as an effort to begin to deal with the problems of the poor; as the best that could be carried through

This essay is based on a larger study, *Poverty As a Public Issue*, edited by Ben B. Seligman, published by the Free Press in 1965. The study was aided by a grant from the Stern Family Fund.

Congress, considering other pressing requirements (like that of keeping federal expenditures to less than $100 billion); as a set of programs that has some chance of success and is likely to improve and expand over the years. They are concerned with the pragmatics of political possibility.

Fundamentalists (those concerned with the necessities of long-run change) and pragmatists talk past each other and, in the process, become principled, conscientious objectors to each other's contrasting visions of progress. One states the case for large-scale, sweeping change in terms of the analysis of long-term developments; the other talks of gradual movement in terms of political feasibility. Pragmatists run the danger of tailoring their analysis of long-term developments to what is feasible now, a futile attempt to remake the image of the future to meet the needs of today. Programs can be modified to encourage action, but if analysis is stunted in its vision it becomes merely an apologia for previously determined policy, rather than a contribution to new directions. At the same time, fundamentalists cannot be permitted the easy advantage of criticizing everything as insufficient; their pessimism about the present does not guarantee the accuracy of their vision of the future.

Present-day social criticism in the United States lacks a middle-ground, a "skeptical idealism," which bridges the gap between a concern with the long-term drift of society and the pragmatic possibilities of politics. If we assign George Meany as the symbol of the pragmatists and Paul Goodman as the symbol of the long-termers, there is relatively little analysis being done that cannot be assigned to one or the other of them.

Our aim is to contribute to the construction of a middle-range social and policy analysis, informed by an understanding of the trends of society and relevant to, but not bound by, present-day policies and programs. Treacherous as it is to operate at this level, such analysis is increasingly important in a society in which great economic power can easily abate symptoms without eradicating causes. We seek to present a critical view which is helpful both to the administrators of programs and to their fundamentalist critics. This level of analysis, although it will seem too "hard" to one group and too "soft" to the other, is desperately needed to enable us to move the possible ever closer to the necessary.

UNLIMITED WAR

One of the difficulties in assessing the war on poverty is the lack of agreement on what it includes. Should it be restricted to the Economic Opportunity Act of 1964? Should the tax cut be included, the Area Redevelopment Administration, the Civil Rights Act, etc.? We think it advisable to have a broad view. It permits a varied choice of programs and different attacks on the problem of poverty. It encourages recognition of the need for coordinating the programs to deal with poverty and solve the range of problems created for the poor through the impact of the American economy.

We cannot attempt here a full review of all the measures that make up the current program of poverty-reduction. We shall try to place the Economic Opportunity Act in a broader and more encompassing perspective by touching on other actions and inactions that impinge on poverty.

It is hard to see why 1964, a year of unprecedented prosperity when the gross national product approached two-thirds of a trillion dollars, saw a declaration of war on poverty, a condition affecting a minority of our population. Neither President Johnson's desire to have a liberal program which he could claim as his own, nor questioning of our economic course by liberal intellectuals, although undoubtedly influential, seem sufficient to explain it. Civil rights demonstrations were probably the most important political event propelling interest in helping the poor, yet the bulk of the United States poor are white, and the bulk of the funds will probably benefit the white rather than the Negro poor. Nor can sizable unemployment—exacerbated by a rapidly expanding young labor force—suffice to explain the inauguration of a war on poverty. Indeed, one of the most striking features of the antipoverty campaign is its development *without* backing from the strong interest groups which usually initiate and promote such legislation.

The war on poverty was not propelled by the organization of the poor in rural areas or in large cities demanding their economic rights. Nor do the prospective political demands of the poor seem great enough to require the launching of a war on poverty in 1964. If the program had not been presented, we doubt whether there would have been mass pressures for such activity in 1964 or even in 1965.

The war on poverty is a political novelty—it does not emerge from the political pressures of the day. This is the achievement of the war; this is also its weakness. The absence of a strong, organized, well-directed movement demanding more effective measures for the poor has resulted in the formulation of a weak bill and its further weakening during the journey through Congress.

One can either be disappointed that a talking horse prevaricates when it says it won the Kentucky Derby or be astonished to find a horse that talks. Our astonishment should not eliminate the need for judging what is *done* with the unusual capacity; still, its very unusualness should not be ignored. We make these remarks because much of the strong criticism of the poverty legislation—which we believe is unfortunately accurate—overlooks the possibilities of the legislation and the need for understanding how it might be made more useful.

The war on poverty can be a sop to the poor to discourage them from asking for more effective programs. That is its danger. Its hope, despite its severe limitations and the shortsighted vision of its program, is that the war is a beginning, that it can lead to increasingly more effective measures to help the poor. To move in these directions requires the development of a political constituency that will push for more appropriate programs as well as a clearer vision of what will help the poor.

A NEW "NEW DEAL"?

The war on poverty is not just the New Deal in new dress, even though it takes over some New Deal programs like the CCC (Civilian Conservation Corps) and the NYA (National Youth Administration). Taken at its potential best, it moves in new and very significant directions.

The New Deal was aimed at providing minimal maintenance to relieve want and distress; it provided a floor of security, whether in terms of minimum wages or old-age assistance and insurance. The war on poverty, however, is aimed at expanding choices (of jobs and education) and thereby enlarging human freedoms. Its goal is not the construction of a floor but the opening up of doors into the main edifice of our economy. Poverty in a time of affluence and economic boom requires different programs from poverty in a time of scarcity and national economic failure. This new perspective represents a dramatic and bold departure from the welfare policies which spurred our legislation in past decades, though it is in the American tradition of expanding educational opportunities.

When a call for the extension of opportunity goes beyond the established consensus, it summons forth the great range of criticism with which the war on poverty has been greeted. The conservatives fear not only the expenditures, but the possibility that expansion of choice for all will reduce the freedom of some. The wider role of government enhances the possibility of basic changes, reducing the advantages of some advantaged, at least in the short run.

Those in favor of extending the scale of opportunity are disappointed by the meagerness of the initial investment. It would cost $11 billion just to bring all families in the United States up to a minimum level of $3,000 income per year; clearly an expenditure of less than $1 billion is unlikely—even with the multiplier effects of governmental expenditures—to make a deep change. A billion dollars looks like a token, not a program.

The Economic Opportunity Act appears to be little more than an umbrella for securing the passage of proposals that had previously been blocked in Congress—the domestic Peace Corps, the Youth Employment program, the Work-Study program. And these programs do not seem adequate to meet the challenge of the preamble of the Economic Opportunity Act, namely, to give "to everyone the opportunity for education and training, the opportunity to work, the opportunity to live in decency and dignity."

What prevents the Act from accomplishing its stated mission are the assumptions which underlie its programs. We shall examine seven such assumptions: the concept of poverty; the fixing of a poverty line; the use of characteristics as causes; the comprehensiveness of the program; the concentration on youth; education as the opportunity vehicle; and inviolate institutions and violate man.

CHANGING THE CONCEPT OF POVERTY

The Act assumes that poverty is a short-run phenomenon. The task is to bring everyone up above a relatively fixed line which can be adjusted for price and other minor changes. It is important to shed this fixed-line orientation in defining poverty. As John Kenneth Galbraith has declared, the "poor" are those who have fallen behind the rest of society. In this view, the poverty line is always relative to time, place, possibilities. As the conditions of society change, so does the concept of poverty:

> No matter what standard is selected and what phrases are used to describe it—maintenance, health and decency, modest but adequate, comfort—the specific goods and services that comprise that level of living change over time (Lenore A. Epstein, *Research Report No. 3*, Social Security Administration, 1963).

People live below the poverty line when the social positions they occupy are so unprotected and unrewarded that they do not advance with the rest of society. As new conditions emerge, new groups are recruited into poverty. The most striking case of the new poor today are the aged who were not poor during their working lives but who become poor in their retirement. Modern cybernation may lead to another category of new poor—formerly well-off workers who will be displaced into long-term unemployment by productive servomechanisms.

Even those who do not suffer any absolute decline in their condition may be poor in tomorrow's circumstances; men in jobs which do not provide long vacations or adequate old-age pensions fall behind as more and more jobs provide these benefits. If the war on poverty is to keep pace with social change, it must build escalator improvements into the various social groups so that they can advance as society advances.

The reason the program lacks these needed escalator improvements is that it tends to ignore the problem of inequality. There is increasing evidence that inequalities in the distribution of income, wealth and social services are prominent and may be growing in the United States. Robert J. Lampman's data show that the concentration of wealth has been increasing in the United States since 1948; the share of income going to the bottom 10 percent has probably decreased since World War I; the income spread between the diploma elite and those who have not graduated from college has been widening. Though the suction power of World War II produced a social revolution reducing inequalities of income and wealth, there is a new rising tide of inequalities. The poverty programs, even taken most broadly, make no effort to reduce inequalities.

Tax legislation illustrates the point: the Kennedy-Johnson administration inadequately defended tax reform and readily capitulated to Congressional pressure in order to win a tax cut. In an effort to account for the declining rate of economic growth, the persistent rise in unemployment, and the greater frequency of recessions, the Council of Economic Advisors developed the concept of "the full employment surplus" or, more simply, "fiscal drag." Tax rates were retarding economic growth; as economic activity quickened, "tax revenues rose rapidly and soon began to operate as a check to growth." Two solutions were possible: much higher government spending or a huge tax cut. In today's political climate the administration opted for the tax cut. The tax cut, because it is intended to generate new jobs, is in President Johnson's view an important aspect of the war on poverty.

In its present unreformed state, our tax-reduction policy is based essentially on a trickle-down theory which assumes that as business prospers, the rewards trickle down—more or less equitably—to all sectors of the society. We believe a more frontal assault on the reduction of inequality is needed. A policy of redistribution not only of income and wealth but of services—especially education and health—is needed if poverty is to decline very markedly.

Despite the inadequacies of a long-term strategy of poverty reduction based on a fixed income line, some fixed standard is necessary to measure present-day needs and assess the adequacy of policies. The question then is: Where shall the poverty line be placed? The Council of Economic Advisors opted for a single standard—$3,000 yearly family income—despite the diversity in family size and in living costs in the United States. With present-day statistical sophistication and with the wealth of basic data, this decision seems unfortunate. It opens the war on poverty to the criticism that farm families of two are not necessarily poor if they have income of $3,000, and it removes the possibility of educating us to the existence of poverty among families with four or more children and incomes above $3,000.

The Council of Economic Advisors justifies its choice of a fixed $3,000 standard by the statement that "the analysis of the sources of poverty, and the programs needed to cope with it, would remain substantially unchanged" wherever the line is set. This assertion is inaccurate. Mollie Orshansky of the Social Security Administration has completed an important reanalysis of the characteristics of poverty in the United States based on a variable standard of poverty which takes into account farm and nonfarm residence, age and sex of family head, and number of children. The use of a variable rather than a fixed standard substantially alters the character of poverty, with important implications for policy and action. For example, the number of families headed by an aged person is halved, from 3.1 million to 1.5 million, while the number of children in poverty rises by more than one-third, from 11 to 15 million children. This grim statistic means that one of every four children in the United States lives in a family that is poor.

THE CAUSE-CONSEQUENCE DILEMMA

The 1964 Economic Report of the President, which presents

the analysis made by the Council of Economic Advisors, examines the incidence and composition of poverty in terms of aging, educational level, female-headed households, race and so on. This approach is useful because it underlines the diversity of the poor and the need for varied programs to deal with their differing needs and possibilities. (We will develop this point later, in the discussion of the comprehensiveness of programs.) But because it is not effectively linked to economic and other structural elements, the analysis does not offer an explanatory theory for the phenomena it describes.

This emphasis on the characteristics of the poor is a psychologizing of poverty; it makes the problem one of individual rehabilitation rather than social change. For the known vulnerable categories—the aged, the Negro, the family headed by a female—this approach fails to relate their plight to the character of our economic and social welfare institutions. For those outside the recognized categories—the more than 50 percent of the heads of poor families who are employed but do not earn a sufficient income—this approach can offer no solution at all. If we are going to categorize the poor, it makes much more sense to group them in terms of their relationship to the labor market, as done by Elizabeth Wickenden of the National Social Welfare Assembly. She talks about those groups who are employed but getting low wages; other groups who are actively interested in work but are unable to secure it and so on.

When we treat the characteristics of the poor as causes of their poverty, it is difficult to know what is consequence and what is cause. We do not know to what extent the characteristic subculture of the poor has developed as a protective response to living in poverty. If we view this subculture as the cause of their poverty, we may be simply blaming the poor for having adjusted to their environment.

Perhaps we are reading too much into the theory which underlies the war on poverty, but we do not believe so: Those who think of characteristics of the poor as causes of poverty, and of "the culture of poverty" as the main barrier to escaping from poverty, are much more likely to be sanguine about the course of the war on poverty than those who emphasize economic and social welfare programs as the main levers of change. Assumptions about the nature and causes of poverty have consequences in the choice and conduct of programs.

Let us consider, for example, that two million families, about 28 percent of all families in poverty, were headed by a person who worked full-time throughout the year. Low wages is the major cause of their poverty. It is common today to account for their low wages by their low productivity—the poor are unskilled, poorly educated and poorly motivated. Such an analysis implies that we must upgrade the skill and educational levels of the poor while leaving the economy untouched. But a more probing account—as suggested by Gabriel Kolko—of the prevalence of low wages must recognize that wages are also a function of the industry's competitive position in the economy, the capital investment ratio required to enter business, and the proportion of total operating costs which must go to wages. Textile industries cannot afford to pay high wages while the automotive and the steel industries can. This kind of analysis suggests solutions dramatically different from reeducating and retraining the poor.

The war on poverty, even it its broadest terms, does not provide wide coverage for all of the poor, as pledged in the preamble to the Economic Opportunity Act. Despite the concern with the characteristics of the poor, the legislation has not sensed the need for varied programs to meet the diversity of the poor. Rather, the initial thrust is toward those who are disaffected from work, as though this were the core of the problem of poverty in the United States.

S.M. Miller, linking cultural, family and economic variables, has outlined four categories of the poor:

> The *stable poor*, who are somewhat below the poverty line and have a stable family unit;
>
> The *copers* or the *strained*, who are in economically painful circumstances but have a stable family condition;
>
> The *skidders*, who are close to the economic level of the stable poor but suffer a good deal of internal family conflict;
>
> The *unstable poor*, who are in great economic and family difficulty.

The categories of the stable poor and the copers contain many aged; presumably Medicare, when enacted, will be part of the poverty war and will certainly help the aged poor. But there is little attention to overhauling the social security system in order to provide a decent floor for the aged which will be automatically adjusted as economic conditions change.

Many of the poor do not suffer from low job motivation, but from the inadequate number of available jobs. This is especially true of the stable poor and the strained. The war on poverty, at least initially, pays inadequate attention to these sizable groups, and the tax cut—the primary employment measure—is inadequate for the task of job creation. The emphasis on increasing employability rather than assuring employment is not enough for today's poor.

The 23 percent of the poor who are on welfare are sprinkled through all four of Miller's categories, but are probably more likely to be in the strained and unstable groupings. (The aged welfare poor are more likely to be in the stable poor.) The war on poverty has only the most limited programs to deal with those on welfare. These provisions, like the 1962 amendments to the Social Security Act, assume that professionalization of local welfare personnel and extension of casework services would basically attenuate the problems of the welfare poor and reduce the number of cases. We doubt that this is true, and we fear that in trying to fulfill this promise social work will be forced to forsake the humane principles on which casework is premised. More attention should be given to benefit levels, which in many states are fantastically low and must be raised, at least to the state's own definition of budgetary need. Stigma must be erased and the right to welfare assured if welfare is not to be debilitating to many. Self-help activities and social services should be separated from the provision of financial aid, so that they will not serve as punishments or infringements of legal rights.

Title V of the Economic Opportunity Act does, however, provide for work experience to increase the employability of those on public welfare. Whatever the intent of this legislation, such services are still work relief, and with 100 percent federal reimbursement they are likely to expand. The danger is that in the interest of reducing dependency, such services expand the discretionary judgments of the welfare bureaucracy and threaten the principle that assistance will be administered as a legal right, where individuals in similar circumstances are treated alike and where both eligibility and benefits are objectively determined. Consider the case which the American Civil Liberties Union recently appealed and won in New York (*People v. LaFountain*, May 19, 1964). Six men in the upstate New York city of St. Lawrence were criminally indicted because they refused to engage in a work relief project which required them to cut brush in below-freezing weather, knee deep in snow.

"No other long-range governmental program for the poor," observes Edward Spero, director of legal services at Mobilization for Youth, "has been torn by as much dispute and doubt on that which is a matter of legal 'right' and that which is a matter of charitable 'privilege.' " The legal services provided by Mobilization and other community action programs seek to provide counsel to welfare recipients to reduce administrative discretion, to enlarge the freedom of choice of clients, and to protect the principle of the legal right to assistance. Elizabeth Wickenden has observed that it is somewhat paradoxical that the poverty program, which provides no legal entitlement to its services, should spawn legal services committed to protecting the legal rights of the poor to welfare services.

YOUTH IN A TEST TUBE

The Economic Opportunity Act focuses almost exclusively on youth, probably as a result of both the American emphasis on education and our continuing fears of juvenile delinquency. "Poverty" measures of this sort can easily obtain Congressional approval.

The danger in the heavy focus on youth poverty is that it encourages the feeling that the problems of poverty are easily solvable, since young people can be trained relatively quickly for existing or expanded niches in society. The emphasis on youth perpetuates the myth that most poor people are misfits, unwilling or unable to work. It leads to an underemphasis on insuring the availability of jobs for those who want to work—the bulk, we suspect, of the nonaged, male poor—and on those who do work, but earn low wages or only obtain part-time employment.

Even within their own bailiwick, the youth programs have an ambiguity about their goals which may obscure a commitment to the eradication of poverty. Our concern with youth unemployment, it must be candidly acknowledged, is in part a concern for the social control of youth; it derives from our fear that they will cause social problems, whether of delinquency or rioting. Youth programs may not be considered failures if they just take care of youth for several years in an "aging vat" called a work camp or training program. If this becomes the fate of the programs, there is justice in the charge made by some that the war on poverty is a cloak for a war on the poor.

If the young people fail to enlist in the war, or—failing to see a payoff in real jobs—desert in great numbers, or fail to get decent jobs later despite their training, we may charge that it is something about *them* that is the obstacle. If we concentrate on youth as the source of failure, then we ignore the kind of analysis which might lead to new, more effective programs. In a difficult task, failures always occur. It is what they do to us and what we do about them that becomes significant in the longer-term picture. The great danger is in looking at failure only in terms of the inadequacy of the clientele and not in terms of the tasks of society.

The emphasis on youth, of course, has its attractive side—to rescue the young before they have fallen into apathy and despair; to provide new life for this rising generation and for the generation which they will father. But to speak of the "culture of poverty," and at the same time to be optimistic about small programs changing the outlook and life-prospects of the youth of this culture, implies that one does not really believe in the analysis. We cannot have it both ways. We cannot believe both that the culture of poverty is the problem and that hope can be injected into the situation with relative ease—through a training program, for example. The culture of poverty theme is terribly overplayed and underbelieved.

We are not confident that spending poverty funds on training programs that are separate from improving the economic conditions of families and neighborhoods is justified. It is quite possible that increasing the income of a poor family would do as much to increase the children's interest in further advancement. With training programs, some youngsters would escape more easily than before from poverty, but we think that it is important to change the conditions of groups as a whole, rather than providing a career open to the talented few of the impoverished.

The firmest element in the American consensus is the central role of education in pulling people out of poverty or in maintaining them above the poverty line. The analysis of the sources of poverty gives heavy emphasis to the greater incidence of poverty among families whose heads have had less than a grammar school education. The emphasis on education in high-industrial society is accurate, but it slurs over a number of important points about educational achievement levels and expenditures. We strive to get dropouts to graduate from high school at a time when high school graduates are suffering economically, especially relative to college and graduate school alumni. In the high-education society toward which we are moving, it is likely that high school graduates will continue to fall behind college graduates in income and security, and will have the vulnerabilities now characteristic of dropouts.

The question is not only the total amount spent on education, but on whom it is spent. While the poor have one-fourth of the children, they probably receive as little as one-tenth of the $28 billion spent on education in the United States. Morgan reports that children in the lowest income families attend schools where the expenditure per child is at least 13 percent below the national average.

As in many other realms of American life, a redistribution of expenditures is needed so that the poor benefit *more* than other groups. If the educational level or quality of the poor advances, but only as rapidly or less rapidly than the more advantaged groups, they will at best be getting only marginal increments in their ability to compete in the labor market. Despite the increase in educational expenditures, it is not at all clear that the low-income groups are differentially gaining. We cannot make a definitive statement because we do not have adequate data in this crucial area, but it is the impression of many that the overall increase in educational expenditures in the United States has not meant that a higher percentage of the expenditures is benefiting the low-income groups who most need the help. This impression may be inaccurate, but what is significant today is not only the total level of expenditures on education but the share allotted to the poor. Expanding educational expenditures will undoubtedly help the poor, but the contribution may not be substantial.

There is also the sad fact that giving more money to starved educational institutions will not be sufficient. True, they desperately need money; but many close observers of the American educational scene are convinced that great changes are needed in the conduct of education, changes which do not depend primarily on funds but on goals, selection, organization and pedagogy. New funds must be used in ways that improve the quality of education. The Vocational Education Act of 1963, which supports vocational education but redirects it away from home economics and farming, is a step in the right direction.

The recently enacted Elementary Education Act and the proposed Higher Education bill move in the right direction of spending more on education and hopefully on the education of the low-income population. But they fail to provide much impetus to move away from "educational business as usual." By placing a great deal of emphasis on state "planning" and "coordination," these educational measures are likely to create further red-tape obstacles to significant change. Nor would the higher education measures remedy the inadequate supply of places in colleges and universities today.

Political difficulties obviously intrude in developing a national educational policy, and we all must acknowledge the strength and spirit provided the U.S. Office of Education by Commissioner Francis Keppel. But the urgency of educational reform (as well as funding) requires that we move much more strenuously in this area than before.

THE WRONG TARGET

The primary thrust of the war on poverty is to improve the opportunities of the poor by changing them rather than the institutions which shape them. The rehabilitative programs in work training assume that if the poor are further trained, motivated and remotivated, they will be able to increase their chances in the main economy. The employing institutions are not major targets of change—whether through subsidies, direct governmental expenditures or investments—to insure the employment of the poor.

Our refusal to face social change is also revealed in our unreserved willingness to give funds to institutions that have time and again failed with the poor. Most educational systems. employment services and social agencies have a sorry record of inadequate and low-quality service to the poor—and frequently, to the nonpoor as well. Providing additional funds to financially starved institutions may improve their services, but not drastically. The need is for change—in goals, in organization, in personnel, in practices. Money helps achieve this, but does not guarantee *qualitative* improvement. Bureaucratic and professional encrustations in educational and social service organizations must be overcome if the kinds of services that will really improve the situations of the low-income population are to be produced. Monitoring programs, aimed only at insuring fiscal accountability or immediate placement, will be insufficient. Existing agencies and professions are not geared to working effectively with the poor. They need to be jogged, led, helped, checked, pressured into doing effective work. New kinds of agencies will have to be developed; new kinds of service occupations will have to emerge. The war on poverty cannot exempt from change the agencies that dispense its largesse. If it does, even large sums will have no impact.

The responsibility is always that of the program and its administrators to provide activities that are effective. Individuals do not fail to satisfy the needs of programs, but programs do fail to satisfy the needs of individuals. Programs are in the service of individuals.

The fundamentalist critics of the war on poverty raise a value issue which goes deeper than any disability of specific segments of the program. They ask whether our aspirations in this war are limited merely to moving more people into the economic mainstream of the United States, or whether we intend to modify the character of our society by changing the prevailing pattern of squalid public services and opulent private goods.

The pragmatists rightly reply—not everything in a day. The "Great Society" theme moves in the fundamentalist direction. But if that theme is to be more than a slogan of hope, it will have to lead at some point to questions about basic changes in American society.

Social Action
on the Installment Plan

MARTIN REIN AND S.M. MILLER

Programs of social change—like all government programs—usually come under political and budgetary scrutiny early in their lives. No matter how comprehensive and ennobling the proponents of a program say it is, the program must still run a political and economic gauntlet to prove its effectiveness and its value. With billions of dollars being allocated to meet changing social needs, we urgently need methods of effecting change that are speedy, appropriate, rational and inexpensive. Many planning bodies, both in and out of government, believe that the "demonstration" or "demonstration-research" project is one of the most powerful methods of bringing about change.

A demonstration project is a small program, founded for a definite period of time (its counterpart in industry is usually called a pilot project). It has specific objectives and approaches which are subjected to critical scrutiny; it serves a select area and population with the fervent hope that the lessons it learns and demonstrates, through the rigors of scientific research, will somehow lead to large-scale adoption and major shifts in the aims, styles, resources and effectiveness of major social service organizations and programs.

It is seldom made entirely clear how this transfer will actually come about. This is probably its chief failing. When an industry runs a pilot program to test or gather information on a new process or campaign, it will usually follow through on its findings. If it fails to be responsive to changing preferences and new technology it may find its profit margin shrinking and its very survival threatened. Social service agencies, however, are not governed by the rules of a competitive economy. As a result they will seldom institute major internal changes—even when feasibility is demonstrated—without outside prodding from government agencies, foundations or other fund-givers or policymakers.

To add to or change existing services means to alter direction and effectiveness; therefore, the analysis of the demonstration project means analysis of social needs and of institutional resistances to change. To examine change is to assess present function —and it forces reexamination of the basic outlook and ideas of social services.

John Kenneth Galbraith has called the demonstration "the modern device for stimulating action without spending money." It is the current "in" thing in social services. A conservative estimate of the cost of demonstration projects in 1964 probably runs about $50 million. In a variety of guises they appear in the war on poverty, manpower retraining, welfare programs, public health, juvenile delinquency, vocational rehabilitation, public housing, education and area redevelopment.

The following are two examples of demonstration projects:

In the slums of one city an advanced preschool program has been set up for the benefit of a few children in a few schools in a neighborhood that does not have enough kindergartens. The hope is that its success, if any, may lead to a major change in the preschool and kindergarten training for disadvantaged children in the area and throughout the city school system.

In a high-crime neighborhood of another city, three social workers on special assignment set out to reach three juvenile gangs considered unreachable by the traditional settlement houses and the police. They were successful, as special assignment workers have been in other cities. But the program was dropped when completed, was never implemented, and most of the recommendations were not followed.

HOPE AND DESPAIR

The name itself—demonstration-research—is both a confession of despair and a profession of hope. There is despair because the needs and problems are so vast, the weight of past failure so oppressive, and what to do next so uncertain. But there also is hope that goals will be defined, the project might work, and research might lead to truth—and that when the right answers are found, rational men will adopt or expand them.

Demonstrations seem to be a way to get action. They spark flurries of activity; they are highly visible; things seem to be happening; private agencies and government bureaus that would not grant funds for operating projects will grant them for demonstrations.

The defects are equally glaring. Demonstrations are also a way to *dodge* action or *postpone* major change—relatively little money is spent, relatively few people are affected, the real problem is hardly touched. Public criticism concerning needed improvements is blunted, at least for a time. And if public interest has drifted when the demonstration finishes, the whole idea of squarely facing major needs can be allowed to die quietly.

This contradiction indicates uncertainty and lack of clear policy. We want to achieve desired social aims—but avoid unnecessary cost. How? We also know that institutions must change. But again, how? For example, should school boards concentrate on integrated schools or quality schools? In dealing with poverty, should we concentrate on the young or the old? Since we have no national social welfare policy, the demonstration project, allowing trial without apparent commitment, is very attractive. Further, it can conveniently meet a major political problem by a token activity which may not solve it, but will not lose votes either.

The emphasis on research carries the aura and prestige of science and rigorous testing into social policy. (After all, if science can conquer space, why can't it conquer poverty?) The scientific aura often masks value judgments by seeming to transform them into technical questions. Is school integration really important because of its effect on learning, as many analysts believe—or because it fosters desegration, as many others believe? The desirability of research should be recognized—but not overemphasized.

The major purpose of the demonstration is to test the validity of ideas which claim to improve the services and policies of established institutions (schools, welfare and health departments, training centers). As long as change is approached through experimentation and small-scale innovation, judgment must be reserved, and condemnation for failure cannot be severe.

The demonstration project is an instrument of change; but it does not severely threaten the established institutions and it demands no immediate action. Peter Marris describes it as "the middle ground between conforming . . . and uncompromising reform." He feels that the demonstration project is an attempt "to professionalize social reform." By means of it the need for change is met in a way that established organizations can live with—perhaps even control.

In broad sum, the assets of the demonstration project are that it is fashionable, politically attractive, rationally appealing, inexpensive and not binding.

THE LIABILITIES

Are we justified in placing so much hope in demonstration projects? Their very virtues are also their defects. Doesn't the professional control of discontent obscure the dramatization of issues that are often necessary for significant change? Reform can be self-limiting and incoherent if it proceeds only when it can secure the cooperation of the institution which it seeks to reform. The weaknesses of a broad commitment demonstration program become obvious in practice:

1. They often promote unequal distribution of money and resources;
2. They distract from national policy;
3. They overemphasize success and they tend to disregard or play down failure.

By their very limited and experimental nature, demonstrations favor some people, some organizations and some locations over others. Some slum children get to go to well-organized nursery schools while those a few blocks away do not even have kindergartens; the poor young residents on the lower East Side of Manhattan get aid programs from Mobilization for Youth which are not available to similar groups in the rest of Manhattan, much less the Watts section of Los Angeles.

Generally, this differentiation is defined as a social good; some help, somewhere, is better than none, anywhere; and it is only by contrast with a control group that the worth of an experimental program can be established. What happens nationally, however, is that whether people in similar situations get the help they need depends on local success in getting demonstration money from funding agencies, plus local willingness to invest the necessary resources, time, skill and effort. The social services flourish in those cities willing and able to experiment; they languish in other cities. A new source of social injustice emerges—between those fortunate needy who happen to live in the cities rich in demonstration projects, and those who do not.

Since demonstrations emphasize local initiative, they work against the establishment of national standards and national agencies of assistance. Entrenched local interests often vigorously oppose liberal welfare benefits—many of the important changes in public policy have come about because it was necessary to deliberately overcome local interests that preferred low taxes to adequate welfare. Therefore, a program that serves a limited population in a small corner of a city at whatever cost (Mobilization for Youth in its first three years of operation cost more than $12 million) may be simply distracting from the major tasks needing to be done. Critics such as Harvey Perloff contend that social planning must be part of a national policy—controlled by a national planning organization like the President's Council of Economic Advisors. Local demonstrations can quickly become misplaced do-goodism. They can easily become permanent substitutes for vital broad-based programs. Demonstrations are now being used to train unemployed youths to qualify for jobs. As far as this goes, it is all to the good; but any retraining program with national meaning requires a major reform of public vocational high schools—not just demonstration-research.

A good idea, however well demonstrated, does not always drive out a bad one, or lead to more good ideas. It may, instead, prevent the use and adoption of better ideas which happen not to have been tested yet. Of course, action cannot be held up indefinitely in the hope of perfection; but we should not immediately adopt any idea because it is "better than what we have" if this means closing off potentially more promising avenues. (In fact, improvement should never stop at any terminal goal, no matter how good. The ideal is open-end adaptability—continuing improvement to meet changing circumstances.)

Since demonstrations are by definition small-scale interventions, they may be too small in scope to discover and bring about the major changes that might need to be made. For instance, a demonstration testing whether more social workers offering greater individualized services will rehabilitate and give more self-respect to relief recipients will not mean much if the welfare requirements themselves humiliate and degrade recipients by continued invasion of privacy and implied moral criticism.

While demonstrations can fail because they are too small in scope, they can also fail if too large. If too much money descends too quickly on a small operation dedicated to radical change. it can soon suffer hardening of the bureaucratic arteries and become a vested interest which will fight change.

YARDSTICK OF SUCCESS

The ultimate test of the success of a demonstration is whether it can actually influence long-term and large-scale policy. It is not enough to have proven that an idea will work if that idea then dies and is interred in a report. But the fundamental question of how a successful demonstration will lead to major policy changes is usually left obscure. The question is seldom even raised—yet nothing in planning can be more important. The comfortable slogan that "nothing can resist an idea whose time has come" avoids the crucial factor in social planning: How can success on a small scale become a means for change, improvement, and greater effectiveness in major institutions?

Three questions are fundamental to the strategy of the

demonstration and must be answered: What kind of influence do the promotors of the demonstration intend to have? Whom do they hope to influence? How will they exert that influence?

What is the demonstration demonstrating? Influence can be exerted and expressed in several ways:

Spread. Do the promoters want their project duplicated exactly elsewhere as needed?

Continuity. Do they want the original project continued on a more permanent basis—perhaps with more money and on an expanded scale? (Continuity is often used as a first stage, to be followed, hopefully, by spread. Usually there is more money available for demonstrations than program expansion; so administrators learn the art of grantmanship and keep applying for new demonstrations and the continuity of the old ones as a means of expansion.)

Spillover. Is the purpose of the demonstration simply to attract attention to a problem—to show that something must be done about it (the solution not necessarily being the same as developed in the demonstration)? In spillover the demonstration serves merely as catalyst, not as model. The goal is the creation of a desire for reform and experimentation.

Those responsible for demonstration projects are often uncertain about who should do what. The President's Committee on Juvenile Delinquency and Youth crime, for example, tried on the one hand to impress a national audience with the necessity of learning and doing something about delinquency—and tried, on the other, to select projects that could make the greatest local changes. Consider the implications of this confusion. Money must come from somewhere, and on a reliable basis. If the demonstration is trying to convince Congress or the state legislature that delinquency, or a preschool program for children, is a federal or state responsibility, then the state or federal governments should appropriate the money. If they are trying to convince local authorities that it is the community's responsibility to keep its own services going, then plans must be made to expand the local tax base or secure revenue from other local sources. It is difficult to see how all of these audiences can be satisfied simultaneously, without developing some priorities.

While vagueness reduces the need for immediate choice,

postponement may only encourage, in the end, a monumental passing of the buck. Consider Project Head Start. If the summer demonstration program proved to be, as President Johnson suggested, "battle-tested" and "worthy," then, as Fred Hechinger, education editor of the *New York Times*, recently asked, "Why is it that so little effort is being made to move in the Head Start direction with local funds?" This question certainly suggests a rather fundamental ambiguity as to who should do what.

TARGETS AND STRATEGY

Whom is the demonstration supposed to influence? Most people assume that they act from rational motives and that what they approve of is "objectively good"; but businessmen, politicians and professionals have different ideas of what constitutes "good." By what criterion do you judge the success of a demonstration in an urban school? Do you measure pupil performance? Adjustment? Cost? What audience was the project aimed for?

Questions of strategy must be answered, because the likelihood of failure to implement successful demonstrations is strong. Established institutions have a vested interest in their own survival, and a built-in resistance to serious change. To get institutions to recognize and incorporate reforms, demonstrations must first be successful. But a successful program is one that is accepted—and established institutions will not readily accept anything threatening. They favor change in small doses—regular, logical steps, built firmly on the foundations of existing programs. But the next "logical" step may never come to grips with the problem, and be far too conservative from any but a purely local viewpoint. Nevertheless, planning organizations and professionally inspired reform must often settle for those programs likely to win financial support from those with local influence. In the resultant political maneuvering and mutual accommodation, the innovations and the problem that needs solving, may come out second best. The necessity to survive usually results in abandoning the strategies for promoting spread and spillover.

In practice, spread often occurs when national funders implement their own policy before the demonstration results are all in—and the pressure is strong for demonstrations merely to prove that they were right. The Amendments to the 1962 Social Security Act are a case in point—the policy of rehabilitation to reduce dependency was first inaugurated with only scattered evidence to support its validity; demonstrations were then set up to prove its worth. Preschool programs for the poor followed a similar pattern. The federal government has, unexpectedly, rescued these demonstrations by serving as a mechanism—through Operation Head Start—for encouraging spread. But frequently it has done so by undermining the very purposes of the demonstration—to implement policies already rationally tested. Thus we appear to have achieved spread, at the cost of rationality.

While funders of demonstrations have given little attention to the strategies of promoting spread and spillover, they have developed an approach for assuring continuity of the life of the demonstration. Three crucial elements of this strategy can be identified: participation, money and knowledge. Let us examine these in turn.

Participation. Some projects try to develop a local board of directors with "clout"—power and influence. In theory, if the board becomes convinced of the correctness of a position, it will have the power and will to do something about it. The demonstration then becomes a strategy for educating the board. One difficulty with this premise is that people with power and influence are very often opposed to spending money for social welfare. They believe in fiscal containment—for them, holding down expenses is the greatest public virtue. They know that voluntary philanthropy cannot do the job alone, but they are philosophically unwilling to expand public participation, which must, in the end, mean increased taxation.

Why should anyone expect a powerful board of busy people to vigorously promote continuity? How much actual involvement can result from formal monthly meetings in which highly selective agendas screen out or postpone most controversy? Yet the belief that participation must lead to commitment remains a persistent and almost cherished myth about how to promote change. It reflects the professional bias which defines change as a process of self-education.

Money. What about financial involvement? Many funding bodies, like the Ford Foundation and various governmental agencies, require "matching funds," money that the community itself must put up as a sign of good faith and commitment. This is supposed to insure that the community will follow through on those demonstrations that work in order not to lose its initial investment.

In practice, however, funders often accept "matching" funds which do not match. A city may simply say that parts of its regular budget outlays for vocational schools, or playgrounds, are "matching funds" for a retraining or delinquency project—and the funder may accept this although in fact the city has spent nothing additional. The President's Committee on Juvenile Delinquency has accepted a Ford Foundation grant as a community's matching fund—and the Ford Foundation has in turn accepted the committee's grant to meet *its* requirement. The community involved here escaped unscathed financially. Such fiscal participation is unlikely to yield a deep commitment to the demonstration.

Besides, matching funds are only for the demonstration. What about the morning after the wedding? Who will pay for felicity during the long years ahead, at steadily increasing prices? Cities have limited tax bases. Boards shy away from projects with increasing budgets—the standard of efficiency is often measured by low cost, not high yield. Who will keep the project going?

If the who, what and how questions are not answered with clarity and determination, a demonstration program, no matter how successful, can easily turn out to be a ritual where change is measured by activity, not by performance.

The power of knowledge. At its best, a demonstration is supposed to be planned, based on and proven by the crucial ingredient of research. Sponsors have firm conviction that the results will be so definite, clear-cut and dramatic that organizations will be impelled to find the opportunity to apply the innovations on a large scale.

Such hopes are like the search for the philosophers' stone. In practice, findings are usually inconclusive and nondramatic; and even if they are overwhelming, there is no assurance they will change anything. Nonetheless, the bread-on-the-waters approach prevails, with firm faith that good ideas must inevitably prevail, and repay a hundredfold.

Consider the early experience of the President's Committee on Juvenile Delinquency, which put great emphasis on research. Often the two research functions—policy making and evaluation —were confounded. The time needed to gather and interpret data that would influence policy was underestimated—with the inevitable result that, since action had to proceed if the program was to survive, the research became an after-the-fact justification of decisions already taken.

Often the whole point of the research was lost. The basic purpose was to test whether social institutions throw up barriers to achievement, and thereby bring about the very alienation and delinquency they deplore. But the researchers hired for the purpose wanted to be rigorously scientific; they fell back on standard techniques of examining individuals—the failings of persons rather than the failings of institutions. Relevance was sacrificed to rigor.

Under the best circumstances, evaluation of results is distressingly difficult. A demonstration project breaks new ground, or should. If it must include a great many unknowns, as in the case of comprehensive demonstrations, how then do you define exactly what is being demonstrated? Moreover, in the absence of clearly defined goals—the norm and not the exception in social action programs—how can effectiveness be measured? But even if the output measures could be clearly defined, often the time required to secure relevant information is much greater than the funders are willing to accept. For example, if we establish an innovative nursery program on the assumption that it will reduce delinquency or poverty, then a valid test requires that we should follow these youngsters through their school careers to adolescence or even to young adulthood. Even if we ask a more limited question about whether nursery programs facilitate later school adjustment, we would need to wait at least five years for reliable answers.

As a result of these difficulties, evaluation research alone can seldom serve as the primary justification for continuing a project. Perhaps this is just as well. Research findings are much more likely to show that expectations were unrealistic, rather than to prove them worthwhile. For instance, a decade and more than a million dollars has gone into research trying to evaluate how effective social case work is. Perhaps the only trustworthy inference to emerge is that more research is needed. Barbara Wootton has observed that the positive achievements of the social sciences have largely been negative: "Up until now the chief effect of precise investigation into questions of social pathology has been to undermine the creditability of virtually all the current myths."

Put bluntly, present-day research methodology is simply inadequate for evaluating comprehensive demonstration programs, which are subject to the vagaries of political expediency.

We turn now from the strategy which the funders have used to promote continuity, to consider the often-implied strategies by which demonstrations might produce institutional change. Clearly, all of these strategies—infiltration, duplication and pressure—are not equally appropriate to the various aims of the demonstration—spread, continuity, and spillover. Selecting a strategy designed to achieve the objectives of the demonstration is obviously one way of strengthening it as an instrument of change.

Infiltration from within. Sometimes a small demonstration is set up inside an established institution (the experimental preschool program within an existing school system) in the hope that the larger will someday come to adopt the innovation of the smaller. How this will come about is not clear, but presumably by the force of good example, or by the tendency of a host organism to eventually develop toleration for a foreign body. Here again, if faith is placed in the power of knowledge to create change then results must be dramatic and unambiguous to be effective. Unfortunately they seldom are.

Also, the demonstration must be able to fit into the larger institution, while trying to change it. This is very difficult. If its concerns are peripheral to the host, it will have little influence. (A preschool program tacked onto a school system which never had one will not affect the higher grades.) If its concerns are fundamental, it will be resisted. The host has control; it is composed of various subgroups which have needs and interests which compete with the demonstration. In practice, in order to avoid confrontation, innovations usually get watered down.

Various methods may be used to keep the demonstration project from seriously changing the host organization. It can become a walled-off enclave able to go its own way as long as it doesn't bother people outside the walls, who go their own way. It can concentrate on remedial programs—remedies are always popular because they patch up old sores (and may even hide them)—rather than perform surgery. Indeed, as a general rule, any demonstration project concentrating on providing remedial service for an established institution has announced its inability to affect deep change, for instance, providing remedial reading services rather than changing the teaching of reading.

In short, as long as the host organization has control, significant change can be resisted. If sponsoring or funding organizations want it to achieve its goals, they should retain some control over its progress, but the more control they exercise the more alien the project becomes to the host.

Under some circumstances the infiltration tactic will work—a foreign body has been introduced into a system, and it must bring on some reaction. The energy, concern, enthusiasm and moral indignation of former Peace Corps volunteers in one school system has disturbed the old equilibrium and shaken up the teachers, destroying a few shibboleths in the process. They also, however, raised resistance and resentment, which in the end undermined the changes they wanted to bring about. The art, then, with such infiltration tactics, is to find the chemical balance that can release great energy and innovation without creating explosion.

Duplication from without. One attractive way to get around an institution's resistance to change is to build a parallel institution which duplicates some or all of its functions, doing them better, in the hope that the established institution will modify its operation accordingly. Duplicate structures have the potential advantage of starting from scratch, unhampered by the dead hand of old practices and rigidities.

In Philadelphia, for example, Opportunities Industrialization, an organization led by Negroes, is attempting, with support from the mayor, the Ford Foundation, and the Office of Economic Opportunity, to set up a system of vocational schools separate from and parallel to the public vocational schools. Recently the Ford Foundation announced a grant to the Church Federation of Chicago which will develop programs that duplicate the activities of a local community action program.

But duplication is an open indictment of the old institution. Obviously, sponsors would not set up parallel facilities if they did not think the old needed change, or if they had much faith in its ability to change itself. The established institution may, therefore, consider paralleling as a declaration of war, inviting swift retaliation. The old institution usually has superior resources for combat and greater experience. Cooperation may be superficial; guerrilla war may develop. It can ask embarrassing questions at high levels (why was the duplication thought necessary?) that can subject the demonstration to constant and pitiless criticism, exposure and examination.

Duplication also bears the vice of expense. To set up a separate school system, for example, is enormously costly, especially if we want high quality. Nevertheless, its virtues should not be overlooked. As Charles Frankel says, we must have "deliberate planning to provide alternatives." We need to invigorate existing agencies to create new ones whose function is to be a thorn in the side of existing bureaucracies—agencies that bear witness to what might be, that animate, enrage and discipline the public imagination. Such agencies could give the public a better chance to choose what it wants and, indeed, to discover what it wants. But if the strategy for promoting spread and spillover is not effective and only continuity is achieved, then duplication can further reduce the coherence of an already fragmented local system for delivering services to people.

Pressures from without. Another way to get action toward implementing demonstration findings is to organize citizen groups—especially those with a personal stake in improving service—to put pressure on local officials or institutions.

Those affected usually know whether they have been getting the services they need, and can, if organized, be useful in seeing that they do get them. Saul Alinsky's Industrial Areas Foundation has been using such tactics for some time and it has inspired others, like the Syracuse Community Development Association, to use them. The Syracuse project is a federally financed antipoverty demonstration program to develop techniques for organizing the poor. Organizers have " 'provoked' the poor to take action in their self interest . . . they have helped organize sit-ins, pickets, and campaigns to protest everything from garbage collections to welfare procedures " (*New York Times*, December 3, 1965).

Social change through citizen action has become increasingly necessary and important. It has many advantages; but it has the great disadvantage that it may quickly build up a backlash of resentment that can make almost any cooperation or alternative strategy impossible. This happened to Mobilization for Youth (MFY) when it organized and encouraged mothers to put pressure directly on school administrators for better conditions for children. The principals, enraged, counterattacked MFY, accusing it of irresponsible agitation. Future cooperation, obviously, became very difficult. The Syracuse project is at present fighting a decision of the Office of Economic Opportunity to cut off its independent financing and force it to apply for funds to the city's official antipoverty program.

The purposes of the strategy are often obscured, for it is at once conceived: as a form of social therapy—people change when they try to change their environment; as a form of protest whose chief aim is to promote institutional change and achieve a more equitable distribution of resources; and as a way of promoting democracy itself—people should be involved in making decisions which affect their lives. But the tactics required to promote the goals of therapy, change and democratic participation often conflict.

The use of citizen pressure, if it fails, may close off the opportunity for other strategies. Moreover, the bitter opposition which such programs create from established institutional powers may serve to reaffirm the powerlessness and helplessness of the poor, and thus defeat their very purposes.

IMPROVING THE ODDS

How can demonstrations become better agents of change? Here are some suggestions:

1. Funders should insist not only that the demonstration be relevant to the social problem involved, but that the staff also be clear on questions of social policy. Few things are more subversive than a good question. What proof is there of real innovation? Who supports the innovation? How exactly will the community employment and retraining program be reorganized? Are there enough resources and "clout" to push the program through in spite of resistance from established institutions?

2. Greater clarity of purpose is necessary. A major problem is not technology but ideology—what is the goal? Is it to achieve continuity, spread or spillover? A demonstration that knows where it is going almost inevitably becomes involved in implementation, in making its recommendations effective. When purposes are unclear not only is direction and momentum lost, but outcomes are difficult to evaluate. How can "results" be judged unless the demonstrator knows whether he is planning to provide choice, planning for coordination, planning for accountability, planning for innovation, or making a master plan, to be used as a model?

3. The funders must stay with the projects, not quit when the going gets rough. The demonstration cannot last or be effective if it is constantly swept with rumors that the funds will stop, and the backers quit backing. The best available evidence suggests that large-scale community planning takes at least seven to ten years—there is no known way to hurry this process. Funders who give way easily to fads, impatience or politics cannot give adequate leadership.

4. The funders must be more concerned with getting and maintaining quality. This may require more monitoring (though not meddling, admittedly a fine distinction). One way of building in accountability—a central necessity for improving social service—would be to set up a public review

board of experts, chosen for knowledge, perspective and integrity.

5. New methods of reporting and accountability would be useful in many ways. Merely requiring better reporting can make agencies more accountable, fostering reform and innovation. Ernest Gruenberg describes a state department of mental hospitals that began to send out a monthly questionnaire to each hospital, asking how many patients were still being kept in straitjackets—and found that the number declined sharply every month. Similarly, Peter Blau reports that when interviewers in an employment service were required to report how many Negroes got job referrals, the rate immediately went up. In both cases all the administrators wanted initially was information; but reporting brought immediate reform. Projects should therefore be required to make reports which permit more accountability of the products they produce. Simply having to describe and break down the numbers and kinds of youths contacted and served or rejected in a delinquency or training program might give administrators a clearer idea of how effective they were, and inform those who shape policy whether the tough cases were being rejected in order to "cream" the easy. The statistics could also be used for large-scale planning concerned with the entire lives of youths, rather than a specialized function.

6. Choices must be made. A program cannot promise, or achieve, everything. (This is related to the clarity and selection of goals and means.) The adoption of a policy is a commitment which itself shapes the development of an organization, and it must be carefully chosen. A proliferation of goals in a program usually reflects low confidence in major achievements. Multiplicity and alteration of goals often substitutes for effectiveness of action.

7. Demonstrations should call for continuous change. While the goal should be definite, it should indicate a direction, a focus, and not a terminus at which everything comes to a stop. As an experiment yields information, a feedback

mechanism should operate which allows continuous modification. Mechanisms must be built which are continually
sensitive and adaptive to new problems and new weaknesses.

8. Demonstration staffs must be prepared for, and learn to live
with, conflict. They should not seek it out; they should try
to minimize it; but they cannot do their job without
challenging existing practices and stirring up resistance. Too
little conflict may very well be proof of failure rather than
success. Since they must work and contend with established
institutions, they should have some sophisticated knowledge about the internal nature of organizations and professions. Organizations are not monolithic; even when they
seem to be "consensus establishments," there is always a
restless underground willing to go in another direction; and
progress and cooperation depends on finding and strengthening those who support the demonstration policies or can
suggest new directions.

There is no sure way of getting desirable results—each
action provokes reaction and involves risk. But the primary
talent in running a successful demonstration is not technical
but administrative and political. It is not enough to know
what is best to do—the administrator must be able to
organize forces to get things done.

9. Research should be broadened to make it relevant to all
social needs and to the whole service world. What is
important here is not only the understanding of a single
service, but of the overall pattern. Research can be vital in
probing the consequences that flow from the present
organization of social services. And since much of what we
are doing is attempting to learn what is useful to do,
research can help in the search for usable goals. This effort
requires new kinds of links and tensions between programs
and research.

Demonstration projects are not supposed to accept the easy
answers. If they are concerned with usefulness rather than
"success," they must ask the tough questions, probe for the basic

issues, regard the accepted decisions with a sceptical eye. In the great debates on national social policy now under way, they can serve as what Peter Marris has called "moral witness" to the accepted social and welfare services.

The New Mythology of Housing

MICHAEL A. STEGMAN

Good housing can make good people, even out of poor people. Such, cruelly compressed, was the cherished belief of housing reformers as they campaigned 30 years ago for low-rent public housing for the urban poor. By now, needless to say, that belief has been exposed as a myth. It has been shown to rest on faulty assumptions not only with respect to why poor people are poor, but also about what can be done to make them "better." As one student of urban affairs put it:

> Once upon a time, we thought that if we could only get our problem families out of those dreadful slums, then papa would stop taking dope, mama would stop chasing around, and Junior would stop carrying a knife. Well, we've got them in a nice apartment with modern kitchens and a recreation center. And they're the same bunch of bastards they always were.

This is to state the disillusionment rather crudely, to be sure; but that is exactly the trouble with founding public policy on mythic grounds. The poor are held to be incurable. The reformers who helped spread the faulty gospel are crucified as false prophets or fade away as the public action they helped get going fails to solve the "problems." But, worse than this, their failures never seem to stimulate any attempts to correct the myths or modify the procedures. Rather, they serve only to weaken subsequent efforts to rally political support for further public action. In the case of low-rent public housing, the whole purpose of the program—the provision of decent shelter for the poor—was smeared along with the exposure of its guiding myth.

Today, the public housing program goes without its traditional liberal and intellectual support; it goes without union support; and it goes without any broad demand among the electorate. And as for the poor, they go without decent housing. As John P. Dean wrote 20 years ago in a review of our disappointing efforts in housing reform "... in the meantime, the patient has continued to sicken."

What I want to do here is take a hard look at what I believe are the *emerging* myths concerning community development and housing. It is only prudent to acknowledge that it would be much less risky to wait another decade or so to pass judgment. Yet by discussing the emerging myths before they become crystalized, I may be able to raise some fundamental questions about their utility as a basis for public action. Moreover, the time seems particularly ripe now that the federal government has passed a multibillion dollar housing bill.

The Model Cities program provides a sophisticated example of current thinking about the complexities of the slum housing nexus. Its pronouncements at least indicate a heightened awareness that housing and social service needs are closely interrelated and might best be met simultaneously with a global attack. This is a far cry from the "good housing = good people" theory of years past, but I still get the nagging feeling that the emerging housing reform myths are going to be equally counterproductive.

The old myths developed as justifications for direct federal intervention in an area previously dominated by the private sector. The new myths are rationalizations for particular federal responses to housing problems that have remained unsolved in spite of earlier governmental involvement. These myths, which are concerned more with notions of how the problems can be solved than with their basic causes, can be characterized as follows:

Myths surrounding the nature of the owners of substandard housing;

Mythical explanations of the potential role of nonprofit sponsors in solving the nation's housing problems;

Myths involving the potential value of adopting a systems approach to neighborhood renewal;

Myths surrounding emerging efforts to involve unemployed ghetto manpower in the rehabilitation of slum housing;

Myths explaining why low-income *ownership* programs should be expected to solve those same social problems that the previous low-income minimum *rental* programs could not solve.

MYTH 1: SLUMLORDS

... the slumlord, that small body of landlords [who] are out to squeeze every last dollar out of the property as quickly as they can, regardless of the consequences in terms of human life, suffering and sickness. It is against this small minority that battle must be given—constant, unremitting and unrelenting battle.—*Former Mayor Robert Wagner of New York*.

Believers in this specimen myth frequently wind up their "argument" with the observation of David Hunter that all owners of substandard housing "look as though they had spent their childhoods drowning their playmates" and then grew up to play that same deadly game as adults—only now in more subtle and painful ways.

This amateurish personality profile of the "typical slumlord" tends to confuse the real issues and has served to distort our national housing policy since the end of World War II. It has encouraged a myopic view of the housing problem, and it has demonstrably provided an outright faulty basis for public action. The stereotype of the slumlord strongly implies that the owners of substandard housing are largely responsible for our chronic housing problem, simply because they are evil men. This is not so for at least four reasons.

First, the stereotype doesn't stand up statistically. There are upwards of six million substandard housing units in our nation's cities and literally hundreds of thousands of individual landlords. Can *all* their owners match the above grotesque? Surely it is more reasonable to assume that their personal characteristics distribute in a pattern similar to that found in any large sample of population.

Second, slumlords and tenants enjoy, if that's the word, a perfectly symbiotic relationship; that is, they need each other. The owners need the poor and troubled because few others would consider living in depressed housing; and who but the poor and troubled must seek the cheapest possible shelter? Yet, this is no justification for blaming the owners for creating the shortages in decent low-rent housing that mark the inner cores of our cities. The notion that owners of substandard units cause the sickness and suffering that plague the unfortunate families who dwell there sounds suspiciously like an inversion of the "good housing = good people" theory.

Third, the charge that most owners of slum properties are making excess profits may be seriously questioned, both within the real estate industry and in comparison with other major industries. While financial information on slums is extremely scarce, such relatively recent works as Woody Klein's *Let in the Sun* include some economic data that will disconcert liberal believers in the bloated slumlord myth. For example, the 36-unit tenement Klein wrote about grossed nearly one-half million dollars over a 60-year period ending in 1966. The New York City Planning Commission has estimated that such structures generally return around 36 percent of gross revenues on a net basis. With respect to the building in question, then, aggregate net revenues for the 60 years would have amounted to approximately $180,000, or an annual average of $3,000. Since fixed expenses (taxes, water and sewer charges and insurance) of such substandard tenements average 25 percent of gross revenues, it's obvious that when you then add on fuel and minimal maintenance costs, there will be little left over for major repairs. In fact, Klein estimates that in order to bring the tenement up to the standard specified in New York City's housing code, annual operating expenses would have to increase by $4,000 per year, which means an annual loss of $3,278. Undermaintenance therefore may be not only a rational, but a necessary means of survival in an industry beset with increased unionization and its concomitant, rising costs, as well as tenant incomes that remain either the same or fall over the years and the same or lower levels of occupancy.

Fourth, it is an incontrovertible fact that almost half (47 percent) of our national housing inventory was built before 1929. Our cities are getting older. And in housing, as in humans, aging causes problems, but it seems naive to place the responsibility for such problems at the feet of the landlord. Old structures are found in old neighborhoods, and more and more of them are becoming slums. Data from the South Los Angeles area show that the proportion of substandard units in that community increased from 18 percent to 34 percent between 1960 and 1965. In New York City the number of slum housing units went from 475,000 in 1960 to an estimated 800,000 in late 1968. The Department of Labor estimates that 600,000 rural and semirural individuals are migrating into large urban areas each year. The housing crisis will surely increase as greater pressures are exerted upon an already aged and obsolete housing stock.

By adopting the myth of the slumlord, the public forecloses any consideration of an alliance with the owner of substandard housing in an attempt to find an enlightened approach to the problem. Also written off is much of the huge investment locked into the existing low-rent private housing stock.

MYTH 2: NONPROFIT SPONSORS

Top housing officials have apparently accepted the myth of the slumlord. They have washed their hands of the individual low-rent property owner. A measure of their disenchantment is the increasing federal attention being paid to such nonprofit institutions as churches, foundations, fraternal organizations and labor unions in their low- and moderate-income housing efforts.

In fact, a program was initiated in 1961 which could be interpreted as designed to stimulate such housing efforts. Known by the call letters 221(d)(3), it provides mortgage monies at low interest rates to nonprofit sponsors. Yet at this writing only 1,568 rental units have been rehabilitated under 221(d)(3), while only 46,565 new units have been built.

The meager contributions of 221(d)(3) can be readily explained. First, there has been an insufficient and uneven flow of federal funds to purchase below-market mortgages. Second, Congress cannot make up its mind whether the Federal Housing Authority should continue to broaden its social perspective, or model its role on that of a conservative Back Bay banker. Third and finally, the federal requirements for obtaining the financing are so complex and difficult to satisfy, that only the most energetic and well-staffed sponsors can succeed in getting any. The 221(d)(3) program requires filing forms for preapplication, application, precommitment processing, preinitial closing, initial closing and final closing stages—more than 40 forms in all. Urban America, Inc., recently published a guide to the program which is 359 pages long.

Simply put, the concept of nonprofit sponsors such as churches developing housing throughout the nation's urban areas on a scale large enough to have any measurable impact is basically ill conceived. When one considers the incredibly large number of steps involved in the residential development process, one has to conclude that the average church is just not prepared to carry the burden of solving even a fraction of our national housing problem. And as for the typical Negro church in the ghetto, the most appropriate potential sponsor for low-income housing, it unfortunately has even less resources and know-how.

It is true that some housing has been constructed under the 221(d)(3) program. The Kate Maramount Foundation in Chicago, the sponsor of nearly half of the 1,568 rental units rehabilitated under the program to date, has certainly mastered its technicalities. Yet, if Maramount were to concentrate all its future activities on Chicago's West Side, and if it were able to rehabilitate 500 units a year under the program, which is highly unlikely, it would take 100 years to eliminate substandard housing in that community alone—assuming that no additional units became substandard in the interim. Obviously, there are not enough Maramounts, nor is there sufficient time for them to act. The scale of the problem is simply too great to be handled in the manner implied in the program.

There are two additional difficulties with this approach that do not show on paper, but which we must anticipate lest they pop up when unsuspecting organizations attempt to duplicate the work of Maramount. First, the open market is a hostile environment for anyone—private developer, church, nonprofit institution or whoever—whose stated objective is to develop housing for black families outside the established ghettos. Frequently it becomes extremely difficult for indigenous institutions such as churches to secure appropriate project sites, sites that meet governmental specifications for mortgage insurance. Zoning, too, becomes a problem. It is most often necessary to secure changes in zoning laws before a project can be begun.

Second, the management of an efficient and financially sound housing development conflicts with the social goals of those institutions which might undertake such an enterprise. Management would have to screen potential tenants to avoid problem families, and it would have to evict families who could not pay their rent. If management begins to wink at rental arrears and is forced to downgrade its maintenance program, it would fall into a vicious cycle. Rental arrears lead to less maintenance. Less maintenance leads to infrequent occupancy. Infrequent occupany leads to reduced revenue. Reduced revenue leads to still less maintenance. QED, the churches become the owners of tomorrow's slums.

The Maramount effort can never be sustained on more than a demonstration basis. The government will commit funds only to the most well-prepared groups to let them show the world what can be done. The irony of this lies in the assumption that this is supposed to highlight what others can do. In reality, when various organizations and institutions in low-income communities across the country hear about the program and become excited about its potential, they are forced to admit in time that they cannot possibly surround themselves with the personnel necessary to bring the needed housing into their communities. This is an illustrative example of the mythic quality of the nonprofit sponsor. On paper, anyone can do it; in reality, very few.

The role of the nonprofit institution in housing is still quite confused. The federal government has not loosened its purse strings, has not reduced the red tape, has not adjusted its mortgage insurance specifications, and has not helped the churches and other institutions prepare for a major role in the redevelopment it apparently wanted to stimulate.

What then is the true purpose of such a policy? Everyone would agree it is worthwhile to encourage such stable and committed institutions as churches to do their part in easing local housing problems—even though they are not yet well equipped for the job. But since the policy has not been enacted on any grand scale, the heart of the matter must lie elsewhere. It lies in the basic unwillingness of the federal government to give serious consideration to why private developers are not dealing in the low- and moderate-income sectors, and in its refusal to provide incentives to encourage such activity. The government has made a tradeoff—it has accepted the cleaner, less tainted nonprofit sponsor and has given up housing units.

MYTH 3: AEROSPACE SYSTEMS PANACEAS

There has been much recent speculation about how efficient community renewal might be if urbanologists and systems analysts jointly planned and implemented broad programs in our cities. Conceiving the neighborhood as a subsystem of interrelated physical, economic, social and political dimensions, which is related in turn to the larger urban system, the integrated approach obviously has value. Yet upon close examination, it reveals serious shortcomings and inaccuracies. The particular advantages of the aerospace systems approach to renewal are more managerial and administrative than they are substantive. Thus, the push for employing multidisciplinary teams and large-scale computers in rebuilding the cities cannot be but one of the most flagrant of the emerging myths of housing reform.

The problem of renewal is money. In the eight major cities recently surveyed by the U.S. Civil Rights Commission, "almost half of the families surveyed received incomes solely from sources such as welfare, AFDC, unemployment compensation or other nonemployment sources." What improvements could come from a sophisticated, fully programmed, multidisciplinary approach to community renewal in those cities? There are hundreds of communities in 42 states where welfare payments fail to meet the states' own standards of the minimum income required for families to live. It is ludicrous to assert that we need a systems approach to reveal that a mother with three children needs $237 a month to live and can be provided through welfare with a maximum of only $126. The basic problem here is lack of money. That is obvious; yet there is no reason to suppose that Congress will show any more willingness to deal with the fundamental problems of poverty than it has in the past.

Another problem is racism. A sophisticated analytical framework cannot be expected to eliminate racial conflict. What could a systems approach accomplish in the Bayside District of Oakland, for example, where the under- and unemployment rate is more than 30 percent? One cannot use a managerial tool and expect to redistribute income. Without basic economic and social reforms, the glamorous aerospace approach to renewal cannot possibly accomplish the ends for which it is intended. Yet Congress has demonstrated that it is far more prepared to sponsor the development of a city technology under the auspices of the aerospace industry than it is to deal with the fact that the poor lack money, that they are the victims of racial discrimination, or that their "assistance programs" are falling apart.

Like the more familiar task forces and blue ribbon commissions empaneled to identify the obvious, the systems approach to community renewal promises to be used as a politically valuable delaying tactic by those who refuse to commit themselves to the necessity of righting wrongs and reversing social or economic injustices.

Systems analysis has of course made many unique, highly visible contributions in the amply funded, high-priority realm of national defense. It is preposterous to expect that this expensive method will yield comparable results in a traditionally low-priority area where Congress is particularly tight-fisted. The systems approach to the physical and human renewal of neighborhoods and communities promises to make much more efficient use of existing resources. It would avoid the piecemeal efforts of earlier renewal programs. Yet the Vietnam experience illustrates the system's failure to take into account the human and political variables. Racism and class conflict are the human and political variables of the cities; it can safely be predicted that systems analysis will be as little effective here as it has been in Vietnam.

MYTH 4: SELF-HELP HOUSING

The systems approach is being sold to Congress as the new urban panacea of the 1970s. It is an attractive panacea, suggesting the efficiency and reliability of moon shots and the like. But how well will it work in practice? While it is an obviously intelligent way to go about doing certain things, one may well wonder how well it will function on limited resources. Only time will tell.

As for public service and community facilities, the black ghettos have been the last to get the least. If one peruses a random sample of Model Cities program applications he will quickly learn that cities of all sizes are now quite willing to admit that their policies have been discriminatory. In response, the black community is now demanding direct and meaningful involvement in making policy and running programs designed to improve the quality of life in the ghettos. Most recently they have demanded the inclusion of low-income, low-skilled, unemployed ghetto men as workers in the construction and rehabilitation of low-income housing.

The myth is that housing programs can provide employment for the ghetto resident, and on paper it looks sound. Unemployed ghetto residents would be prepared for jobs in the building trades even as they are helping to alleviate the chronic housing problems in their neighborhoods. It would provide residents with a meaningful experience and a sense of contributing to neighborhood development. And maybe it would even reduce the vandalism in the houses being rehabilitated. All this is fine. Yet it is also, I think, naive to expect that a large share of the greater than six million substandard units in our metropolitan areas can be brought up to standard through such efforts.

Urban self-help housing has not yet assumed the stature of a major myth, but it is gaining increasing exposure and support as Model Cities monies become more available. I do not doubt that such efforts will result in rehabilitated housing; nor that unskilled labor can be trained in the building trades. However, as long as self-help housing is localized in the relatively few communities that have the talent and organizational base to push it, the number of units involved will remain small. And, as long as the rehabilitation efforts are headed by undercapitalized Negro contractors who do not pose overt threats to organized labor, it is a safe bet that direct involvement of black manpower in the rebuilding effort will fail to crack labor's stranglehold on the ghetto.

Localized self-help training programs seem too small a threat to the unions to warrant large mobilization against them. No better evidence need be sought than the fact that black workers themselves recognize the meagerness of these programs. Blacks are now demanding entry into the Chicago, Detroit and Pittsburgh construction unions. This marks the beginning of a much-needed and long-awaited national confrontation between the blacks and the buildings and trades unions. It also raises the conflict to a level beyond the point where training programs might have been an issue. Even were they to become an issue, the unions seem to have the procedural equipment to appear good guys. Consider the following scenario:

The unions select and deal with relatively small and isolated black contractors in scattered communities. They allow a certain number of trainees to work on the otherwise unionized rehabilitation jobs. If pressures for reform of the union arise, or if blacks made concerted efforts to penetrate the union ranks, the union local can then threaten to slow up or close down the rehabilitation job. As this would spell certain disaster to the usually undercapitalized black contractor, he would find ways to short-circuit the whole procedure. In the end, by permitting a scant few nonunion blacks to work on rehabilitation crews in a few ghetto communities, the unions appear progressive while still excluding blacks from where the main action is, in the unions themselves.

Yet, this issue seems to have the potential to escalate into a major conflict. A Negro contractor working in Cleveland's Hough district claims that "a union carpenter brought up in new construction is no better equipped for rehabilitation work than a raw man. . . . We can train a laborer to set up our prefab partitions in two hours. He can learn faster than a veteran carpenter because he isn't set in his ways and has no old work habits to overcome." If unskilled ghetto labor is capable of being trained to do rehabilitation work in significantly less time than the unions are willing to admit, and this appears to be the case, then massive training programs could be initiated. Such a new labor pool would be highly mobile and a threat to the unions. The unions would probably offer stiff resistance to such a development, so these self-help training programs may prove to be yet another false expectation.

With all these forces eddying around direct involvement in ghetto redevelopment, it is likely that a highly limited program will be enacted, which is tokenism at its worst. The myth is subtle. It plays upon the need and desires of the minority poor for a stake in the action. At the same time it guarantees that institutional changes in organized labor will be minimal or nonexistent, that the buildings and trades unions will not have to open their ranks to black labor on a large scale—because "they" will have their self-help training programs.

MYTH 5: HOME OWNERSHIP FOR THE POOR

Congress recently considered more than 24 low-income home-ownership bills; its action resulted in Section 235 of the Housing Act of 1968. The purpose of the program is to broaden the base of home ownership in an already predominantly home-owning nation through the provision of interest rate subsidies to low- and moderate-income families. The proponents of this program expect it to accomplish all the socially desirable ends that the welfare reformers of 30 years ago had hoped their public housing programs would achieve. Today public housing has come to represent a patronizing dole, they reason, while home ownership involves a stake in a piece of property, a sense of pride in one's home. Belief in this myth persists mainly because the public and the legislators see in home ownership a device to prevent more and greater rioting.

The myth of low-income home ownership is vulnerable on many counts. The most glaring error is that such programs are based on the projection of middle-class values onto a nonmiddle-class culture. Moreover, it is perceived as a solution, a salve to balm the wounds caused by discrimination, cultural starvation and the structural problems of our national labor market. But there are several difficulties with this romanticized notion of what ownership can accomplish.

There was and is nothing about a publicly supported low-rent housing program that would necessarily rob a man of his pride or sap him of his self-respect. Nor is there anything about owning one's home that guarantees that pride and self-respect will spontaneously spring up in the owner's breast. As far as the actual low-income ownership programs are concerned, they may amount to little more than saying that everyone should have a title to his slum.

Realistically speaking, one cannot expect much more than a limited low-income home-ownership program. The entrenched and anachronistic National Association of Real Estate Boards (NAREB) is making visible efforts to avoid opening up the market to Negroes. A recent NAREB circular was distributed to presidents of local real estate boards entitled, "Some Questions (and Their Answers) Suggested by a Reading of Title VIII of Public Law No. 90-284 Related to Forced Housing." It was an exploration of means to circumvent the provisions of the federal open-housing bill. In spite of recent federal legislation in this area, and the Supreme Court's ruling that an almost-forgotten law enacted in 1866 is effectively a sweeping fair-housing bill, a truly open housing market seems highly unlikely in the foreseeable future.

Moreover, to stimulate hopes for home ownership without moving toward reducing levels of unemployment and underemployment might be the cruelest hoax yet perpetrated on the low-income population. Let us assume that the program provides for monthly carrying costs equal to 20 percent of monthly income. I feel the average low-income family participating in the program would find it extremely difficult to pay for its housing-related needs (operation, maintenance, taxes, water and insurance) as well as its nonhousing needs from its limited budget. Consequently, such a program might provide the family a piece of middle-class America, but only a little piece—a piece obtained at the cost of accepting the increased pressures that go along with internalizing middle-class values, with only a fraction of the economic resources with which to play the game.

It is of paramount importance to remember that the *style* in which a program is administered has direct impact upon the quality of life of the participants. For example, if a project is administered in a paternalistic manner, that is, if the local authority sits in judgment of the moral suasion of tenant families, the project becomes the enemy. As David Hunter has observed:

> The projects in Harlem are hated. They are hated almost as much as policemen and this is saying a great deal. And they are hated for the same reasons; both reveal, unbearably, the real attitude of the white world. . . .

The way in which the program is administered could conceivably be as important as the housing it makes available to participating families. While the proponents of ownership for low-income families ceremonially chant incantations about the ideals that such an experience instills in one's soul, someone must begin to work out solutions to the many problems. How can the market be opened in the face of organized opposition? How can the low-income family be expected to absorb the hidden costs of ownership on a marginal budget? How can a home-ownership program improve the pride and self-respect of the participants? How can such a program be administered in a fashion that does not duplicate the inexcusably high-handed manner with which we have administered our low-rent housing programs throughout the country?

In the next generation we will have to build as many houses to accommodate population growth and normal replacement needs as we have built in our entire history as a nation. Yet we have seriously underestimated the extent and depth of our current housing crisis.

I cannot recommend a course that can eliminate existing inhuman housing conditions throughout the nation: I do not think that anyone can. The problem is too firmly rooted in our society. It is too much a part of our economic system. It is too closely related to such fundamental issues as the distribution of wealth and income to be dealt with in terms of housing alone. I would like to give serious consideration to several points that I believe are neither myths nor misconceptions, and that must be recognized in the development of any viable strategy to deal with the chronic shortage of decent housing.

First, uneven and underutilization of existing housing is a contributing factor to the perpetuation of the slum housing problem. Vacancy and abandonment rates are increasing in our small towns as well as in our large and congested cities. Therefore slum formation can no longer be equated solely with the unending crush of new arrivals forced to seek living space in already overcrowded and overutilized housing.

Second, the slumlord of myth does not exist. In his place is a many-headed hydra, the hundreds of thousands of individuals who own the slums. These people all have varying economic resources, motives for entering the slum market, and knowledge of the dynamics of the market. But the owner of slum property is not as sophisticated and professional as many of us have been led to believe, nor is he as unintelligent as many of us would like to think. In his study of slum properties in Newark, George Sternlieb found that "more than half the parcels are owned by people to whom real estate represents a trivial supplement to income . . . to a considerable degree this reflects the comparatively amateur kind of holder who predominates in the market . . . many are . . . owners by default rather than by purchase; are owners by inheritance, or lack of purchasers to buy unwanted properties; or by a relatively trivial investment which is not too meaningful in terms of overall capital or income."

The owner of substandard housing is aware that the government frequently provides meaningful incentives to stimulate housing programs. He is also aware that recent incentives have been largely limited to developing luxury housing or to aiding nonprofit sponsors. Until a meaningful program is developed for low-income housing, he will continue to shy away from government programs ostensibly designed to assist him to improve his housing but which will end up reducing the value of his investment, based upon existing market conditions.

Third, and in light of the above discussion, it is urgent that we devise a means for accumulating current and accurate information of the economics of slum ownership. Many owners of slum properties do not keep reliable financial records of their holdings. Without these, differences in the circumstances of various segments of the ownership pool makes it virtually impossible to devise meaningful programs to help renew our inner cities. Therefore I suggest that the public perform an audit or accounting function in the low-income sector of the market. We could require, as a possible way to do this, that every renter-occupied dwelling unit found to be substandard in the course of routine inspection be subjected to financial analysis by independent auditors employed or secured by local licensing and inspection departments.

This information would allow us to develop a multiplicity of plans for the various sectors of the substandard market. Matching each plan to its appropriate situation seems to be the only meaningful way to renew the existing housing inventory. Obviously the needs of an elderly widow without any capital except a five-unit substandard tenement are not the same as those of a real estate broker who owns 60 parcels and maintains a work crew to service them. Nor, of course, are their motives or knowledge of the market the same. Governmental policies and programs must reach both extremes; families living in units owned by the widow must not be penalized because the government has chosen to assist the broker.

Furthermore, if we can obtain the economic data to build a repertoire of programs, we will then be in a position to penalize those owners who fail to respond to the offer of aid. Outright public purchase would be justified, as would government assistance in the transfer of ownership from a recalcitrant owner to one who will cooperate.

In brief, I suggest we develop a data-gathering mechanism for an analysis of the economic patterns of slum ownership, that we develop a repertoire of solutions to the various problems, and that we stimulate property improvement by enforcing penalties upon those owners who fail to respond to the offer of aid. Should this plan fail, and the rate of deterioration of the existing stock continue unabated or increase in the future, some emergency measures should be adopted. I propose that we give serious consideration to the multifaceted implications involved in declaring this nation's existing inventory of low-rent housing a public utility. The basis for such a declaration would be the nation's compelling interest in maintaining the health, safety and social well-being of hundreds of thousands of American families living in substandard housing in the cities and the nation at large.

Such a proposal obviously includes, among other things, consideration of the regulation of profits, subsidies to those owners who cannot earn a reasonable return on their investment, the movement of structures into and out of the regulated sector, and the problem of defining the sector of the inventory to be covered. I offer this suggestion as an alternative approach to safeguarding the shrinking supply of privately owned low-rent units. It is indicative of the gravity with which I view the housing crisis.

The Business of Urban Reform

PETER WILEY AND BEVERLY LEMAN

In 1967, some of the country's largest corporations from the ranks of *Fortune*'s 500 announced their commitment to the social reclamation of urban America. Since then corporate magnates such as Henry Ford II have taken a personal interest in ghetto affairs and have not hesitated to contact black representatives of nationalist as well as established organizations. In setting up reform programs they have made particular efforts to work with militant groups (like CORE).

However, corporate interest in reform has affected more than representative groups in the black community. The liberal reformer, who plans and administers programs from the labyrinths of government bureaucracies, is witnessing the usurpation of the supposedly sacrosanct rights of the welfare state by the direct intervention of corporations in local affairs. Until now the liberal reformer regarded corporate capitalism as a necessity that could only be humanized by the countervailing effort of government. Through various forms of legislation the reformer protected the

This essay first appeared in *Leviathan*, March 1969. Copyright © 1969 *Leviathan*.

less fortunate from the system's occasional "aberrations," while the businessman directed his efforts toward making profit. Today, however, corporate aggressiveness is upsetting this division of labor by moving in where the government has failed to keep pace with the system's no longer occasional aberrations. As the National Advisory Commission on Civil Disorders reported:

> The spectacle of Detroit and New Haven engulfed in civil turmoil despite a multitude of federally-aided programs raised basic questions as to whether existing 'delivery systems' are adequate to the bold new purposes of national policy. Many who voiced these concerns overlooked the disparity between the size of the problems at which the programs are aimed and the level of funding provided by the federal government.

Since this report, Congress has responded to the urban crisis by *reducing* appropriations for reform programs. The Model Cities Program was cut by more than half and the size of the Neighborhood Youth Corps, a program to cool the ghetto by hiring black youths in the summertime, was reduced from 400,000 to 230,000. Election year austerity and the bottomless pit of Vietnam expenditures contributed to the spree of budget-trimming, but much of the impetus came from Congress' punitive response to the black rebellion.

The corporations responded to the crisis in a different way. In August 1967, an influential group of businessmen met with leaders in labor, civil rights, the church and local government to form the Urban Coalition. This new "superlobby" discussed three major goals: 1) expansion of the private sector's efforts to employ and train the poor; 2) emergency federal work programs; and 3) long-range plans for the physical and social reconstruction of the cities. Local coalitions were set up in major cities across the nation to implement these aims and involve the local business community.

In the coalition, business was represented by a formidable lineup: Roy Ash, president of Litton Industries, the prototypical corporate conglomerate and a leader in aerospace; Henry Ford II, chairman of the board of Ford Motor Company; David Rockefeller, president of Chase Manhattan Bank; Frederick J. Close, chairman of the Aluminum Company of America; Andrew Heis-kell, chairman of Time Inc., to name a few. The black community was represented by the old standbys, A. Philip Randolph, Roy Wilkins and Whitney M. Young, Jr.

During this period, corporate leaders also manned the Advisory Panel of Private Enterprise set up by the National Advisory Commission on Civil Disorders. Charles B. ("Tex") Thornton, chairman of Litton, headed the panel. He was assisted by John Leland Atwood, president of North American Rockwell, another aerospace giant; Walter E. Headley, senior vice-president of the Bank of America, the largest bank in the world; and Louis F. Polk, Jr., a vice-president of General Mills. The panel argued that massive monetary incentives could lead to "maximum utilization of the tremendous capability of the American free enterprise system." Drawing on the experiences of several corporations (particularly aerospace) involved in job corps camps and other crash programs, the panel recommended that business focus on job training, especially among the hard-core unemployed.

THE UNIQUE PARTNERSHIP

Although President Johnson supported the business effort, he never responded warmly to the Urban Coalition, which had been initiated by New York's Republican mayor, John Lindsay. Instead he set up the National Alliance of Businessmen (NAB), headed by Urban Coalition member Henry Ford II.

Before announcing its formation, the Johnson administration examined several pilot projects in which federal contracts were awarded companies to hire and train the poor and set up plants within slum areas. Johnson sent Hubert Humphrey to Watts to examine one such project begun by AeroJet-General, an important aerospace firm and a subsidiary of the conglomerate, General Tire and Rubber. AeroJet, sensing federal contract monies, assigned its vice-president, William E. Zisch, to the post of special assistant to the Secretary of Commerce to help work out similar projects. Subsequently, training programs were set up in five cities, and contracts were awarded to four aerospace firms including AeroJet. Once these projects were underway, Johnson officially announced the formation of the NAB (January 1968) as a "one-step service for businessmen in dealing with the Federal Government."

In line with this program, government subsidies for job training and housing construction were introduced and promised to make corporate reform profitable. Federal agencies such as the Small Business Administration were eager to provide guarantees against the risk of ghetto investment. And government approval of such nongovernmental organizations as the Urban Coalition and the NAB would prevent what the Advisory Panel on Private Enterprise called the "loss of management prerogatives over the productive process." Following the lead of AeroJet, other corporations placed key men in government positions to ensure that the centers of political power would pay close attention to their interests. For example, IBM's Robert M. McAuliffe became head of the Department of Housing and Urban Development's new Office of Business Participation.

Urban Coalition chairman John Gardner, former Secretary of Health, Education, and Welfare, explained to the public that "there isn't one American in a hundred, perhaps a thousand, who has a clear grasp of the unique partnership that is evolving between public and private instrumentalities in this country."

BLACK POWER AND BLACK CAPITALISM

While this partnership was being cemented in Washington, business began a massive attempt at social engineering intended to foster black capitalism and remake the ghetto in the image of white America. First, however, the corporations needed an environment stable enough to ensure profits; blacks had to be discouraged from burning down the cities. Then corporate leaders could direct their attention to the development of a black administrative hierarchy that would be attuned to the interests of business.

Recognizing that the NAACP and the Urban League were no longer keeping pace with the black community, and that new, more responsive political forces were emerging, businessmen turned their attention to the more militant blacks. They hoped to channel the new militants away from attacking the presence of white business in the inner city, and toward reforms aimed at restoring and expanding urban markets, and, in effect, increasing that presence. To achieve this, however, it was necessary to create the illusion of political self-determination (community control).

In the new equation of reform, black power meant black capitalism. According to corporate reformers, black capitalism would provide aspiring blacks with a "model of achievement" and a "sense of their own worth." Black entrepreneurship was encouraged mainly through the establishment by corporations of ghetto subsidiaries staffed by blacks. When Eastern Gas and Fuel Co. in Boston received a $32 million contract from FHA and the Boston Rehabilitation Corporation for 3,200 housing units, Eastern formed a black firm in Roxbury, Sanders Associates, to share the work. In Baltimore, B. Green and Co., a major grocery wholesaler, found that many retail supermarkets had been burned out during the ghetto rebellion. Because the white owners were reluctant to return to black areas, Green selected small merchants from among its black retail customers and formed partnerships with them to take over the white supermarkets. If all its ghetto retailers were black, B. Green and Co. felt it would have a measure of protection, and new captive customers were gained in the bargain.

To carry their programs to black people, the corporate reformers attempted to cultivate a new political vanguard. They wanted a group of ambitious black leaders who could combine a militant, populistic style with political "flexibility." Robert Allen of the *Guardian* reported that after a series of meetings in the summer of 1967 involving the Ford Foundation, the NAACP and the Urban League, and at which SNCC and black power were discussed, Ford made its decision to fund CORE. CORE had credibility with blacks—it had played a major role in the Southern freedom struggle—but it remained "flexible" and had not taken the path of SNCC. A few months prior to Ford's decision, CORE director Floyd McKissick had said to a senate committee, "You tell us to live under the capitalist system. Well, brother, give me a chance to make it in the system."

Cleveland was selected as the pilot city to develop corporate relations with black militants. The Ford Foundation had been working there since 1961 without much success, despite contributions to the NAACP, the Urban League and the Negro Industrial and Economic Union, whose best-known members were Jimmy Brown and Carl Stokes. Now $175,000 was given to CORE, mainly for voter registration. In effect, Ford was financing the election of Stokes as mayor.

Ford's confidence in CORE's "flexibility" and in its own policies was also confirmed by CORE's program on the national level. In July 1968, emphasizing that Negroes should have a full partnership in capitalism, CORE announced support of a legislative program entitled the Community Self-Determination Act. The measure was given support by 82 legislators, ranging from Jacob Javits to John Tower of Texas. It also coincided with the interests of corporations involved in urban reform; in December of 1968, CORE director Roy Innis and Joseph C. Wilson, chairman of the board of Xerox, both announced plans to campaign nationally for CORE's program.

The act's intention is to use government power to attract business to the ghetto. The government is to grant tax incentives to investors from the outside, while guaranteeing bonds issued by neighborhood corporations working with the investors. The justification is that once the investor has made a profit (which would be easy since costs are deducted from taxes), the plant will be sold to its employees.

Efforts to involve black militants in business reform schemes will undoubtedly be successful as long as the militants are not opposed to capitalism as such. However, the end result cannot be an independent black capitalism. A look at the economics of any major ghetto reveals the real nature and potential of black capitalism.

In Harlem, more than a quarter of the business enterprises are black owned, but these are almost entirely marginal operations like barber shops, repair shops and laundromats. In fact, in all of New York City there are only 12 black-owned or managed businesses that employ more than ten people. Alongside the traditional small owners, a new black administrative class is now emerging. These are the men who run government programs in the ghetto, the official militants from major black organizations, the managers of "black" subsidiaries of white-owned corporations, and the owners and managers of "independent" black enterprises (like Sanders in Roxbury) which are dependent on white financing or are captives of white corporations because they produce a product for only one purchaser.

Using the rhetoric of black power, corporate leaders talk as if they were creating an independent and parallel economic system that will recapitulate the historical development of American capitalism. In reality, independent black capitalism never has and never will pass the small shop stage. Even these marginal businesses are now threatened (along with their white counterparts) by the extension of large corporations like the supermarket chains into the ghetto. What is really developing is a subordinate economic system run for the benefit of white corporations by a black managerial class.

There may be other advantages for business in the development of black administrators. Having such a force allied with nonghetto interests will direct some of the hostility now reserved for "whitey" back toward members of the black community. The resulting conflicts may provide opportunities to pit one group against another and blunt a united black attack on the "white power structure."

The goals of the corporate reformers also include the expansion of the black working class through job training and employment programs. Soon after the NAB was formed, it joined with the Urban Coalition to announce an "intensive campaign" to hire and train blacks. At the same time, the National Advisory Commission on Civil Disorders called for the creation of two million new jobs in three years.

The advocates of these programs argued that a job is a stake in society, and can thus serve as an antidote to "instability." They also pointed out that training for blacks could help relieve the strains on the skill capacities of the work force caused by rapid technological change. In many industries, skilled workers are in short supply while blue-collar jobs are increasing slowly, if at all. Many corporations, particularly in the aerospace industry, feel that public-controlled vocational training is not being upgraded fast enough. They are convinced they can do a better job, that is, as long as the government provides the subsidies.

In this instance, the government was willing to cooperate. According to Labor Secretary Willard Wirtz, "the campaign to give jobs to unemployables got underway in cities where tight labor markets made employers desperate for help." Blacks provided both a more convenient and a cheaper source of labor than whites; the pressures of unemployment, lack of mobility and lack of unionization all worked to keep ghetto wages low. (AeroJet-General once candidly reported that it had originally planned to locate its new Watts subsidiary in the South in order to avoid high wages.)

There are difficulties involved in training workers from the ghetto—absenteeism, high turnover and frequent failures to complete the program—but these do not entail risks for the corporations. They have made it clear that they will not participate in the job training programs unless they are assured of a profit. They have requested and are receiving higher compensation to offset training costs. For example, while the Labor Department spends $2,000 to $4,000 per trainee, the employers who ran the pilot program preceding the formation of NAB received $2,880, and business-run job corps camps receive as much as $5,500.

In general, however, corporations have responded only half-heartedly to the NAB job-training and employment campaigns and NAB itself has proved more adroit at manipulating figures than in finding jobs. In August 1968, when NAB was claiming it had placed 40,000 hard-core unemployed and 100,000 teenagers, an Associated Press survey of the ten largest cities found that NAB's claims were a hundred times higher than what was being claimed at the local level. Watts Manufacturing, the showcase ghetto employer, hired only 530 of 5,500 applicants in an area where 25,000 are unemployed.

The poor response to these programs is not surprising. As William Zisch, AeroJet's advisor to the government, explained, hiring the unskilled poor violates a fundamental business principle because it requires hiring the least productive members of the work force. In view of the unpredictability and inefficiency of government agencies and the limited amount of available funds, subsidies are not adequate to offset the disadvantages for most corporations.

However, corporations in the vanguard of job-training and investment programs view the problem from a broader perspective. They see an opportunity to break ground in the ghetto and stake out a base of operation in order to reorganize the whole urban complex.

AN URBAN MASTER PLAN

For these corporations, the black rebellions conveniently drew attention to a crisis that had been maturing for years, and provided the opportunity to develop long-range plans for dealing with the decaying urban community. These companies view the reconstruction of the city as a life and death matter. As Charles Adams of Raytheon explained, "The American business community is sharply aware of the fact that the commercial world cannot exist without the market place, and that the strength of the market place is in the city. Thus, when the social and economic sickness of the American ghetto affects the commercial health of the population centers, it also gnaws away at the tissues and bones and living cells of American industry."

By 1967, this crisis seemed severe enough to jeopardize the entire urban economy. A major factor has been the exodus of the white working and middle classes to the suburbs; and many industries have followed or encouraged this demographic shift. At the same time, the need for greater inner-city expenditures on housing, education, police, transportation and welfare have far outstripped the cities' ability to pay. Since 88 percent of locally raised revenue comes from property taxes, the growth of the suburbs has further undermined the cities' ability to deal with increasing urban decay.

The decline of the cities has coincided with a more fundamental crisis in the corporate system. Although the cold war and the ensuing arms race alleviated the threat of another crippling depression, by the early 1960s the economy again appeared to be slowing down. According to a June 1964 *U.S. News and World*

Report, "The feeling grows that the U.S. market, while huge, is relatively saturated." Many corporations turned to foreign markets, where the return on investments was often higher.

The aerospace industry was particularly anxious about the lack of new markets. Aerospace epitomized the new corporate relationship with government; giants like Litton, founded in the early fifties, were products of the cost war. They were virtually created by the government's rapid development of a nuclear war machine, and they felt threatened by the possibility of peace and reduced defense spending. By the early sixties the consensus in the aerospace industry was that the "governmental environment" was not right. Defense spending was not increasing fast enough, and the government was not creating alternative domestic markets through other types of spending.

By 1966, aerospace had begun to look to the socioeconomic market and the business of urban reform. In California, where slim aerospace profit margins were a problem, several urban planning studies were prepared, but they did not result in the anticipated expenditures, and AeroJet-General bemoaned the fact that efforts to introduce systems analysis into the field of domestic reform seemed premature.

At the same time other, less forward-looking industries were recognizing that their immediate interests were also threatened by the cities' decay. David Rockefeller explained to a Senate committee that commercial banks were heavily invested in urban real estate and mortgage loans; the Bank of America has more than half its funds invested in this area. Prudential Insurance company expressed another concern: the threat of ghetto rebellions to investments in plant and equipment—for Prudential, $40 million in Newark alone.

Thus, special concern with the ghetto rebellions resulted in a convergence of government and corporate interests. The former were confronted with the obvious failure of federal programs at a time when their credibility was seriously threatened unless they could cool the ghetto.

Corporate intervention presented the only alternative to traditional reform programs, but this promised to change the very structure of reform. The corporations insist that the new programs have to be profitable, and that they be given the widest possible range of control over the programs. In effect, they are asking the government to become the financial intermediary that collects funds from the public through taxes and then redistributes them to the corporations.

BEATING LOCAL GOVERNMENT

At the same time, corporate leaders want to eliminate the problems of working with a chaotic complex of overlapping and competing government agencies.

> There are now over 400 grant programs operated by a broad range of federal agencies and channelled through a much larger array of semi-autonomous state and local government entities. Reflective of this complex scheme, federal programs often seem self-defeating and contradictory; field officials unable to make decisions on their own programs and unaware of related efforts; agencies unable or unwilling to work together; programs conceived and administered to achieve different and sometimes conflicting purposes (*National Advisory Council on Civil Disorders*).

As an antidote to these arrangements as well as a tonic for the urban economy, many corporations are supporting the national modernization trend toward regional and metropolitan planning and government. This move away from local government is being carried out through the establishment of quasipublic (business-government) corporations at the state and regional levels.

For example, in New York State Governor Rockefeller helped push through legislation in April 1968, which established the Urban Development Corporation (UDC), a nongovernmental agency with a nine-member board of directors. Four board members will be state commissioners of commerce, banks, insurance and planning; the remaining five will be appointed by Rockefeller from the private sector. Edward Logue, who headed the Boston and New Haven redevelopment agencies, has been chosen to be president of the board. One of his functions will be to attract private capital.

The UDC was given virtually unlimited powers and huge sums of untaxed capital to buy whatever land it wishes. Using its power to override the objections of local government and local zoning regulations, it will condemn land, purchase it from local owners and resell it at low prices to new investors. Tax breaks as well as cheap land will encourage investment in housing, industrial and shopping complexes, recreational facilities, transportation, etc. The taxpayer will pick up the tab; his money will make up for the revenue lost in corporate tax deductions, pay the interest on UDC bonds to New York bankers, and finance the tax losses accrued by selling land cheaply.

In short, UDC ensures investors a profitable entry into the city proper. But more significantly, UDC and other such quasipublic corporations provide the machinery with which to implement new metropolitan and regional areas. It not only restricts local autonomy, but has the powers to rezone an entire area. It is more than a coincidence that as blacks become a majority in and threaten to take control of the central cities, regional agencies are being created and funded by state and federal governments to administer programs in larger and whiter areas.

Regional governments will give corporations greater control in reorganizing the urban marketplace by limiting black political power in the inner city and by preventing a further division of suburb from city. Moreover, corporate planners are eager to reunite the city and its suburbs through overarching (regional) institutions. The white middle and working classes have fled the cities to escape both the sprawling black ghetto and to find better housing, services and lower taxes; but in the process the urban market, work force and tax source have been widely disseminated. With regional structures the market and labor force will be reconstructed, and the government will be able to extract new taxes (i.e., commuter taxes) from suburbanites for regional programs that will affect both city and suburb.

Although plans for regional structures are just getting underway, other plans to reintegrate the middle class into the city through urban renewal programs have been operative for years. In every major city, low-income housing has been replaced with downtown shopping complexes and middle-income housing, both of which are designed to concentrate and organize the middle-income consumer market. Prudential Insurance in Newark provides a good example. One of the contributing factors to the Newark uprising was the state's plan to displace ghetto families to make way for a new medical college. As part of a billion dollar program sponsored by the insurance companies, Prudential remains intent on investing in a $4.5 million co-op to house the medical students and staff. While Prudential claims its fee of $27 per room is comparable to rents in the surrounding tenements, it is obvious that the $800 deposit places the housing well beyond the reach of the people who are being dispossessed.

In some cities—for example, St. Louis—urban renewal has resulted in the dissolution of traditional ghettos and their reconstruction on the edges of town. In all cases, black families are pushed from one decaying area to another with ruthless indifference. The "housing problem" is simply swept under the rug.

PROFIT VS. REFORM

When all the programs for ghetto reclamation are examined from the perspective of the ghetto inhabitant, it is clear that they will have very little impact. A small number of blacks will become administrators for white corporations, some will be brought into the labor force, and many will be relocated. But in general blacks will continue to experience high unemployment and poor housing in a decaying environment.

In contrast, the corporations that participate in reform plans stand to do well. Their claims that they are forgoing more profitable forms of investment should be greeted with skepticism. In each specific project risk is virtually eliminated by government guarantees, and returns from reform investment are as good if not better than returns in the so-called free market. Consequently, the insurance industry is investing a large portion of its one billion dollars in FHA mortgages guaranteed by government. By law they do not pay more than 6 percent, but according to *Fortune* this is still better than the return on mortgages in most company portfolios. In New York City, Robert Kennedy's

Bedford-Stuyvesant program called for the government to pay a supplemental tax-free 6 percent return to construction companies, which would have brought their annual yield to between 12 and 19 percent.

But for the corporations, there is a more important problem: will the government be able to spend the amount necessary to finance the ambitious plans to remake America? Reconstruction must be made profitable, and *Business Week*'s estimate of the necessary government expenditure corresponded to the amount set in the Martin Luther King Freedom Budget drawn up by Bayard Rustin. Large-scale corporate-administered reform would intensify, not alleviate the government's current fiscal crisis, exemplified by the near bankruptcy of the large cities.

The need for greater expenditure comes at a time when more spending can further endanger the international economic position of the United States. The quest for foreign markets and the construction of a nuclear war machine prevented economic depression after World War II, but forced the United States to defend the international market system from collapse in Europe and from revolutionary communism in Asia. The costs of this policy are now coming home. Expenditures to defend the empire have resulted in a permanent balance of payments problem. Vietnam has brought inflation and diverted funds from domestic reform. Today, rising costs resulting from inflation are jeopardizing America's competitive position in foreign markets at a time when the economy most needs those markets. Large monopolies like the steel corporations are accustomed to passing on higher costs to consumers in the form of higher prices. But now the steel industry has begun to price itself out of the international market; even American corporations are importing cheaper steel from Germany and Japan.

In short, to keep the economy expanding, new markets must be created, largely through government spending in areas like foreign aid, military equipment and domestic reform. But the expenditures themselves contribute to inflation, weakening the competitive position of the United States. Moreover, the international market system rests on the dollar, and when the dollar is in danger, the whole system is threatened.

The only way to protect the dollar, according to the *Wall Street Journal*, is to keep interest rates high and to cut spending. But a decrease in spending sufficient to reduce the rate at which prices are rising will cause an 8 percent increase in unemployment. Corporate plans for "massive monetary incentives" are coming precisely at a time when government is under strong pressure to cut spending.

Whether or not all this results in a recession, blacks will continue to lose out. Capital spending will focus on labor-saving technology to combat rising costs. If spending is cut, increased unemployment will affect newly hired blacks first, and "luxury" projects like job training will be the first to be terminated.

If funds do become available, for example, as a result of a slowdown in the Vietnam war, the corporate schemes at their best can do little to ameliorate ghetto conditions. The needs far outstrip the corporations' most grandiose plans, and more important, the priorities determined by profit-making, like the creation of black subsidiary firms, are not in the interests of the vast majority of ghetto residents.

IN WHITE AMERICA

In effect, the corporate attempt to reorganize the urban market and restructure the black community will touch all elements of the metropolitan complex—reaching beyond the central city into the suburbs, the new home of many of the white working class. The development of a mass consumption society since World War II meant that many white workers have become suburban homeowners. As a result, important segments of the population are defining their political position with respect to their role as consumers as well as producers. Despite this apparent change in status and despite rising real incomes, the suburbanite still feels his social position is precarious; new pressures, such as consumer debt, have been added to a sense of instability in the workplace caused by rapid technological change. And to the working-class suburbanite, blacks and their imagined allies in the federal government are deemed responsible for their precarious position. When increased tax revenues are allocated for Great Society reforms, the programs are viewed as depriving the suburbs of needed facilities such as schools in order to support "shiftless niggers" in the ghettos.

There is also the real and imagined competitive threat of black workers in the labor market. White workers bitterly resent what they consider the favoritism displayed toward blacks in hiring and training programs. White workers feel threatened not only by the "lawlessness" of underclass blacks, but by the remote and unresponsive centers of political and economic power in the factory, the city and in "their" unions. These are the fears which lie behind the popularity of the Wallace campaign, and the formation of paramilitary organizations in many white neighborhoods.

Although the lines are rapidly being drawn, a radical polarization is not inevitable. The white working-class outlook is a confused potpourri of racist and populist attitudes (although informed by none of the anticapitalist attitudes of earlier populist movements). Many workers genuinely fear blacks, knowing them only as the raised fists and looters presented by the mass media. But workers also recognize and resent manipulation and control from afar which does not originate in the ghetto: a long, senseless war, corrupt politicians, etc.

What is clear is that white suburbanites are responding to the same pressures that are politicizing blacks: deteriorating suburban services, rising prices, growing indebtedness and rapid technological change which threatens important segments of the work force. Moreover, as the corporations rezone new areas to reintegrate the city and its suburbs, these pressures will increase. In many neighborhoods people have begun to draw together against those who appear to jeopardize their lifestyle. And although they have wrongly identified the enemy as the black militants, they unwittingly stand in vigilant opposition to the modernization trends of urban America.

Much depends on the white Left. In the ghetto, attempts by corporations to extend their hegemony by taking over where government has failed will release opposing political forces. Attempts to bring potential opponents of the system into a black administrative class have already fragmented many existing black organizations. But the corporation's loud promises and constant presence in ghetto affairs may confront blacks with the real protagonists more rapidly than if corporations had continued to operate from behind the screen of an apparently neutral government. By forcing a class polarization in the ghetto, corporations may help win converts to anticapitalist groups like the Black Panthers.

In white communities these trends are not apparent. The white Left is just beginning to divest itself of outworn dogma and romantic conceptions of the working class. If the white Left can extend its political influence into working-class neighborhoods on a large scale, by relating to the *real* situation in these areas, they can take advantage of the transformation of the urban complex before it is well underway. Although plans are just beginning to be implemented, the tensions they generate are already becoming evident (witness suburban response to the small New York City commuter tax).

This situation provides the Left with a unique opportunity to take the offensive, anticipate the problems, and challenge the plans before they are executed.

Guaranteed Income Plans—
Which One Is Best?

CHRISTOPHER GREEN

As the war on poverty enters its Valley Forge, there is increasing discussion about whether the poor should receive guaranteed annual incomes. Among the issues is *which* guaranteed-income program would be best. Despite the controversy, however, my own analysis has shown that all the major guaranteed-income proposals are similar in their essentials. Choosing among them is as much a social and political issue as it is an economics issue.

In general, the proposals fall into two categories:

Social-dividend taxation would see to it that all families, rich and poor, receive a stipend. These stipends would fill the whole poverty gap and substantially alter the distribution of income.

Negative-income taxes (or, more precisely, negative-rates taxation) would close a portion of the poverty gap and benefit the poor exclusively. The government would make payments, based on negative rates, to people with incomes below some specified line—while collecting positive taxes

This chapter is extracted from *Negative Taxes and the Poverty Problem* by Christopher Green. Copyright ©1967 The Brookings Institution.

from people whose incomes are above that line.

These two "transfer-by-taxation" plans, despite their obvious differences, have many things in common. They aim to supplement the present antipoverty program—by using the federal tax system to help close the gap between the poor family's income and the income a family needs to remain above the poverty line. In addition, they stress a family's income in determining its eligibility for financial aid, rather than age, physical disability, work history, dependent children and so on. These plans also make use of the federal tax system as a vehicle for redistributing income. Finally, the economic principle behind all social-dividend taxation and negative-rates taxation plans is the same—as the following review and analysis of a few of these various plans will demonstrate.

In 1943, Lady Juliette Evangeline Rhys-Williams, the mother of transfer-by-taxation plans, proposed that a "social dividend" be paid weekly to every man, woman and child in Great Britain. All welfare services operated by the state, she suggested, should be combined into a single comprehensive system that would give stipends to all, not just those in need.

Her idea grew, in part, out of her discontent with unemployment insurance, which tended to reduce incentives to accept jobs. "The lion in the path of curing want by means of social insurance," she wrote in *Something to Look Forward To*, "is the fact that if the standard of unemployment pay is raised to a level at which real want is banished, ... then the advantages of working for wages largely disappear." As a solution, she advocated the abandonment of the existing social-insurance system and its philosophy that the state helps only the destitute and sick. The new philosophy she advocated was based on "the democratic principle that the state owes precisely the same benefits to every one of its citizens." However, she recommended that any able-bodied unemployed who refused a job not be given benefits.

At the time of Lady Juliette's original proposal, the British government was seriously considering family allowances, a program that—like most other industrial nations—it eventually adopted. Lady Juliette's social-dividend plan and family allowances are similar in that both provide payments to families regardless of their need. They differ in that the family allowances adopted have generally been restricted to families with children, and Lady Juliette's plan explicitly tied the welfare system to the tax system.

Her proposal never received great support in other North Atlantic nations, but the simplicity of her solution to the problem of poverty attracted the attention of a few postwar economic thinkers.

While C.E. Ayres has not developed a comprehensive plan, in *The Industrial Economy* (1952) he does propose a social-dividend plan for industrialized nations like the United States. He would have every member of the community receive a "basic independent income, the same for all, and just sufficient to cover the 'minimum of subsistence.'" Ayres notes that all taxpayers already receive a subsidy—through exemptions for their dependents—and that it is only a step from tax deductions to direct payment.

Robert R. Shutz's plan, which he calls "continuous taxation," is very like Lady Juliette's plan. He, too, recognizes that paying poor families the difference between their own incomes and the incomes they need might reduce the productivity of workers with incomes below the guaranteed income.

D.B. Smith, a manufacturer writing in the *Canadian Tax Journal* (May-June 1965), would provide $1,000 for every adult and $200 for everyone 21 and under. His rationale is that "our society is changing so fast that it passes large numbers of our citizens by." These citizens represent "overwhelming personal disasters," each an "infinitesimal part of a national disaster in the making." Smith's plan would eliminate other Canadian welfare programs, including family allowances and all subsidies.

The cost of the social-dividend plans—because they guarantee a minimum income to all families, and not just the poor—is very high. I have estimated that individual social-dividend plans would run as high as $50 billion. All the plans would be financed by taxes on all income, and a flat tax rate might have to be as high as 40 percent.

One way to avoid the high cost of social-dividend plans, without creating major deterrents to working for a living, is to confine the programs to the poor and fill only *part* of their income gap. This is the essence of negative-income taxation.

In a sense, negative-income taxation is really a watered-down version of social-dividend taxation: it would meet only part of the poor's cash needs. Its limited coverage reflects recognition of the fact that, in the United States, the poverty-stricken are a dwindling—although a disturbingly large—minority.

HOW NEGATIVE TAXATION WORKS

The principal advocates of negative taxes in the United States are Milton Friedman, Robert J. Lampman and James Tobin. But they are by no means the only economists who have suggested that the income-tax rates could be extended below zero to negative levels in order to pay transfers, or negative taxes, to low-income families. In the early 1940s, there was apparently some discussion of this proposal within the Treasury Department itself. Later, James Buchanan wrote in *The Public Finances* (1960) that taxes could be imposed on those considered as "receiving excessively high incomes, and the proceeds would be used to pay subsidies (negative taxes) to those considered to be receiving excessively low incomes." Earl Rolph and George Break, in *Public Finance* (1961), suggested a similar approach if a "nation-wide program of assistance to all low-income groups" is found desirable.

A year later, Friedman's *Capitalism and Freedom* urged a negative-income tax as an alternative to present welfare programs. Briefly, Friedman's plan would work like this: each head of a family and his dependents would continue to receive the $600 tax exemptions as well as all standard deductions. Then, if the family's total of exemptions and deductions—say, $3,000—exceeded its adjusted gross income—say, $2,000—by $1000, the family would receive 50 percent of the difference, in this case, $500. In short, Friedman would apply a 50 percent negative tax rate to the unused exemptions and deductions of families with no taxable income. Since families with no taxable income are presumably poor, Friedman notes, society could be assured that it was building a floor under the income of poor families—and not subsidizing families that were not poor. Friedman writes:

The advantages of this arrangement are clear! It is directed specifically at the problem of poverty. It gives help in the form most useful to the individual, namely, cash. It is general and could be substituted for the host of special measures now in effect. It makes explicit the cost borne by society. It operates outside the market. Like any other measure to alleviate poverty, it reduces the incentives of those helped to help themselves, but it does not eliminate that incentive entirely, as a system of supplementing incomes up to some fixed minimum would. An extra dollar earned always means more money available for expenditure.

Lampman differs from Friedman in considering negative-income taxes as only one way to reduce poverty. He agrees that really poor families—especially those with children— don't recieve the full benefit of personal exemptions and deductions. By applying a tax rate to unused exemptions and deductions, as Friedman has suggested, the present tax system would be more equitable, Lampman asserts. However, he stops short of Friedman's view that the negative-income tax should *replace* existing social-welfare programs, including farm subsidies and public housing. To Lampman, the negative-income tax should complement existing welfare programs (which, however, because of a negative-income tax, could be reduced).

In a recent paper, Lampman explored the philosophy and mechanics of a negative tax. The poor need help, he believes, and the present income tax discriminates against the poor. For instance, a family of four with no income pays no tax; neither does a family of four with a $3,000 income. Also, he argues, neither cuts in the tax rates nor more liberal exemptions and standard deductions do much for the poor. The tax system would be much fairer, according to Lampman, if negative-tax rates were added. But fairness would presumably result from a 14 percent tax rate, the present positive rate for the lowest bracket. If *more* than fairness is desired, if welfare is to be of prime importance, the negative tax rate should be closer to 50 percent.

Lampman has told me that if the negative rate is to be above 25 percent, the poverty-income gap should be used as the negative-tax base—not unused exemptions and deductions. He reasons that, if simple fairness plays second fiddle to welfare or antipoverty goals, this weakens the argument that negative taxes would provide a further rationale for the individual income-tax systems. It would be preferable, then, to use the poverty-income gap as a base—because the poverty gap would produce greater equity in the treatment of poor families of different sizes.

Another allowance proposal, which seems to be a cross between the negative taxation and social-dividend plans, has been advanced by James Tobin, writing in *Daedalus* (Fall 1965). Essentially, his plan would provide a basic allowance of $400 a year for every man, woman and child. But the seventh and eighth members of a family would get $150 apiece—and no stipends would be provided for additional family members. No family would get more than $2,700.

The Tobin plan uniquely merges the negative tax with the present positive-tax system—and assures that no one would pay more taxes than he is now paying. It would work this way: A family of four (with an allowance of $1,600) would be subject to a 33.3 percent tax rate on income other than the allowance—up to the income level ($6,306 here) where the net tax, under the Tobin plan, equals the tax liability of the present positive-tax schedule. (The net tax is the basic allowance minus the income-tax liability.) Above this income level ($6,306), the existing income-tax schedule would apply.

The net cost of the Tobin plan would be about $14 billion, about twice the cost of the aforementioned negative income-tax plans, the costs of which range from $6 billion to $8 billion. Tobin evidently assumes that $14 billion is modest enough to be financed out of the rising revenues produced by economic growth.

FACTORS IN THE EQUATION

All of the transfer-by-taxation plans designed to close or eliminate the poverty gap are basically similar in that each contains three basic factors, any two of which determine the third:

1. A guaranteed minimum level of income, which varies with family size or composition or both;
2. A tax rate or rates applied against a tax base;
3. A break-even level of income where the tax liability equals the allowance guaranteed.

The links between these factors can be clarified by simple illustrations. If a family is guaranteed $3,000, and a negative tax rate of 50 percent is applied against income, the break-even point will be $6,000. That is, at $6,000 the family's income-tax liability of $3,000 (50 percent of $6,000) equals the guaranteed allowance. Suppose the family's break-even point were set at $3,000 and $1,500 was guaranteed. Then the transfer-tax rate would be 50 percent, or some combination of rates averaging 50 percent. Finally, a break-even point of $3,000 and a 25 percent tax rate would produce a guaranteed income of $750 (25 percent of $3,000). Only if the guarantee is $750 will the net allowance be reduced to zero by a flat 25 percent negative tax rate when income reaches $3,000.

Once it becomes clear that the essentials of transfer by taxation can be reduced to three basic factors, it is easy to understand that the only important variations between plans lie in the magnitude of the guaranteed minimum income or allowance, the level of the tax rate, and the break-even point.

All the social-dividend schemes begin with the choice of a guaranteed income, which varies with family size, and the choice of an income-tax rate, which will finance the plan. These choices determine the magnitude of the third factor, the break-even point. This does not mean, however, that the break-even point is not a matter of concern for policy-makers. It simply means that social-dividend taxation is characterized by emphasis on a guaranteed minimum income and a tax schedule that, at some point, reduces the guaranteed payment to zero. This is true of Tobin's plan also, although his differs from pure social-dividend plans in its more modest proportions and his failure to specify how the cost is to be financed. It is true of tax-credit schemes as well, which would convert the personal exemptions under present tax systems into a refundable tax credit financed by a tax on income.

NO BASIC DIFFERENCES

The emphasis in negative taxation is somewhat different. First, the break-even point is determined. In the case of Friedman's plan, the break-even point is the value of exemptions and deductions allowed a family; in Lampman's, it is the family's poverty line. When the break-even point is combined with a negative-tax schedule, a guaranteed minimum-income level is determined. Thus, the stress is on a break-even point and a guaranteed minimum income, and the outcome is the negative tax rate.

The tax base, at first glance, would seem to separate negative-taxation plans from social-dividend plans and the Tobin mixture. In negative-tax plans, the tax base is the gap between some standard—such as the values of personal exemptions and minimum standard deductions allowed a family, or the family's poverty line—and the family's income. In social-dividend taxations and Tobin's plan, the tax base is the family's income before allowance.

Table 1: ALLOWANCE FOR A FAMILY OF FOUR UNDER TWO TRANSFER-BY-TAXATION PLANS

Type of Plan	Family's Income Before Allowance				
	$ 0	$ 500	$1,000	$2,000	$3,000
Negative Rates Taxation					
1. Poverty-income gap or unused EX-MSD*	$3,000	$2,500	$2,000	$1,000	$ 0
2. Allowance based on 40% of poverty gap or unused EX-MSD	1,200	1,000	800	400	0
Social-Dividend Taxation					
3. Basic allowance guarantee of $1,200 (equal to 40% of poverty line)	1,200	1,200	1,200	1,200	1,200
4. Tax liability with 40% income tax rate	0	200	400	800	1,200
5. Net allowance (3)-(4)	1,200	1,000	800	400	0

*Both the Lampman poverty line and the value of exemptions and minimum standard deductions (EX-MSD) are $3,000 for a family of four.

But this difference, in fact, is superficial. It is easy to show that a negative-tax plan that fills x percent of a family's poverty gap is the same as a plan that guarantees a minimum income equal to x percent of the family's poverty line and taxes the family income at an x percent rate. An example is shown in Table 1. The first plan shows what would happen under a typical negative-tax plan with a negative-tax rate of 40 percent applied against the family's poverty-income gap or its unused exemptions and deductions. The second resembles a social-dividend plan in that it guarantees the family $1,200 (40 percent of $3,000) and taxes family income at the same rate. The second and fifth lines show that both plans, given the family's income, produce identical results.

Does *any* plan that guarantees a minimum income differ, in principle, from a transfer-by-taxation plan? That is, if a plan completely unrelated to the tax system is devised, will it be, in substance, the same as a transfer-by-taxation plan?

The answer would seem to be Yes. If, for instance, some federal bureau were established with the duty of assuring all families a minimum income, it would necessarily have to draft guidelines, including a "tax rate" and a break-even point of income, in addition to the guaranteed minimum. This is because the bureau would be forced to decide on a rate at which the guaranteed allowances are reduced as a family's income rises. Once this is determined, the rate or rates, in conjunction with the guarantee, will determine a break-even point. In addition, the bureau would have to obtain financing, even though the means of financing might be completely unrelated to the plan itself.

Guaranteed minimum-income plans have been proposed by Robert Theobald, an English-born social economist, and Edward E. Schwartz of the University of Chicago School of Social Work. They urge raising the income of poor families to some predetermined level. This really means equating the minimum-income guarantee and the break-even level of income. The outcome is a 100 percent tax rate on the nonallowance income of allowance recipients. But modifications can be made to mitigate somewhat the potentially powerful deterrent to work produced by a 100 percent tax on earned income.

Theobald has suggested bringing all incomes up to an adequate level, with a small premium added to mitigate the deterrent effects on working for a living. If a family is guaranteed $3,000 a year, under his plan, and has earnings of $2,000, it might be allowed $1,000, which would fill the poverty gap, plus (perhaps) 20 percent of its earned income.

The difficulty with this scheme is that it produces what tax experts call a "notch" problem. It is possible that the payments to some families below but near the poverty line will make them more affluent than others near but *above* the line.

Table 2: THE SCHWARTZ PLAN

Earned Income	Tax on Income	Allowance	Total Income
$ 0- 999	60%	$3,000-2,400	$3,000-3,399
1,000-1,999	70	2,399-1,700	3,399-3,699
2,000-2,999	80	1,699- 900	3,699-3,899
3,000-3,999	90	899- 0	3,899-3,999
4,000-4,499	100	– 0 –	4,000-4,499

Source: Edward Schwartz, "A Way to End the Means Test," *Social Work*, Vol. 9 (July 1964), page 9.

Schwartz's plan would pay families the difference between their incomes and a federally guaranteed annual minimum of $3,000. It would remedy the notch problem by extending eligibility for an allowance to families whose income, before taxes, is somewhat above $3,000. Under his modification (outlined in Table 2), as earned income rises, the allowance is reduced until a break-even point is reached at $4,000.

In sum, simply filling the poverty gap is equivalent to a negative-tax plan with a 100 percent negative rate. If the deterrent-to-work effect of such a plan is to be avoided without producing a notch problem, the resulting plan will resemble a social-dividend plan. The same analysis may be applied to public-assistance, social-insurance and family-allowance programs designed to guarantee a minimum income.

THE PLANS' MERITS AND DEMERITS

Negative-income taxation and social-dividend taxation, one

can conclude, do not really differ in principle. But each raises different issues and problems.

Social-dividend plans would make payments to all segments of the population. They are a more sweeping, systematic method of redistributing national income and wealth. They would help the poor—but not single them out for special treatment—and help others as well. They would also avoid deficiencies in defining poverty on the basis of annual income. But financing such a program would present great problems because of the great costs.

Negative-income taxation, on the other hand, is an offshoot of social-dividend taxation and a less radical proposal—because it is much less expensive and it is confined to a minority of society. In the form presented by Friedman and Lampman, it represents a way of attacking poverty with a minimum of income redistribution. Unlike many other forms of assistance, it would allow beneficiaries to increase their disposable income by earning more; and it would avoid an implicit marginal-tax rate of 100 percent, in contrast with present welfare programs that generally reduce payments by a dollar for each dollar earned.

There are, however, thorny problems in negative taxes. The trade-offs involved in choosing the income guarantee, the negative-tax rate, and the break-even point involve some inescapable arithmetic. As I noted earlier, any two of the three basic factors determine the third in an uncomfortable manner. For example, the objective of a high guaranteed minimum income, combined with a tax rate that keeps deterrents to work low, is not compatible with an objective of confining allowances to the poor. Conversely, a low break-even point, and a reasonably low negative-tax rate, is not compatible with a high guaranteed minimum. Something has to give. If a schedule of rates averaging much above 50 percent would not be politically acceptable, either the guarantee will be relatively low (even compared with public-assistance minimums in many states)—or the break-even point will be too high to confine benefits to the poor.

Nevertheless, the adoption of even a small negative-income tax plan would mean that the meager incomes of the poor will be supplemented—and that the poor will benefit from the tax cuts if the reductions include an increase in the negative-tax rate, or a rise in personal exemptions. And in this age of general economic affluence and Keynesian economic policy, a means by which the poor can benefit directly from both affluence and economic policy should certainly be sought.

FURTHER READING

The symposium on negative income taxation in *Industrial Relations* (February 1967) is worth referring to. The three articles are:

"Schemes for Transferring Income to the Poor" by Christopher Green and Robert J. Lampman. Describes and evaluates nine methods of transferring income.

"Second Thoughts on the Negative Income Tax" by George Hildebrand. A discussion of the shortcomings of negative income-tax plans, including the difficulties in administering them.

"The Case for a Negative Income Tax Device" by Earl R. Rolph. A proposal for the general redistribution of income.

The Relief of Welfare

FRANCES FOX PIVEN and RICHARD A. CLOWARD

Aid to Families with Dependent Children (AFDC) is our major
relief program. It has lately become the source of a major public
controversy, owing to a large and precipitous expansion of the
rolls. Between 1950 and 1960, only 110,000 families were added
to the rolls, yielding a rise of 17 percent. In the 1960s, however,
the rolls exploded, rising by more than 225 percent. At the
beginning of the decade, 745,000 families were receiving aid; by
1970, some 2,500,000 families were on the rolls. Still, this is not
the first, the largest or the longest relief explosion. Since the
inauguration of relief in Western Europe three centuries ago, the
rolls have risen and fallen in response to economic and political
forces. An examination of these forces should help to illuminate
the meaning of the current explosion, as well as the meaning of
current proposals for reform.

Relief arrangements, we will argue, are ancillary to economic
arrangements. Their chief function is to regulate labor, and they

do that in two general ways. First, when mass unemployment leads to outbreaks of turmoil, relief programs are ordinarily initiated or expanded to absorb and control enough of the unemployed to restore order; then, as turbulence subsides, the relief system contracts, expelling those who are needed to populate the labor market. Relief also performs a labor-regulating function in this shrunken state, however. Some of the aged, the disabled and others who are of no use as workers are left on the relief rolls, and their treatment is so degrading and punitive as to instill in the laboring masses a fear of the fate that awaits them should they relax into beggary and pauperism. To demean and punish those who do not work is to exalt by contrast even the meanest labor at the meanest wages. These regulative functions of relief are made necessary by several strains toward instability inherent in capitalist economics.

LABOR AND MARKET INCENTIVES

All human societies compel most of their members to work, to produce the goods and services that sustain the community. All societies also define the work their members must do and the conditions under which they must do it. Sometimes the authority to compel and define is fixed in tradition, sometimes in the bureaucratic agencies of a central government. Capitalism, however, relies primarily upon the mechanisms of a market—the promise of financial rewards or penalties—to motivate men and women to work and to hold them to their occupational tasks.

But the development of capitalism has been marked by periods of cataclysmic change in the market, the main sources being depression and rapid modernization. Depressions mean that the regulatory structure of the market simply collapses; with no demand for labor, there are no monetary rewards to guide and enforce work. By contrast, during periods of rapid modernization—whether the replacement of handicraft by machines, the relocation of factories in relation to new sources of power or new outlets for distribution, or the demise of family subsistence farming as large-scale commercial agriculture spreads—portions of the laboring population may be rendered obsolete or at least temporarily maladjusted. Market incentives do not collapse; they are simply not sufficient to compel people to abandon one way of working and living in favor of another.

In principle, of course, people dislocated by modernization become part of a labor supply to be drawn upon by a changing and expanding labor market. As history shows, however, people do not adapt so readily to drastically altered methods of work and to the new and alien patterns of social life dictated by that work. They may resist leaving their traditional communities and the only life they know. Bred to labor under the discipline of sun and season, however severe that discipline may be, they may resist the discipline of factory and machine, which, though it may be no more severe, may seem so because it is alien. The process of human adjustment to such economic changes has ordinarily generated mass unemployment, distress and disorganization.

Now, if human beings were invariably given to enduring these travails with equanimity, there would be no governmental relief systems at all. But often they do not, and for reasons that are not difficult to see. The regulation of civil behavior in all societies is intimately dependent on stable occupational arrangements. So long as people are fixed in their work roles, their activities and outlooks are also fixed; they do what they must and think what they must. Each behavior and attitude is shaped by the reward of a good harvest or the penalty of a bad one, by the factory paycheck or the danger of losing it. But mass unemployment breaks that bond, loosening people from the main institution by which they are regulated and controlled.

Moreover, mass unemployment that persists for any length of time diminishes the capacity of other institutions to bind and constrain people. Occupational behaviors and outlooks underpin a way of life and determine familial, communal and cultural patterns. When large numbers of people are suddenly barred from their traditional occupations, the entire network of social control is weakened. There is no harvest or paycheck to enforce work and the sentiments that uphold work; without work, people cannot conform to familial and communal roles; and if the dislocation is widespread, the legitimacy of the social order itself may come to be questioned. The result is usually civil disorder—crime, mass protests, riots—a disorder that may even threaten to overturn existing social and economic arrangements. It is then that relief programs are initiated or expanded.

Western relief systems originated in the mass disturbances that erupted during the long transition from feudalism to capitalism beginning in the sixteenth century. As a result of the declining death rates in the previous century, the population of Europe grew rapidly; as the population grew, so did transiency and beggary. Moreover, distress resulting from population changes, agricultural and other natural disasters, which had characterized life throughout the Middle Ages, was now exacerbated by the vagaries of an evolving market economy, and outbreaks of turbulence among the poor were frequent. To deal with these threats to civil order, many localities legislated severe penalties against vagrancy. Even before the sixteenth century, the magistrates of Basel had defined 25 different categories of beggars, together with appropriate punishments for each. But penalties alone did not always deter begging, especially when economic distress was severe and the numbers affected were large. Consequently, some localities began to augment punishment with provisions for the relief of the vagrant poor.

CIVIL DISORDER AND RELIEF

A French town that initiated such an arrangement early in the sixteenth century was Lyons, which was troubled both by a rapidly growing population and by the economic instability associated with the transition to capitalism. By 1500 Lyons' population had already begun to increase. During the decades that followed, the town became a prosperous commercial and manufacturing center—the home of the European money market and of expanding new trades in textiles, printing and metal-working. As it thrived it attracted people, not only from the surrounding countryside, but even from Italy, Flanders and Germany. All told, the population of Lyons probably doubled between 1500 and 1540.

All this was very well as long as the newcomers could be absorbed by industry. But not all were, with the result that the town came to be plagued by beggars and vagrants. Moreover, prosperity was not continuous: some trades were seasonal and others were periodically troubled by foreign competition. With each economic downturn, large numbers of unemployed workers took to the streets to plead for charity, cluttering the very doorsteps of the better-off classes. Lyons was most vulnerable during periods of bad harvest, when famine not only drove up the cost of bread for urban artisans and journeymen but brought hordes of peasants into the city, where they sometimes paraded through the streets to exhibit their misfortune. In 1529 food riots erupted, with thousands of Lyonnais looting granaries and the homes of the wealthy; in 1530, artisans and journeymen armed themselves and marched through the streets; in 1531, mobs of starving peasants literally overran the town.

Such charity as had previously been given in Lyons was primarily the responsibility of the church or of those of the more prosperous who sought to purchase their salvation through almsgiving. But this method of caring for the needy obviously stimulated rather than discouraged begging and created a public nuisance to the better-off citizens (one account of the times describes famished peasants so gorging themselves as to die on the very doorsteps where they were fed). Moreover, to leave charity to church or citizen meant that few got aid, and those not necessarily according to their need. The result was that mass disorders periodically erupted.

The increase in disorder led the rulers of Lyons to conclude that the giving of charity should no longer be governed by private whim. In 1534, churchmen, notables and merchants joined together to establish a centralized administration for disbursing aid. All charitable donations were consolidated under a central body, the "Aumone-Generale," whose responsibility was to "nourish the poor forever." A list of the needy was established by a house-to-house survey, and tickets for bread and money were issued according to fixed standards. Indeed, most of the features of modern welfare—from criteria to discriminate the worthy poor from the unworthy, to strict procedures for surveillance of recipients as well as measures for their rehabilitation—were present in Lyons' new relief administration. By the 1550s, about 10 percent of the town's population was receiving relief.

Within two years of the establishment of relief in Lyons, King Francis I ordered each parish in France to register its poor and to provide for the "impotent" out of a fund of contributions. Elsewhere in Europe, other townships began to devise similar systems to deal with the vagrants and mobs cast up by famine, rapid population growth and the transition from feudalism to capitalism.

England also felt these disturbances, and just as it pioneered in developing an intensively capitalist economy, so it was at the forefront in developing nationwide, public relief arrangements. During the closing years of the fifteenth century, the emergence of the wool industry in England began to transform agricultural life. As sheep raising became more profitable, much land was converted from tillage to pasturage, and large numbers of peasants were displaced by an emerging entrepreneurial gentry which either bought their land or cheated them out of it. The result was great tumult among the peasantry, as the Webbs were to note:

> When the sense of oppression became overwhelming, the popular feeling manifested itself in widespread organised tumults, disturbances and insurrections, from Wat Tyler's rebellion of 1381, and Jack Cade's march on London of 1460, to the Pilgrimage of Grace in 1536, and Kett's Norfolk rising of 1549—all of them successfully put down, but sometimes not without great struggle, by the forces which the government could command.

Early in the sixteenth century, the national government moved to try to forestall such disorders. In 1528 the Privy Council, anticipating a fall in foreign sales as a result of the war in Flanders, tried to induce the cloth manufacturers of Suffolk to retain their employees. In 1534, a law passed under Henry VIII attempted to limit the number of sheep in any one holding in order to inhibit the displacement of farmers and agricultural laborers and thus forestall potential disorders. Beginning in the 1550s the Privy Council attempted to regulate the price of grain in poor harvests. But the entrepreneurs of the new market economy were not so readily curbed, so that during this period another method of dealing with labor disorders was evolved.

Early in the sixteenth century, the national government moved to replace parish arrangements for charity with a nationwide system of relief. In 1531, an act of Parliament decreed that local officials search out and register those of the destitute deemed to be impotent and give them a document authorizing begging. As for those who sought alms without authorization, the penalty was public whipping till the blood ran.

Thereafter, other arrangements for relief were rapidly instituted. An act passed in 1536, during the reign of Henry VIII, required local parishes to take care of their destitute and to establish a procedure for the collection and administration of donations for that purpose by local officials. (In the same year Henry VIII began to expropriate monasteries, helping to assure secular control of charity.) With these developments, the penalties for beggary were made more severe, including an elaborate schedule of branding, enslavement and execution for repeated offenders. Even so, by 1572 beggary was said to have reached alarming proportions, and in that year local responsibility for relief was more fully spelled out by the famous Elizabethan Poor Laws, which established a local tax, known as the poor rate, as the means for financing the care of paupers and required that justices of the peace serve as the overseers of the poor.

After each period of activity, the parish relief machinery tended to lapse into disuse, until bad harvests or depression in manufacturing led again to widespread unemployment and misery, to new outbreaks of disorder, and then to a resuscitation and expansion of relief arrangements. The most illuminating of these episodes, because it bears so much similarity to the present-day relief explosion in the United States, was the expansion of relief during the massive agricultural dislocations of the late eighteenth century.

Most of the English agricultural population had lost its landholdings long before the eighteenth century. In place of the subsistence farming found elsewhere in Europe, a three-tier system of landowners, tenant farmers and agricultural workers had evolved in England. The vast majority of the people were a landless proletariat, hiring out by the year to tenant farmers. The margin of their subsistence, however, was provided by common and waste lands, on which they gathered kindling, grazed animals and hunted game to supplement their meager wages. Moreover, the use of the commons was part of the English villager's birthright, his sense of place and pride. It was the disruption of these arrangements and the ensuing disorder that led to the new expansion of relief.

By the middle of the eighteenth century, an increasing population, advancing urbanization and the growth of manufacturing had greatly expanded markets for agricultural products, mainly for cereals to feed the urban population and for wool to supply the cloth manufacturers. These new markets, together with the introduction of new agricultural methods (such as cross-harrowing), led to large-scale changes in agriculture. To take advantage of rising prices and new techniques, big landowners moved to expand their holdings still further by buying up small farms and, armed with parliamentary Bills of Enclosure, by usurping the common and waste lands which had enabled many small cottagers to survive. Although this process began much earlier, it accelerated rapidly after 1750; by 1850, well over six million acres of common land—or about one-quarter of the total arable acreage—had been consolidated into private holdings and turned primarily to grain production. For great numbers of agricultural workers, enclosure meant no land on which to grow subsistence crops to feed their families, no grazing land to produce wool for home spinning and weaving, no fuel to heat their cottages, and new restrictions against hunting. It meant, in short, the loss of a major source of subsistence for the poor.

New markets also stimulated a more businesslike approach to farming. Landowners demanded the maximum rent from tenant farmers, and tenant farmers in turn began to deal with their laborers in terms of cash calculations. Specifically, this meant a shift from a master-servant relationship to an employer-employee relationship, but on the harshest terms. Where laborers had previously worked by the year and frequently lived with the farmer, they were now hired for only as long as they were needed and were then left to fend for themselves. Pressures toward short-term hiring also resulted from the large-scale cultivation of grain crops for market, which called for a seasonal labor force, as opposed to mixed subsistence farming, which required year-round laborers. The use of cash rather than produce as the medium of payment for work, a rapidly spreading practice, encouraged partly by the long-term inflation of grain prices, added to the laborer's hardships. Finally the rapid increase in rural population at a time when the growth of woolen manufacturing continued to provide an incentive to convert land from tillage to pasturage produced a large labor surplus, leaving agricultural workers with no leverage in bargaining for wages with their tenant-farmer employers. The result was widespread unemployment and terrible hardship.

None of these changes took place without resistance from small farmers and laborers who, while they had known hardship before, were now being forced out of a way of life and even out of their villages. Some rioted when Bills of Enclosure were posted; some petitioned the Parliament for their repeal. And when hardship was made more acute by a succession of poor harvests in the 1790s, there were widespread food riots.

Indeed, throughout the late eighteenth and early nineteenth centuries, the English countryside was periodically beseiged by turbulent masses of the displaced rural poor and the towns were racked by Luddism, radicalism, trade-unionism and Chartism, even while the ruling classes worried about what the French Revolution might augur for England. A solution to disorder was needed, and that solution turned out to be relief. The poor relief system—first created in the sixteenth century to control the earlier disturbances caused by population growth and the commercialization of agriculture—now rapidly became a major institution of English life. Between 1760 and 1784, taxes for relief—the poor rate—rose by 60 percent; they doubled by 1801, and rose by 60 percent more in the next decade. By 1818, the poor rate was over six times as high as it had been in 1760. Hobsbawm estimates that up to the 1850s, upwards of 10 percent of the English population were paupers. The relief system, in short, was expanded in order to absorb and regulate the masses of discontented people uprooted from agriculture but not yet incorporated into industry.

Relief arrangements evolved more slowly in the United States, and the first major relief crisis did not occur until the Great Depression. The inauguration of massive relief-giving was not simply a response to widespread economic distress, for millions had remained unemployed for several years without obtaining aid. What finally led the national government to proffer aid was the great surge of political disorder that followed the economic catastrophe, a disorder which eventually led to the convulsive voting shifts of 1932. After the election, the federal government abandoned its posture of aloofness toward the unemployed. Within a matter of months, billions of dollars were flowing to localities, and the relief rolls skyrocketed. By 1935, upwards of 20 million people were on the dole.

The contemporary relief explosion, which began in the early 1960s, has its roots in agricultural modernization. No one would disagree that the rural economy of America, especially in the South, has undergone a profound transformation in recent decades. In 1945, there was one tractor per farm; in 1964 there were two. Mechanization and other technological developments, in turn, stimulated the enlargement of farm holdings. Between 1959 and 1961, one million farms disappeared; the three million remaining farms averaged 377 acres in size—30 percent larger than the average farm ten years earlier. The chief and most obvious effect of these changes was to lessen the need for agricultural labor. In the years between 1950 and 1965 alone, a Presidential Commission on Rural Poverty was to discover, "New machines and new methods increased farm output in the United States by 45 percent, and reduced farm employment by 45 percent." A mere 4 percent of the American labor force now works the land, signalling an extraordinary displacement of people, with accompanying upheaval and suffering. The best summary measure of this dislocation is probably the volume of migration to the cities; over 20 million people, more than four million of them black, left the land after 1940.

Nor were all these poor absorbed into the urban economic system. Blacks were especially vulnerable to unemployment. At the close of the Korean War, the national nonwhite unemployment rate leaped from 4.5 percent in 1953 to 9.9 percent in

1954. By 1958, it had reached 12.6 percent, and it fluctuated between 10 and 13 percent until the escalation of the war in Vietnam after 1964.

These figures pertain only to people unemployed and looking for work. They do not include the sporadically unemployed or those employed at extremely low wages. Combining such additional measures with the official unemployment measure produces a subemployment index. This index was first used in 1966—well after the economic downturns that characterized the years between the end of the Korean War and the escalation of the war in Vietnam. Were subemployment data available for the "Eisenhower recession" years, especially in the slum-ghettoes of the larger central cities, they would surely show much higher rates than prevailed in 1966. In any event, the figures for 1966 revealed a nonwhite subemployment rate of 21.6 percent compared with a white rate of 7.6 percent.

However, despite the spread of economic deprivation, whether on the land or in the cities, the relief system did not respond. In the entire decade between 1950 and 1960, the national AFDC caseload rose by only 17 percent. Many of the main urban targets of migration showed equally little change: the rolls in New York City moved up by 16 percent, and in Los Angeles by 14 percent. In the South, the rolls did not rise at all.

But in the 1960s, disorder among the black poor erupted on a wide scale, and the welfare rolls erupted as well. The welfare explosion occurred during several years of the greatest domestic disorder since the 1930s—perhaps the greatest in our history. It was concurrent with the turmoil produced by the civil-rights struggle, with widespread and destructive rioting in the cities, and with the formation of a militant grassroots movement of the poor dedicated to combating welfare restrictions. Not least, the welfare rise was also concurrent with the enactment of a series of ghetto-placating federal programs (such as the antipoverty program) which, among other things, hired thousands of poor people, social workers and lawyers who, it subsequently turned out, greatly stimulated people to apply for relief and helped them obtain it. And the welfare explosion, although an urban phenom-

enon generally, was greatest in just that handful of large metropolitan counties where the political turmoil of the middle and
late 1960s was the most acute.

The magnitude of the welfare rise is worth noting. The
national AFDC caseload rose by more than 225 percent in the
1960s. In New York City, the rise was more than 300 percent;
the same was so in Los Angeles. Even in the South, where there
had been no rise at all in the 1950s, the rolls rose by more than
60 percent. And most significant of all, the bulk of the increase
took place after 1965—that is, after disorder reached a crescendo.
More than 80 percent of the national rise in the 1960s occurred
in the last five years of the decade. In other words, the welfare
rolls expanded, today as at earlier times, only in response to civil
disorder.

While muting the more disruptive outbreaks of civil disorder
(such as rioting), the mere giving of relief does nothing to reverse
the disintegration of lower-class life produced by economic
change, a disintegration which leads to rising disorder and rising
relief rolls in the first place. Indeed, greatly liberalized relief-
giving can further weaken work and family norms. To restore
order in a more fundamental sense the society must create the
means to reassert its authority. Because the market is unable to
control men's behavior a surrogate system of social control must
be evolved, at least for a time. Moreover, if the surrogate system
is to be consistent with normally dominant patterns, it must
restore people to work roles. Thus even though obsolete or
unneeded workers are temporarily given direct relief, they are
eventually succored only on condition that they work. As these
adjustments are made, the functions of relief arrangements may
be said to be shifting from regulating disorder to regulating labor.

RESTORING ORDER BY RESTORING WORK

The arrangements, both historical and contemporary, through
which relief recipients have been made to work vary, but broadly
speaking, there are two main ways: work is provided under public
auspices, whether in the recipient's home, in a labor yard, in a

workhouse or on a public works project; or work is provided in the private market, whether by contracting or indenturing the poor to private employers, or through subsidies designed to induce employers to hire paupers. And although a relief system may at any time use both of these methods of enforcing work, one or the other usually becomes predominant, depending on the economic conditions that first gave rise to disorder.

Publicly subsidized work tends to be used during business depressions, when the demand for labor in the private market collapses. Conversely, arrangements to channel paupers into the labor market are more likely to be used when rapid changes in markets or technology render a segment of the labor supply temporarily maladapted. In the first case, the relief system augments a shrunken labor market; in the other, its policies and procedures are shaped to overcome the poor fit between labor demand and supply.

Public work is as old as public relief. The municipal relief systems initiated on the Continent in the first quarter of the sixteenth century often included some form of public works. In England, the same statute of 1572 that established taxation as the method for financing poor relief charged the overseers of the poor with putting vagrants to work. Shortly afterwards, in 1576, local officials were directed to acquire a supply of raw goods—wool, hemp, iron—which was to be delivered to the needy for processing in their homes, their dole to be fixed according to "the desert of the work."

The favored method of enforcing work throughout most of the history of relief was the workhouse. In 1723, an act of Parliament permitted the local parishes to establish workhouses and to refuse aid to those who would not enter; within ten years, there were said to be about 50 workhouses in the environs of London alone.

The destitute have also sometimes been paid to work in the general community or in their own homes. This method of enforcing work evolved in England during the bitter depression of 1840-1841. As unemployment mounted, the poor in some of the larger cities protested against having to leave their communities to enter workhouses in order to obtain relief, and in any case, in some places the workhouses were already full. As a result, various public spaces were designated as "labor yards" to which the unemployed could come by the day to pick oakum, cut wood and break stone, for which they were paid in food and clothing. The method was used periodically throughout the second half of the nineteenth century; at times of severe distress, very large numbers of the able-bodied were supported in this way.

The first massive use of public work under relief auspices in the United States occurred during the 1930s when millions of the unemployed were subsidized through the Works Progress Administration. The initial response of the Roosevelt administration was to appropriate billions for direct relief payments. But no one liked direct relief—not the president who called for it, the Congress that legislated it, the administrators who operated it, the people who received it. Direct relief was viewed as a temporary expedient, a way of maintaining a person's body, but not his dignity; a way of keeping the populace from shattering in despair, discontent and disorder, at least for a while, but not of renewing their pride, of bringing back a way of life. For their way of life had been anchored in the discipline of work, and so that discipline had to be restored. The remedy was to abolish direct relief and put the unemployed to work on subsidized projects. These reforms were soon instituted—and with dramatic results. For a brief time, the federal government became the employer of millions of people (although millions of others remained unemployed).

Quite different methods of enforcing work are used when the demand for labor is steady but maladaptions in the labor supply, caused by changes in methods of production, result in unemployment. In such circumstances, relief agencies ordinarily channel paupers directly into the private market. For example, the rapid expansion of English manufacturing during the late eighteenth and early nineteenth centuries produced a commensurately expanded need for factory operatives. But it was no easy matter to get them. Men who had been agricultural laborers, independent craftsmen or workers in domestic industries (i.e., piecework manufacturing in the home) resisted the new discipline. Between 1778 and 1830, there were repeated revolts by laborers in which local tradesmen and farmers often participated. The revolts failed, of course; the new industry moved forward inexorably, taking the more dependent and tractable under its command, with the aid of the relief system.

The burgeoning English textile industry solved its labor problems during the latter part of the eighteenth century by using parish children, some only four or five years old, as factory operatives. Manufacturers negotiated regular bargains with the parish authorities, ordering lots of 50 or more children from the poorhouses. Parish children were an ideal labor source for new manufacturers. The young paupers could be shipped to remote factories, located to take advantage of the streams from which power could be drawn. (With the shift from water power to steam in the nineteenth century, factories began to locate in towns where they could employ local children; with that change, the system of child labor became a system of "free" child labor.) The children were also preferred for their docility and for their light touch at the looms. Moreover, pauper children could be had for a bit of food and a bed, and they provided a very stable labor supply, for they were held fast at their labors by indentures, usually until they were 21.

Sometimes the relief system subsidizes the employment of paupers—especially when their market value is very low—as when the magistrates of Lyons provided subsidies to manufacturers who employed pauper children. In rural England during the late eighteenth century, as more and more of the population was being displaced by the commercialization of agriculture, this method was used on a very large scale. To be sure, a demand for labor was developing in the new manufacturing establishments that would in time absorb many of the uprooted rural poor. But this did not happen all at once: rural displacement and industrial expansion did not proceed at the same pace or in the same areas, and in any case the drastic shift from rural village to factory system took time. During the long interval before people forced off the land were absorbed into manufacturing, many remained in the countryside as virtual vagrants; others migrated to the towns, where they crowded into hovels and cellars, subject to the vicissitudes of rapidly rising and falling markets, their ranks continually enlarged by new rural refugees.

These conditions were not the result of a collapse in the

market. Indeed, grain prices rose during the second half of the eighteenth century, and they rose spectacularly during the Revolutionary and Napoleonic wars. Rather, it was the expanding market for agricultural produce which, by stimulating enclosure and business-minded farming methods, led to unemployment and destitution. Meanwhile, population growth, which meant a surplus of laborers, left the workers little opportunity to resist the destruction of their traditional way of life—except by crime, riots and incendiarism. To cope with these disturbances, relief expanded, but in such a way as to absorb and discipline laborers by supporting the faltering labor market with subsidies.

The subsidy system is widely credited to the sheriff and magistrates of Berkshire, who, in a meeting at Speenhamland in 1795, decided on a scheme by which the Poor Law authorities would supplement the wages of underemployed and underpaid agricultural workers according to a published scale. It was a time when exceptional scarcity of food led to riots all over England, sometimes suppressed only by calling out the troops. With this "double panic of famine and revolution," the subsidy scheme spread, especially in counties where large amounts of acreage had been enclosed.

The local parishes implemented the work subsidy system in different ways. Under the "roundsman" arrangement, the parish overseers sent any man who applied for aid from house to house to get work. If he found work, the employer was obliged to feed him and pay a small sum (6d) per day, with the parish adding another small sum (4d). Elsewhere, the parish authorities contracted directly with farmers to have paupers work for a given price, with the parish paying the combined wage and relief subsidy directly to the pauper. In still other places, parish authorities parcelled out the unemployed to farmers, who were obliged to pay a set rate or make up the difference in higher taxes. Everywhere, however, the main principle was the same: an underemployed and turbulent populace was being pacified with public allowances, but these allowances were used to restore order by enforcing work, at very low wage levels. Relief, in short, served as a support for a disturbed labor market and as a discipline for a disturbed rural society. As the historians J.L.

Hammond and Barbara Hammond were to say, "The meshes of the Poor Law were spread over the entire labour system."

The English Speenhamland plan, while it enjoys a certain notoriety, is by no means unique. The most recent example of a scheme for subsidizing paupers in private employ is the reorganization of American public welfare proposed in the summer of 1969 by President Richard Nixon; the general parallel with the events surrounding Speenhamland is striking. The United States relief rolls expanded in the 1960s to absorb a laboring population made superfluous by agricultural modernization in the South, a population that became turbulent in the wake of forced migration to the cities. As the relief rolls grew to deal with these disturbances, pressure for "reforms" also mounted. Key features of the reform proposals included a national minimum allowance of $1,600 per year for a family of four, coupled with an elaborate system of penalties and incentives to force families to work. In effect, the proposal was intended to support and strengthen a disturbed low-wage labor market by providing what was called in nineteenth century England a "rate in aid of wages."

ENFORCING LOW WAGE WORK
DURING PERIODS OF STABILITY

Even in the absence of cataclysmic change, market incentives may be insufficient to compel all people at all times to do the particular work required of them. Incentives may be too meager and erratic, or people may not be sufficiently socialized to respond to them properly. To be sure, the productivity of a fully developed capitalist economy would allow for wages and profits sufficient to entice most of the population to work; and in a fully developed capitalist society, most people would also be reared to want what the market holds out to them. They would expect, even sanctify, the rewards of the marketplace and acquiesce in its vagaries.

But no fully developed capitalist society exists. (Even today in the United States, the most advanced capitalist country, certain regions and population groups—such as southern tenant farmers—

remain on the periphery of the wage market and are only partially socialized to the ethos of the market.) Capitalism evolved slowly and spread slowly. During most of this evolution, the market provided meager rewards for most workers, and none at all for some. There are still many for whom this is so. And during most of this evolution, large sectors of the laboring classes were not fully socialized to the market ethos. The relief system, we contend, has made an important contribution toward overcoming these persisting weaknesses in the capacity of the market to direct and control men.

Once an economic convulsion subsides and civil order is restored, relief systems are not ordinarily abandoned. The rolls are reduced, to be sure, but the shell of the system usually remains, ostensibly to provide aid to the aged, the disabled and such other unfortunates who are of no use as workers. However, the manner in which these "impotents" have always been treated, in the United States and elsewhere, suggests a purpose quite different from the remediation of their destitution. These residual persons have ordinarily been degraded for lacking economic value, relegated to the foul quarters of the workhouse, with its strict penal regimen and its starvation diet. Once stability was restored, such institutions were typically proclaimed the sole source of aid, and for a reason bearing directly on enforcing work.

Conditions in the workhouse were intended to ensure that no one with any conceivable alternatives would seek public aid. Nor can there be any doubt of that intent. Consider this statement by the Poor Law Commissioners in 1834, for example:

> Into such a house none will enter voluntarily; work, confinement, and discipline will deter the indolent and vicious: and nothing but extreme necessity will induce any to accept the comfort which must be obtained by the surrender of their free agency, and the sacrifice of their accustomed habits and gratifications. *Thus the parish officer, being furnished an unerring test of the necessity of applicants, is relieved from his painful and difficult responsibility: while all have the gratification of knowing that while the necessitous are abundantly relieved, the funds of charity are not wasted by idleness and fraud.*

The method worked. Periods of relief expansion were generally followed by "reform" campaigns to abolish all "outdoor" aid and restrict relief to those who entered the workhouse—as in England in 1722, 1834 and 1871 and in the United States in the 1880s and 1890s—and these campaigns usually resulted in a sharp reduction in the number of applicants seeking aid.

The harsh treatment of those who had no alternative except to fall back upon the parish and accept "the offer of the House" terrorized the impoverished masses in another way as well. It made pariahs of those who could not support themselves; they served as an object lesson, a means of celebrating the virtues of work by the terrible example of their agony. That, too, was a matter of deliberate intent. The workhouse was designed to spur men to contrive ways of supporting themselves by their own industry, to offer themselves to any employer on any terms, rather than suffer the degraded status of pauper.

All of this was evident in the contraction of relief which occurred in the United States at the close of the Great Depression. As political stability returned, emergency relief and work relief programs were reduced and eventually abolished, with many of those cut off being forced into a labor market still glutted with the unemployed. Meanwhile, the Social Security Act had been passed. Widely hailed as a major reform, this measure created our present-day welfare system, with its categorical provisions for the aged, the blind and families with dependent children (as well as, in 1950, the disabled).

The enactment of this "reform" signalled a turn toward the work-enforcing function of relief arrangements. This became especially evident after World War II during the period of greatly accelerated agricultural modernization. Millions were unemployed in agriculture; millions of others migrated to the cities where unemployment in the late 1950s reached extremely high levels. But few families were given assistance. By 1960, only 745,000 families had been admitted to the AFDC rolls. That was to change in the 1960s, as we have already noted, but only in response to the most unprecedented disorder in our history.

That families without jobs or income failed to secure relief during the late 1940s and the 1950s was in part a consequence of restrictive statutes and policies—the exclusion of able-bodied males and, in many places, of so-called employable mothers, together with residence laws, relative responsibility provisions and the like. But it was also—perhaps mainly—a consequence of the persistence of age-old rituals of degradation. AFDC mothers were forced to answer questions about their sexual behavior ("When did you last menstruate?"), open their closets to inspection ("Whose pants are those?"), and permit their children to be interrogated ("Do any men visit your mother?"). Unannounced raids, usually after midnight and without benefit of warrant, in which a recipient's home is searched for signs of "immoral" activities, have also been part of life on AFDC. In Oakland, California, a public welfare caseworker, Bennie Parish, refused to take part in a raid in January 1962 and was dismissed for insubordination. When he sued for reinstatement, the state argued successfully in the lower courts that people taking public assistance waive certain constitutional rights, among them the right to privacy. (The court's position had at least the weight of long tradition, for the withdrawal of civil rights is an old feature of public relief. In England, for example, relief recipients were denied the franchise until 1918, and as late as 1934 the constitutions of 14 American states deprived recipients of the right to vote or hold office.)

The main target of these rituals is not the recipient who ordinarily is not of much use as a worker, but the able-bodied poor who remain in the labor market. It is for these people that the spectacle of the degraded pauper is intended. For example, scandals exposing welfare "fraud" have diffuse effects, for they reach a wide public—including the people who might otherwise apply for aid but who are deterred because of the invidious connotations of being on welfare. Such a scandal occurred in the District of Columbia in 1961, with the result that half of all AFDC mothers were declared to be ineligible for relief, most of them for allegedly "consorting with men." In the several years immediately before the attack, about 6,500 District of Columbia families had applied for aid annually; during the attack, the figure dropped to 4,400 and it did not rise for more than five years—long after that particular scandal itself had subsided.

In sum, market values and market incentives are weakest at the bottom of the social order. To buttress weak market controls and ensure the availability of marginal labor, an outcast class—the dependent poor—is created by the relief system. This class, whose members are of no productive use, is not treated with indifference, but with contempt. Its degradation at the hands of relief officials serves to celebrate the virtue of all work and deters actual or potential workers from seeking aid.

THE CURRENT CALL FOR REFORM

From our perspective, a relief explosion is a reform just because a large number of unemployed or underemployed people obtain aid. But from the perspective of most people, a relief explosion is viewed as a "crisis." The contemporary relief explosion in the United States, following a period of unparalleled turbulence in the cities, has thus resulted in a clamor for reform. Similar episodes in the past suggest that pressure for reform signals a shift in emphasis between the major functions of relief arrangements—a shift from regulating disorder to regulating labor.

Pressure for reform stems in part from the fiscal burden imposed on localities when the relief rolls expand. An obvious remedy is for the federal government simply to assume a greater share of the costs, if not the entire cost (at this writing, Congress appears likely to enact such fiscal reform).

However, the much more fundamental problem with which relief reform seeks to cope is the erosion of the work role and the deterioration of the male-headed family. In principle, these problems could be dealt with by economic policies leading to full employment at decent wages, but there is little political support for that approach. Instead, the historic approach to relief explosions is being invoked, which is to restore work through the relief system. Various proposals have been advanced: some would force recipients to report regularly to employment offices; others would provide a system of wage subsidies conditional on the recipient's taking on a job at any wage (including those below the federal minimum wage); still others would inaugurate a straightforward program of public works projects.

We are opposed to any type of reform intended to promote work through the relief system rather than through the reform of economic policies. When similar relief reforms were introduced in the past, they presaged the eventual expulsion of large numbers of people from the rolls, leaving them to fend for themselves in a labor market where there was too little work and thus subjecting them once again to severe economic exploitation. The reason that this happens is more than a little ironic.

The irony is this: when relief is used to enforce work, it tends to stabilize lower-class occupational, familial and communal life (unlike direct relief, which merely mutes the worst outbreaks of discontent). By doing so, it diminishes the proclivities toward disruptive behavior which give rise to the expansion of relief in the first place. Once order is restored in this far more profound sense, relief-giving can be virtually abolished as it has been so often in the past. And there is always pressure to abolish large-scale work relief, for it strains against the market ethos and interferes with the untrammeled operation of the market place. The point is not just that when a relief concession is offered up, peace and order reign; it is, rather, that when peace and order reign, the relief concession is withdrawn.

The restoration of work through the relief system, in other words, makes possible the eventual return to the most restrictive phase in the cycle of relief-giving. What begins as a great expansion of direct relief, and then turns into some form of work relief, ends finally with a sharp contraction of the rolls. Advocates of relief reform may argue that their reforms will be long-lasting, that the restrictive phase in the cycle will not be reached, but past experience suggests otherwise.

Therefore, in the absence of economic reforms leading to full employment at decent wages, we take the position that the explosion of the rolls is the true relief reform, that it should be defended, and that it should be expanded. Even now, hundreds of thousands of impoverished families remain who are eligible for assistance but who receive no aid at all.

FURTHER READING

The Village Labourer by J.L. Hammond and Barbara Hammond (London: Longmans, Green & Company, 1948) contains evidence from English history on the relationship of economic change to the rise of disorder, and on the role of relief-giving in moderating disorder.

Captain Swing by E.J. Hobsbawm and George Rude (New York: Pantheon Books, 1968) is a detailed study of one series of English rural disorders in the 1830s.

Aid to Dependent Children by Winifred Bell (New York: Columbia University Press, 1965) is the best and most candid account of this American relief program which has lately become so controversial.

Poverty Programs
and Policy Priorities

MARTIN REIN AND S.M. MILLER

The war on poverty is financially boxed in—on the one side, by the military priorities for the war in Vietnam, and on the other, by conservative domestic politics and assaults. In this state of siege, its progress is limited. But even if the conflict in Vietnam—and in Congress—were to end tomorrow, the anti-poverty program would still face major battles and possible defeat. For success in any program depends on strategy as well as resources. Given vastly greater funds and lowered political opposition, basic questions would still have to be answered: Which projects should the government support? How well are they planned? What can they realistically accomplish? What goals come first?

It is not the purpose of this article to recommend specific programs, whether old or new, which should be continued or started. Rather, we are concerned with helping to construct a workable framework for making such decisions—a framework needed under any circumstances of war or peace.

To set up priorities, we must consider what is wanted (values), what could be effective (rationality), and what is politically and organizationally *feasible*. We must not only know what benefits we seek, and why, but what we are willing to pay, or give up, to achieve them. Goals very often conflict; to promote one may not only mean neglecting others, but even working against them. Values must not be buried under technical considerations—the "whys" lost sight of because of the "hows." The kind of nation and life we think worthwhile—our view of the good society—must help determine the programs we choose.

There are no final or absolute answers here. Rather, let us explore what choices are available, how people choose, and how they should go about choosing.

Most programs for reducing poverty to date, whether in the planning or implementation stage, fall under six major headings: amenities, investing in human capital, transfers, rehabilitation, participation and economic measures.

Amenities. These are concerned with supplying services that strengthen and enrich the quality of life, that directly modify the environment of the poor. They serve as increments to personal and family welfare, whether as household help, child-care facilities or information centers. They extend the quality of living; if the poor have them, they are less poor in the sense of being without services. Alfred Kahn calls them "social utilities" and considers them as necessary as such public utilities as water and roads. They should not be considered remedies for a disease, but a normal and accepted service.

Investing in Human Capital. Investment of wealth is a means of creating more wealth. Investments in "human capital" (an "in" term among economists) concentrate resources on making the poor more self-sufficient and productive: schooling, job training, health care, and various techniques of fitting them into the job market. Theodore W. Schultz believes that "changes in the investment in human capital" are the basic and most effective means for "reducing the inequality . . . of personal income," rather than such devices as progressive taxes.

But what is a good investment? The purposes of "investments in human capital" are not as clear-cut as the parallel with investment in physical capital implies. What purposes, for instance, are educational programs in the war on poverty designed to accomplish? There is considerable confusion about this. In the nineteenth century, the emphasis in the charity schools was on inculcating character—good work habits and such traits as industry, promptness and reliability—rather than in teaching the specific skills and abilities necessary to rise in the world. The Job Corps and Neighborhood Youth Programs frequently seem intent on following this nineteenth-century model. The rhetoric of these programs implies that the goal is increasing lifetime earnings rather than conformity. On the other hand, "good character" seems to be a prerequisite for higher salaries.

Transfers. Transfers provide cash to the poor (and to other groups in society). Devices include the proposed negative income tax, fatherlessness insurance, children's allowances, guaranteed income and various cash subsidies. They are a means of redistributing income outside the marketplace. Cash transfers to the poor could be provided in a way that promotes self-respect and perpetuates the myth that they, like the farmer or subsidized industry, are actually helping the country by accepting the money. Transfers emphasize a way to build up and assure total income, instead of the 1930s emphasis on replacing income lost because of illness, unemployment, accident or old age.

But American public policy has been biased against the use of transfer payments to reduce poverty. We seem continually haunted by that legacy of Victorianism that a guaranteed income (for the poor) must increase shiftlessness, immorality and illegitimacy. Subsidy payments to farmers or industry rouse few doubts about the danger to the moral fiber of their recipients. Public assistance programs seem less concerned with whether the poor get enough as the harm it might do them if they did. The prevailing orthodoxy (see Title V of the Economic Opportunity Act and the 1962 amendments to the Social Security Act) is committed to change sources of income rather than to increase it, to "get people off the dole" by work training and the amendments by social services.

Rehabilitation. This approach concentrates on changing people, usually by psychological means, to restore social functioning. It ranges from guidance and counseling, through casework, to psychotherapy and psychoanalysis. Rehabilitation hopes to overcome poverty by overcoming personal and family disorganization and deviancy. Those reclaimed will become more acceptable, more employable, more competent. Rehabilitation, seeking to change the person, accepts the environment as it is.

Participation. Participation includes those activities that try to overcome many of the psychological and social effects of poverty by giving the poor a stake in society and a chance to affect their own destinies. As Alan Haber says:

> American poverty, while it involves considerable physical hardship, is primarily "social poverty." It isolates the individual from the social mainstream, denies him the respect and status of the "respectable" members of the society, and excludes him from mobility opportunities into positions of social worth.

But there seems a confusion of purpose. Is the primary goal and effect of this strategy to help the poor to help themselves, or is it a means to organize them so that they can exert collective power? Warren G. Haggstrom has emphasized the more common concern with participation as a psychological condition of powerlessness. Involvement "provides immediate and compelling psychological returns." But another interpretation comes from Richard A. Cloward: "Economic deprivation is fundamentally a political problem, and power will be required to solve it."

Economic Measures. One economic approach to reducing poverty uses the "dribble-down" concept—if production is stimulated and the nation prospers at the top, some of the benefits will also dribble down to the poor. Another approach favors "bubbling up" the poor into the economic mainstream by programs designed directly to benefit them—new jobs, more low-skill jobs, minimum wages and so on. Which is the best way to promote economic growth and full employment? Some economists emphasize selective training for those jobs that are still unfilled and creation of special new job opportunities (for instance, nonprofessionals in hospitals and agencies). Others believe that the economy as a whole should be heated up so that a near-full employment situation emerges. But the concern with price increases, loosely called inflation, tends to stymie high-level employment, and many of the poor are low-skilled and not likely to be employed except with special inducements to employers.

To sum up, the six intervention strategies can be conceived of as attempts to change environment (amenities); to change occupational chances (investment); to change the pattern of claims on income distributed outside the market (transfers); to change people (rehabilitation); to change the distribution of power (participation); and, finally, to change the performance of the economic system (economic measures).

THE MANY FACES OF POVERTY

This inventory outlines not only a list of policy choices, but also embodies different conceptions about the meaning and causes of poverty. The different definitions of poverty imply different means to overcome it. What appears to be a concern with "poverty" is actually a tissue of sometimes-conflicting agenda. The term "poverty" cloaks the competing objectives. We note six ways to describe poverty, beyond mere lack of money:

Poverty and Social Decency. By this conception, citizens have a right not only to freedom from want, which requires a minimum of income, but also to adequate (and not inexpensive) services. One cannot reduce poverty without providing housing, medical care and recreation. The lack of these amenities is then, by definition, poverty.

Poverty and Equality. Proponents of this view hold that poverty exists as long as the bottom fifth (or tenth) of the population receives a shrinking or stable share of a growing economic pie. Their concern is with inequality—the position of lowest income groups *relative* to the rest of the nation. Improving the absolute level of a group without decreasing the gap between it and other groups may heighten its sense of relative deprivation. Improvement in absolute standards can lead to frustration and discontent, as the case of the Negro in the United States illustrates. Reducing poverty requires reducing inequality.

The goal of equity is not simply a matter of taking from the rich to give to the poor, but requires a searching way of examining the distribution of government largesse. For example, in housing we lump tax concessions with public housing expenditures as forms of government subsidy (as Richard Titmuss suggests), then we reach the startling conclusion that the major beneficiaries of housing welfare policies are the middle and upper classes. Alvin Schorr estimates that subsidies to the upper income fifth in 1962 were twice those to the bottom fifth ($1.7 billion to $820 million). Good housing therefore becomes simply a matter of equal treatment—the poor should receive at least as much from the government as the rich.

Poverty and Mobility. Poverty, according to this conception, is the lack of opportunity to alter one's income, occupational or social position. In a rigidly stratified social structure, those at the bottom, even if above a subsistence level, are still poor: they cannot escape upward. Enlisted men in the armed forces are not in want, and they may receive amenities as a matter of right; but they may be, as William Grigsby has pointed out, nevertheless in poverty if they are forced to remain in a rigid social niche. Similarly the Negro—stuck at the bottom of the social hierarchy —must be considered poor even if he has an adequate livelihood. Whether or not children remain in the same social and occupational classes as their parents, therefore, can be used as a measure of the reduction of poverty and the rigidity of the social order.

Poverty and Social Control. For many, improved income and services cannot be enough—for they are concerned with the social problems associated with poverty: alcoholism, delinquency, illiteracy, illegitimacy, mental illness. In the rhetoric of professionals, rehabilitation contributes to "self-actualization," but in fact it is more often used for social control—getting the poor to behave according to accepted standards. This view frequently merges into a broader concern with social harmony and equilibrium. If reducing poverty among Negroes did not eliminate race riots, the programs would be considered failures.

Poverty and Social Inclusion. In this view, people are poor when they cannot participate in the major institutions of our society, particularly the institutions that affect their lives—that is, when they have little or nothing to say about schools, employment, law enforcement, or even welfare and other social services. "The meaning of poverty," writes Peter Marris, "is humiliation: lack of power, of dignity, of self respect. . . . It is a mark of inferiority, and so more damaging than want itself."

Some experts justify reducing poverty for economic reasons—

the poor will spend their increased incomes for necessities and comforts and improve the economy; if the money went instead to the middle class, more would simply go into savings. Therefore, as the poor prosper, all will prosper. Humanitarian and economic goals coalesce.

But what if they should come to conflict? Then, to follow this concept to its logical conclusion, economic considerations must be given priority. We must prevent inflation even at the cost of preserving, or increasing, poverty; economic growth is more important than redistribution. At these points, the concern with the economy sharply displaces the interest in helping the poor or reducing poverty.

POLICY MODELS

These different concepts lead us to at least three basic models of how to view the overall purposes of social policy:

Allocative Justice. Policy is guided by a commitment to the more equitable distribution of benefits—who gets what, where, why and how. This model emphasizes equal opportunity for investment in career jobs and education and for the redistribution of amenities, income and resources necessary for well-being.

Policy as Handmaiden. This strategy seeks to promote programs that reduce poverty, but these are subordinate to other goals, such as economic growth, social stability or physical renewal of cities. Thus, transfer payments to the poor could be primarily supported because they stimulate the economy. Or services and amenities to the poor could be aimed at reducing social unrest, providing a silent strategy for riot control. Or the major purpose of rehabilitation of the poor in slums could be to make them good tenants and to facilitate the relocation of those displaced by urban renewal programs aimed at increasing the real estate values of downtown areas. These programs are designed to win the joint support of what might otherwise be competing groups. But in case of conflict the secondary role of poverty policy becomes evident.

Policy as Therapy. Many people, including a disproportionate number of the poor, do not behave according to our prevailing, accepted and predominantly middle-class standards. Poverty programs may exact conformity. Rehabilitation programs illustrate this approach.

This analysis leads to four fundamental policy questions: What are the purposes of the programs? How effective are they in achieving them? How feasible are they politically (what are the chances of getting them adopted and implemented)? How do we choose between competing desirable programs or goals?

PURPOSES OF POVERTY PROGRAMS

The question of purpose involves much more than technical classifications. It includes value judgments about goals. For instance, do we consider adequate housing and health programs for the poor *amenities* (to make the quality of their lives more comfortable) or *investments* (good housing to prevent poverty, and good health to reduce unemployment and improve learning in school)?

It is a political question as well: Will legislators vote funds for an antipoverty program unless we contend it will reduce poverty and crime or welfare costs? But a technical and rational question also is involved: What is the evidence that better housing and medical care will prevent poverty? Can we document the charge that the poor are really the most victimized by these insufficiencies?

Alvin Schorr has made an impressive and persuasive attempt to bring together evidence on the relationship between housing and poverty. He concludes:

> The following effects may spring from poor housing: A perception of one's self that leads to pessimism and passivity, stress to which the individual cannot adapt, poor health, and a state of dissatisfaction; pleasure in company but not in solitude, cynicism about people and organizations, a high degree of sexual stimulation without legitimate outlet, and difficulty in household management and child rearing; and relationships that tend to spread out in the neighborhood rather than deeply into the family.

He believes that malnutrition, poor health and inadequate

housing reinforce each other in causing, and intensifying, poverty. As he sees it, it is not the "life styles" of the poor that disable them so much as the lack of means to live properly. What they need is not psychological or sociological analysis but health, housing, adequate incomes.

Others disagree. Their studies indicate to them that improved housing has little effect on such things as deviant behavior or physical illness. Nathan Glazer, for instance, challenges Schorr's assumption:

> The chief problems of our slums are social—unemployment, poor education, broken families, crime. . . . Nor can they be solved by physical means, whether by urban renewal projects or . . . housing directly for the poor.

In fact, Glazer believes that social relationships have more effect on housing than vice versa; that broken families can nullify the effects of even the best housing. The facts Glazer quotes are impressive: Two-thirds of the poorest urban families (under $2,000 a year) do not live in substandard housing; further, most of substandard housing is not occupied by the poorest.

What about the traditional relationship between morbidity and poverty? Charles Kadushin concludes: "A review of the evidence . . . leads to the conclusion that . . . there is very little association between getting a disease and social class, although the lower class still feel sicker." That is, Kadushin says, the poor complain more about illness and stay away from work longer for it, but are not necessarily more ill.

Others challenge Kadushin's interpretation. Further, these data do not provide an argument against the development of health and housing programs for poor people. If health and housing seem unrelated, this may be because of difficult problems of measurement. Are the poor who live in standard housing overcrowded? Do they pay too high a portion of their income for this housing? They may be largely older people living in their own homes, while the families with many children live in substandard apartments. Inadequate statistics can distort the total picture.

Let us consider health in the same light. Even if morbidity rates among the poor are low, infant mortality is high, life is shorter, hospitalization longer, and disability has more severe consequences.

The fact is that we have so little good policy-oriented research that we cannot make any firm conclusion about the relationships between poverty and housing and health care. Consequently, we cannot be sure that better housing and health would help raise the poor from poverty.

But housing and health can be justified on other grounds than reducing poverty. Equality, as noted, is one. Inequalities and loss of dignity might be the crucial aspects of poor housing. According to Schorr: "It makes little difference whether bad housing is a result or a cause of poverty, it is an integral part of being poor." And the psychology of poverty is reinforced by seeing, all about, how the other half lives. By this definition, then, people without adequate housing or access to medical care are poor; adequate amenities reduce poverty. It is not that housing is instrumental to improved education or income; it is a goal in itself.

PROGRAM EFFECTIVENESS

The second policy issue is effectiveness. What good is a program that does not accomplish its purpose? But, in the first place, what is a program's purpose? Anyone who tries to get a straightforward statement of goals from a social agency usually finds that they react as though their very reason for being were under challenge.

But if the agencies will not provide clear answers, what of social science itself? For instance, do present rehabilitation programs actually reduce deviancy? When the score is finally totaled, the answer turns out to be, mostly, no. Social science research generally winds up exploding myths rather than giving solutions. William Kvaracecous, who recently reviewed the literature on delinquency, has reached the gloomy conclusion that nothing works very well. Other studies support him. Social work techniques may make youths and groups more democratic, more willing to join in approved sports and dancing, but they have little effect on lawbreaking. Walter Miller has concluded that delinquency depends largely on age and sex—young men commit most crimes—and therapy will not change these conditions.

Will rehabilitation and counseling help broken or ineffective families or reduce economic dependency? A number of studies—including the most recent analysis of a vocational high school by Henry Meyer and his associates—indicate that intensive casework makes little difference in reducing social problems.

However, ineffectiveness alone is not always enough reason to abandon a strategy. A program can be effective in unplanned ways. Even if rehabilitation does not reduce pathology and poverty much, its ethical, moral and humanitarian value should not be discounted.

Another practical political factor impedes effectiveness. We frequently adopt programs not because of demonstrated validity, but because they are feasible—we can get them adopted and financially supported. "It is always easier to put up a clinic than tear down a slum," Barbara Wootton argues. "We prefer today to analyze the infected individual rather than the infection from the environment." Rehabilitation as a means of reducing dependency has become a national policy. Also, for political reasons we have reversed the usual procedure by starting programs and *then* testing the concepts in demonstration projects. In such situations the pressure to find exactly the answers we are already committed to is hard to resist. Thus, what is politically possible makes a rational analysis difficult.

What of the argument that the poor should, as a policy, be encouraged to achieve power through collective action and pressure? Alvin Schorr has summarized the arguments against such grass-roots involvement:

> Efforts to promote self-organization fail more often than they succeed. . . . First, poor people have learned cynicism from bitter experience. They do not widely and readily respond to efforts to organize them. Second, when they do seek serious ends for themselves, they threaten established institutions or interest groups. At that point they are likely to learn once more that they are comparatively powerless. Third, the professionals who try to help them have, with rare exceptions, one foot in the "establishment." The ethical and practical problems that arise in their marginal situation are not solved simply by an effort of will.

POLITICAL FEASIBILITY

The foregoing leads us to the third policy issue—the feasibility of programs that invest in human resource development. If we say that investment in education or training will result in jobs, can we deliver? Is there a coherent relationship between the learning and the job?

More education or training usually pays off in more and better employment. But how much education—and expense—before the payoff starts? College graduates are better off than others, and the income differences between them and the noncollege population are expanding. But the differences in job opportunities and wages between high school graduates and dropouts are not great, especially for nonwhites. They seem, in fact, to be declining. For males age 35 to 44 in 1939, dropouts earned 80 percent as much as high school graduates; in 1961, 87 percent. As more people get more education, the tipping point for education may come later and later. Investing in human resources may have a limited gain if would-be dropouts do not go to college.

How much education, how good, and how relevant to the job market are all important questions in job training. And on one or more of these counts most of our training programs have fallen down. A study of "successful" exconvicts shows that only 17 percent were working at the trades they had learned in prison. Of 1,700 young people who applied to Mobilization for Youth (MFY) for training, only "roughly one in four eventually achieved competitive employment as a direct result," according to Richard A. Cloward. And these were mostly for marginal jobs, paying marginal salaries. As Herbert E. Klarman says: ". . . in the past the market economy has apparently not absorbed appreciable numbers of rehabilitated persons."

The relationship between occupational training and unemployment is very low. First, whatever its faults, we have done a much better job of rehabilitating people than of preparing society to receive them; and training means little if it does not lead to jobs. The connection between jobs and training is frequently very loose. Second, our training programs are often simply not good or relevant enough. Cloward reveals that the youths who did graduate from the MFY program could not read better than when they started, and had failed to get skills that could qualify them for the higher paying jobs. Training just to improve character or work habits—the intent of many if not most training programs for low-income youth—is a poor investment.

Moreover, employers tend not to take this training seriously, or consider it a legitimate credential of employability. One of the great virtues of a diploma, or even an honorable military discharge, is that an employer will recognize it as a credential of employability and character.

Why train if that training is inadequate, discounted, or if no jobs are available? Real improvement can only come about with changes in our educational, referral and economic institutions—which are untouched by the training programs. In short, unless relevant institutions themselves are changed, even highly promising programs will be frustrating rather than improving prospects. Training can be an effort to evade the issue of job availability.

Few people will argue that better training and more jobs for the poor are not desirable goals. But the stubborn facts are that most training is not good enough, and that the jobs which follow training are too often marginal or scarce. To yield large payoffs, education will need large investments. Are we willing to face these difficulties?

COMPETING GOALS

What happens when goals conflict, whether the conflict is real or apparent, recognized or ignored?

As Isaiah Berlin has astutely observed, there is a "natural tendency of all but a few thinkers to believe that all the things they hold good must be intimately connected or at least compatible with one another." In social policy, as in other fields, this is a delusion; goals often conflict, and we must decide on priorities. Here are four major areas of real or assumed value conflict:

Prices and Poverty. Paul Samuelson and Robert Solow have

concluded that a 5.5 percent level of unemployment is necessary to keep prices stable; anything less must result in inflation. "It may be doubted . . . that we can achieve both a satisfactory level of employment and price stability without major improvements in our antiinflationary weapons." Similarly, the British Labor government has recently discovered, with some distress, that if it strengthens its international economic position, it may have to let unemployment rise and renege on its promise to raise pensions.

In short, we may have to choose between social welfare programs and rising prices. As James Tobin says:

> We are paying much too high a social price for avoiding creeping inflation and for protecting our gold supply and "the dollar. . . ." The interests of the unemployed, the poor and the Negroes are underrepresented in the consensus which supports and confines current policy.

Income Plans and Incentives. Raising incomes through payments can conflict with trying to get the poor into the labor market. Is providing an incentive to work more important than assuring adequacy of income? As Evelyn Burns puts it:

> Workers whose normal incomes are very low and whose economic horizons are very limited may, if social security income is adequate for their modest wants, prefer benefit status to securing an income from employment, particularly if their normal type of employment is arduous or unpleasant, or if they are unmarried with no family responsibilities.

Rights and Misuse. Support programs contain various tests of eligibility, and provisions to punish violators. These are supposed to prevent cheating and make sure that welfare does not interfere with the free labor market and private economic incentives. These goals, however, conflict with those of economic costs and social rights. Obviously, the greater the gap between benefits and wages, the less effectively welfare can serve to increase demands in time of recession, and generally stabilize the economy; and the more rigid the rules and administrative control over welfare payments, the less chance of reducing feelings of powerlessness among the poor, and of establishing social benefits as legal *rights.*

Order and Conflict. The goals of keeping public order and

protecting the well-to-do and of safeguarding the social and constitutional rights of the poor often conflict. We have not only a law about the poor, which seeks to deal with their condition, but a law *of* the poor, based on police powers. As Jacobus Ten Broek has declared, it is "designed to safeguard health, safety, morals, and well-being of the fortunate rather than directly to improve the lot of the unfortunate." The goal is the protection of society against the poor rather than safeguarding the poor from an indifferent or callous society. When we encourage the poor to be militant and independent, to secure and exercise the legal rights to assistance and protection, we tend to sharpen this conflict. If they are to try to shape policy, they may become involved in boycotts, pickets, strikes and other dramatic forms of protest—in other words, in threatening the "well-being of the fortunate." In such areas as school desegregation, the interests of the fortunate will be directly pitted against those of the unfortunate. These are natural conflicts in a pluralistic society.

Thus, the single, seemingly simple aim of reducing poverty hides the many and often contradictory goals deriving from different conceptions of what poverty is. They call for many different kinds of strategy, which cannot hope to satisfy everybody.

COST-BENEFIT ANALYSIS

How do we establish rules to allocate limited resources to promote goals that are in partial conflict? Can we develop more effective methods of making decisions that specifically recognize contrasting objectives and give policy-makers a clearer choice of the costs and benefits of various combinations?

Cost-benefit analysis has become more popular as older decision-making methods have proven inadequate for fighting poverty. The economic market had long been the traditional way of making decisions—automatic, impersonal. More recently, politicians and their administrators have made many important decisions—reflecting the play of political and value preferences. But though it moderated some of the dangers of market decisions, political determination has brought new strains of its own—arbitrariness, and the obscuring of national needs because of political traditions and expediency. Cost-benefit analysis seeks to professionalize decision-making. It offers a rational as opposed to a market or political (value) basis for making decisions. Means are in agreement with goals.

It makes important contributions. But it does not provide a mechanism for superseding questions of value and preference. When used that way, it has important defects. Our criticism of cost-benefit analysis is sixfold: it suffers from technical limitations; it can lead to a quantitative mentality; the issue of operational feasibility is largely ignored; it has no ready-made response to the basic question of what costs and which benefits; goals are difficult to delineate; and it does not deal with the issue of competing goals. The large-scale danger in cost-benefit analysis is that values surreptitiously and inevitably creep in. The covert handling of values limits democratic discussions. Nor does it, we believe, strengthen in the long-run an effective policy of poverty or inequality-reduction.

It implies knowledge and confidence about social data that are ill placed. One does not have to agree with the doubts that we have raised in this paper about the efficacy of housing or the connection between health and poverty to doubt that one can have much confidence in measurements of costs and benefits. Hunches are frequently more important than scientific determination. Obviously, social science will develop and some uncertainties will diminish. But we cannot be confident that all our evaluations are based upon scientific proof and that in the future we will always have a firm scientific basis for choices to be faced.

Another technical problem is the question of the "interest rate." In order to calculate cost and benefits which are received or expended over a number of years, it is necessary to use some way to calculate future benefits in terms of their present value. Since present gains are valued more than future, the latter should be reduced by an appropriate discount. The level of the discount can markedly affect total benefits. For example, cost-benefit analysis of much vocational education would have different results if a higher discount rate were employed than in some present calculations. The appropriate level of the discount is not undebatable.

The result of looking at benefits over a long number of years is, therefore, inevitably an emphasis on youth. The longer individuals can benefit from a program, the greater the return. It pays then to concentrate on youth rather than on the aged. But are there not other reasons for concentrating on older workers?

Cost-benefit analysis tends to emphasize those variables that can be reduced to figures. For example, the inability in urban renewal to assign a monetary value to the aesthetic pleasure of greenery may be a serious difficulty. There is danger of sliding into the position that the only goals with merit and legitimacy are those that are quantifiable and convertible into money. Quantitative reasoning may lead to stressing productivity (return per unit of expenditure) over total results. Productivity can be high while total returns may be less than in some other kind of activity which has a high relative cost per unit of expenditure. For instance, it may be more "productive" to work with the highly educated, "cream" unemployed because it is easier to get them jobs than it is for the hard-core, long-term unemployed individuals. But which activity comes closer to solving the problems of unemployment?

Quantitative reasoning also tends to underestimate the importance of feasibility. Here we do not refer to the political issues, but to the effective implementation of a program. It may be that a particular program is highly productive with a likelihood of a return far outweighing its cost. But this program may be extremely difficult to mount because of manpower or administrative obstacles. Another program may have a much poorer prospect in terms of productivity and costs, but be much easier to implement.

In making these points, we do not argue that the defects cannot be remedied, rather that current practice tends to ignore them. But now we move into issues which are more basic to the long-term difficulties of cost-benefit analysis.

What is a cost and what is a benefit is not so obvious as it seems. To a large extent cost-benefit analysis narrows the definition of both cost and benefit. To what extent are second and third order effects of any action included in the analysis? This is largely a political and value question more than a technical one.

What is the goal? The foregoing analysis has stressed competing goals. Which should have priority is not only a question of rational calculations but of political issues and value preferences. Cost-benefit analysis provides some important kinds of information, but it does not resolve the issues of values, direction, purposes or priorities. Is the goal to bring the poor up to a certain income level? Or is it a larger one of reducing inequalities within society?

Which is preferable cannot be determined by cost-benefit analysis alone. Cost-benefit analysis at best is only a tool. It may be useful, but it also can be misleading when assumed to have greater clarifying power than it actually has.

We must not be lulled into thinking that cost-benefit analysis can rescue us from choice. Three solutions—cost-benefit analysis, the marketplace, the political process—are probably necessary, but none is sufficient alone, or even together. Policy is not all about technical rules for implementing value-neutral hardware. No simple choices are on hand. The crucial issues remain: How do we define a good society? How do we implement it?

These questions must be confronted. Technology must serve purpose. There are several ways to reveal the techniques of policy-making as the politics that they are. One good way may be to create a pluralistic system of advisory planning where many interest groups have their own experts to develop and support their own policies. Herbert Gans suggests that this may have already developed in city planning, where a progressive wing concentrates on social planning and a conservative wing defends "traditional physical planning and . . . middle class values."

Value judgments have to be made—but who, specifically, shall make them? However it is done—overtly or covertly, consciously or unconsciously, democratically or dictatorially—it occurs. The planner is not a value-free technician serving a value-free bureaucracy. The assumption that politics is without content—only efficient or inefficient—is unacceptable. As Paul Davidoff says: "Appropriate policy in a democracy is determined through a political debate. The right course of action is always a matter of choice, never a fact." The search for "rationality" cannot avoid the issues of objectives and ideologies.

There should be many analyses, based on competing outlooks as well as assumptions. In a pluralistic, competitive society the people should weigh competing values, vigorously promoted, before they can make just decisions. But ultimately, after all technical analyses are made, the selection of goals and timing must depend on judgment; and judgment must depend on those brute preferences we call values.

6

LESSONS FOR THE FUTURE

Poverty, Professionalism and Politics

LEON EISENBERG

With all the force of religious revelation, a self-evident truth has erupted into professional consciousness: the earth and its treasures are finite. And from that long-since-obvious proposition spring revolutionary consequences. If it is so obviously true and for so long obvious, why should the proposition have so startling an impact? Because, for the first time in our history, we are beginning to approach the limits of that finitude.

So long as this country had what appeared to be an endless frontier, the ravaged land we abandoned mattered little to us. So long as the marvels of technology promised limitless productivity, the growth of world population was in keeping with the biblical injunction to be fruitful and multiply. So long as we thought that there was more of everything to be had, poverty could be corrected, in principle at least, without taking from the haves to give to the have-nots.

Now we begin to be aware of the moving finger. It is still true that the green revolution could permit us to feed a world population several fold larger than its present aggregate mass. If we were to use Dutch standards of cultivation and nutrition, the arable land mass of the world would support a population of perhaps 28 billion people; if we use Japanese standards, perhaps 95 billion. But what has not been reckoned with, as we dazzled ourselves with our technological virtuosity, is the garbage disposal problem. Whether measured by air pollution, water defilement or radioactive wastes, the limiting condition is not producing goods; it is the present inability of the ecosystem to recycle the artifacts of civilization. The short-run threat to Spaceship Earth is not the birth of more Chinese or Indians or Africans, but the birth of more Americans and West Europeans, each of whom consumes resources and creates wastes at many times the rate of the citizens of underdeveloped countries. Why is the recognition of this relationship revolutionary? Because it is we who must change, not merely others. Because it implies that, even at zero population growth, a condition not likely to be attained soon, the world's resources cannot be expanded sufficiently to attain dignity for all without halting conspicuous consumption. Conventional economic wisdom held that growth in the gross natural product (GNP) would enable us to continue to improve living standards without invading the prerogatives of the privileged. How different is the world as we now see it!

My thesis is oversimplified and overstated in order to sharpen my focus on the challenge that we face. I do not suggest that we have reached the point where no further economic growth is possible. That is far from true. I do not suggest that further technological development will not dissipate some of our present waste disposal problems; there is no reason to doubt that the scientific ingenuity that we have devoted to making war, if applied to virtuous ends, could enable more of us to make love. But even if the economic pie can be made somewhat larger than it is now, my thesis remains valid; namely that, of necessity, we are about to enter a period of slower growth and that the resulting social pressures will force a redistribution of wealth because our capacity for generating new wealth will not suffice to meet all competing needs.

I propose to pursue this theme by citing examples of the ways in which this new state of affairs has begun to affect professionals and thus to penetrate their consciousness. These first examples are far from the most significant for the national welfare but, as they affect the "welfare" of professionals, they bring our own responses to center stage. I will next examine how Americans are being betrayed by false solutions cleverly engineered to offer the appearance of change but actually designed to reinforce the status quo. Finally, I will conclude by stressing the interrelationship between human services and professional responsibility.

The issues that have emerged into professional consciousness are as varied as our specialties. Consider scientific research workers. In the period from the end of World War II to the mid-1960s, federal allocations for research and development expanded at an exponential rate. Indeed, grim humorists have calculated that, had the process continued, in another generation the entire GNP would have been consumed by Science! Surely rational men should have been able to recognize that the cornucopia was not inexhaustible, but, when the decline in appropriations began, the cries of anguish echoed down laboratory corridors. Some statesmen of science had warned that a limit was being approached; few listened to the Cassandras so long as the day of reckoning seemed postponable.

During the period of continuous growth, little thought was given to the formulation of an explicit national science policy; almost everything that was worth doing was supportable. We did not have to make choices between basic and applied research, between organic chemistry and anaesthesia, between health research and space research. I do not mean to suggest that choices were not being made even then, but the determinations were made by a scientific elite who were able to support a promising new development without discontinuing a traditional field of inquiry. Now, with the total science budget in real dollars actually declining or at best fixed, a decision that a new field merits major support has the immediate consequence that an equivalent amount must be subtracted from a previously supported but now less favored discipline. Apart from the jockeying for position that results, such a decision requires a reasoned basis, a basis other than scientific purity (the need to climb the mountain because it's there). Yet, there are dangers to the setting of priorities on the grounds of obvious relevance alone; a preoccupation with immediate results may stifle the far greater benefits that can flow from a research area apparently remote from current crises. Once it is clear that we cannot support everything, we have to have a basis for deciding what we will support. Having avoided formulating a general solution to this problem during the fat years, we are at a great disadvantage in fashioning policy solutions under the gun of budget cuts.

Consider a second example from the academic campus. Universities have grown at an enormous rate. In 1958 there were only ten institutions with an enrollment of more than 20,000 students; they accounted for only 8 percent of the national student body. Eleven years later, there were 65 of that size (of which 26 held more than 30,000 students) accommodating more than a quarter of the total student population. But is bigger really better? A persuasive case can be made that growth beyond a critical size (in the range of 3,000 to 9,000 students) is dysfunctional because of the disproportionate multiplication of administrative structures, decrease in personal interactions, and the resulting alienation of students and faculty in an institution that has lost human proportions. But what is an optimal size? The same question can be raised for the modern teaching hospital with its proliferation of specialty services, its problems of communication and its lack of awareness of the relation between the complex disease problems it manages and the general health of the community it is meant to serve.

In university and in hospital, institutions I choose because I am familiar with both, the approaching moratorium on building and the worsening budget crises pose issues none of us had to face during the past two decades. If a field not represented within the institution is judged to be a major growth point for new knowledge, then how does the dean or the executive faculty go about providing funds and space for the new department when existing departments hold a lien on available resources? Clearly, to start department Z, one has to cut departments X and Y, chosen because they are no longer productive, or else reduce all departments A through Y on a proportionate basis. The first solution requires hard judgments; the second postpones judgment-making for a doctrine of "fairness" that avoids the difficult but inevitable task of assessing relative contribution. Areas of science do play out. It does not require intimate knowledge of the university to write the scenario for the political infighting which develops as each department prepares to resist encroachment on its own turf, a demesne to which it has primary loyalty rather than to the domain of the university as a whole.

The same holds true for welfare agencies within a United Chest; which agency executive or trustee has stepped forward to propose a reduction in his own budget when the need to support a new black community agency becomes evident? As patterns of human needs change (for example, as the result of the prevention or cure of a previously crippling disease), a naive citizen might expect to see categorical agencies close their doors to be replaced by others designed for new problems. Instead, what he observes are obsolescent agencies in search of a "need." Self-perpetuation has replaced service. This illustrates in particularly sharp fashion a prevailing professional dilemma: a growing tendency with time for professional organizations (whether of doctors or nurses, social workers or teachers) to substitute self-serving for the public good they originally functioned to guarantee. Standards, initially fashioned to guard against charlatanism, all too readily become a defense of traditional practice against the unsettling threat of change. An APA, whether psychological or psychiatric, begins to think that what is good for General Motors is good for the nation.

I begin with this unpleasant truth about ourselves as a necessary step in coming to grips with special interests which do not profess to serve the general good. If we behave this way, should we be surprised that suburbanites resist the taxation needed to support the inner city? They do what we do (and what some of us who are suburbanites join them in doing); namely, they develop an elaborate rationale that justifies the protection of enclaves of privilege in the name of noble goals.

Let us turn from these narrow professional myths to issues more central to human welfare. We fight wars, not for aggrandizement or protection of markets, but to "defend democracy." To

lessen our burden of guilt for murder, we dehumanize the
"enemy" into a pseudospecies. We resist welfare budgets, not
because we resent the cost of helping the downtrodden, but to
"curb cheats and chislers." We argue against a guaranteed annual
income, not because it would reduce our own, but to protect the
cash incentive "essential" to a productive economy. To lessen our
burden of guilt, we invent myths, myths that, on the one hand,
dehumanize the poor, myths that, on the other, allege that
income *is* being redistributed for their benefit.

Americans believe that welfare families are loaded with kids
and have kids to get more money. In fact, the typical welfare
family has a mother and three children; since 1967, its birth rate
(like that of the general population) has been dropping. Americans believe that welfare families are black; in fact, the largest
racial group is white. Americans believe that welfare recipients
buy Cadillacs and go to Florida on tax money; in fact, welfare
families in all but four states are kept on a dole well below
poverty standards. Americans believe welfare people are cheats; in
fact, despite repeated efforts to detect fraud, efforts that dissipate public funds, cheating occurs in less than .4 percent of the
total case load nationally. Each of you can make your own
estimate of the cheating on defense contracts, state payrolls and
income tax returns. Just what should we call the ITT contribution to the Republican National Convention? Americans believe
that once on welfare, always on welfare; in fact, the average
family has been on the rolls for less than 23 months. Americans
believe that welfare rolls are full of loafers; in fact, less than 1
percent are able-bodied unemployed males, 55 percent are children, 25 percent are aged or permanently disabled, and 19
percent are women, most of them family heads, four out of five
eager to work if work and child-care arrangements are available.
The enormous discrepancy between relief and reality defines the
magnitude of the task facing advocates of human welfare and
provides a measure of our failure in the public arena.

No less pernicious are the myths surrounding federal, state and
municipal tax structures. Taxes are viewed solely as a means for
generating the revenue needed to maintain essential governmental
services. They are almost never understood for what they are:

instruments of public policy based on implicit values. And we professionals, no less than the general public, have been gulled by public officials adroit in the manipulation of symbols into the belief that we have a progressive tax structure. The facts are strikingly different.

Consider the social security tax; packaged as insurance, it now brings the federal government $64 billion in revenue—two-thirds as much as individual income tax returns ($95 billion) and almost twice as much as corporate income tax ($36 billion). Not only is it not progressive, it is regressive in concept; it does not soak the rich, but does soak the poor. The rate (5.2 percent) is the "same" for all wage earners but only up to $9,000 annual base. Thus, the more money earned, the lower the actual percentage paid in social security tax. If federal, state and local taxes are summed, those in the $2,000 to $4,000 income range are taxed at the same rate (27 percent) as those in the $10,000 to $15,000 bracket. In 1969, 574 Americans with incomes exceeding $200,000 paid no taxes. In 1970, after tax "reform" aimed at the 18,000 wealthy individuals in privileged sanctuaries, payment still was at an overall rate of *4 percent*, and 1,338 with incomes in excess of $50,000 continued to enjoy the status of nontaxpayer! Equally discriminatory but less obvious are the subsidies buried within the tax structure. Mortgage and property tax exemptions available to the middle- and upper-income homeowner subsidize his housing in an amount three and one-half times the federal investment in public housing projects. Again, agricultural subsidies (two-thirds of which accrue to the upper one-sixth of farm owners) exceed the cost of all federal, state and local welfare expenditures. And how shall we classify the $5 billion the public pays for oil import quotas without even reckoning the cost of the oil depletion allowances? We *are* a welfare state, a welfare state for the wealthy. There *are* welfare chiselers: Lockheed and Penn Central are their names, corporations bailed out by a government solicitous, no doubt, of the widows and orphans among their stockholders.

Mythmaking is not limited to the rationalization of tax policy. It is applied with equal skill to the process governing expenditure of public funds. President Nixon, in an effort to obscure the racism of his stand against busing, announced a $1.5 billion program for compensatory education. Analysis of his proposal reveals nothing more than a *relabeling* of funds already allocated so as to imply the availability of new money that isn't there. Similar deliberate obfuscation surrounds the debate on a guaranteed annual income. By appearing to accept the radical view while turning it into its opposite by advocating levels of support well below that now incorporated into the welfare system, Republicans and conservative Democrats alike debase the meaning of language and degrade public understanding.

Slogans have always been cheap. They appeal to both political parties. Remember Johnson's war against poverty? It deserves to be remembered for the role professionals played in it. The con game then was "interrupting the cycle of poverty." Think about that phrase. In bald terms, it meant that the poor were poor, not for so simple-minded a reason as lack of money, but because of their behavior. Society's victims were held responsible for their own victimization. The poor were invested with new labels: "culturally impoverished," "matriarchal," "disadvantaged." They were proffered "help." Redeemers were not lacking—at a consultation fee. Money was transferred—but into professional pockets. The poor remain poor; they still need money.

The Nixon administration acknowledges a crisis in health care, proclaims "bold new initiatives," but is careful to avoid tampering with the privileges of private medical practitioners. Not only are the funds proposed for expanding medical education and for establishing health maintenance organizations grossly inadequate, but federal policy conspicuously fails to address the need for a health care system. Until this issue is faced, nothing will increase except medical costs. Some of us thought we had won a major victory when Medicare was established, but the AMA was the real winner. By incorporating Medicare benefits into the traditional fee-for-service payment scheme, it reinforced the most dysfunctional elements in episodic medical care. Now AMA and administration are allied in attacking basic medical research, as if the diversion of the 2 percent of the total medical costs now invested in research back into the service budget would make a perceptible difference in national health indices. Its one clear consequence will be a tragic reduction in the probability of discovering how to treat and prevent the major causes of death—heart disease, cancer and stroke—and of discovering how to treat and prevent the major causes of suffering—mental disease and drug addiction.

If my examples seem to have strayed over the map, ranging as they do from competition for space and funds among agencies, through inequities in tax policy, to income maintenance and health care, they have been chosen to illustrate the necessity of uniting in a crusade for human services in place of our customary categorical campaigns. It is an absurdity to demand funds for community mental health without at the same time supporting comprehensive health care, effective public schools and income maintenance. It is an absurdity to support taxes for public services without at the same time demanding reform of the tax structure that worsens the inequities it purports to correct. It is an absurdity to fight for a share of the federal budget without at the same time demanding an end to war and preparing for war. What is spent for guns will not be spent for butter.

If ever it was in doubt, it is now clear that we cannot escape active involvement in the political arena if we are to serve our clients. Those who daily confront the victims of social injustice have an inescapable responsibility to bring the meaning of that injustice to public attention whatever the personal cost involved. Narrow professionalism is a perversion of the ends our professions were created to serve. What matters is human welfare.

FURTHER READING

"Taxation and Its Beneficiaries" by R.D. Corwin and S.M. Miller in American Journal of Orthopsychiatry (No. 42, pp. 200-214, 1972).

Blaming the Victim by W. Ryan (New York: Pantheon Books, 1971).

"Uncle Sam's Welfare Program—For the Rich" by P.M. Stern in *The New York Times Magazine* (April 16, 1972) pp. 26-71.

Toward a New War on Inequity

MARC PILISUK

When we view antipoverty measures from the perspective of a society that produces, even requires, poverty, we can understand why the war on poverty has accomplished so little. Ours is an economic system that generates poverty, a social system that prevents a redistribution of wealth even while purporting to fight poverty, and a culture that provides the official myths by which the poor come to be blamed for their own poverty while the accumulators of great concentrations of wealth remain unquestioned.

PUBLIC ASSISTANCE AND SUBSIDY

American society protects the return on investments of its most powerful sectors. To the major corporate investors, the unemployed and the underemployed are a source of low-cost, standby labor. They can be minimally sustained by public assistance or employed, as needed, in periods of war or economic expansion. When the poor are not needed by the economy they are a potential threat. They might demand, or take forcibly, what they need for survival or for equality. This potential threat is quelled, in part, by a host of meagre programs of support—welfare, unemployment insurance, job training, food stamps, even by little wars on poverty. A sizeable group of unemployed can be maintained with little cost to the investors since the major costs for such low levels of public support are paid primarily by working people through taxes.

There is an added bonus to the corporate investors from the pattern of using middle and working class taxes for support of welfare. The bonus is an economic wedge that tends to pit working people against the very poor and to head off united and potentially powerful movements for economic redistribution. Often this division occurs along race lines, which intensifies the hostility between job holders and the unemployed.

Gross federal subsidies are a major factor in the guarantee on investment return. While public attention is called to the myth of the high costs of welfare, the spotlight rarely shines on the far greater subsidies afforded to wealthy corporate interests in defense, aerospace, agribusiness, highways, petroleum and urban housing. Insurgent Congressman Ronald Dellums accurately labeled the difference between welfare and subsidy. "Subsidy is a larger check that goes to fewer people." Such candor about subsidized wealth is rare, however.

EMPLOYMENT

Perhaps the most damaging of the cultural myths, to poor people, is that individual success is earned through competition in the market place of equal opportunity. In some cultures poverty is accepted as a matter of fate, a view which facilitates economic exploitation but which at least does not destroy the individual's sense of worth. In our culture, to be poor is to have failed—in school, in the job market, in the larger world which measures success by consumption. But the association of individual competition with economic success is pervasive. Wide segments of our society associate the ending of poverty with the willingness or capability of the poor to get jobs. Nevertheless, a substantial proportion of the poor cannot work, and for many of those who could work there are no jobs. Others work and still live in poverty.

A large segment of the American poor are the aged, the handicapped or disabled, and mothers of young, dependent children. Many of these people cannot work. Some could work but only with special provisions for child care or flexible hours or in protected workshop settings.

For those who can work there are inadequate job opportunities. The open market now has unemployed professionals in a number of fields. Can this same constricted market be expected to provide jobs for those barely able to work in less skilled capacities? A great decrease in unskilled jobs in manufacturing has led to disproportionately high unemployment rates for minority groups and for young people. It is apparent by now that the problem is deeper than that of temporary dislocation caused by automation. Whole categories of jobs have been eliminated. Growth of production and earnings in the private sector has coincided with a shrinking of jobs. If it were ever possible to create markets at will through advertising, it is now clear that ecological constraints are forcing a limitation on compulsive consumption. Increased production may strangle us in our own wastes, but it will not provide any long term answer for the unemployment problem. An overabundance of goods can be produced by fewer people than ever before and the resultant unemployment shows no sign of vanishing.

Poverty is not, however, restricted to the jobless. Many poor people work for their poverty. The pitifully low federal minimum wage applies to only 60 percent of the nongovernment work force. In New York City alone, over a million workers earned less than $100 per week in 1969. Half of the white families earning more than $5,000 per year do so only because there is more than one wage earner in the family. The giant agribusiness still thrives on subpoverty wages.

PROFITS ON POVERTY

Despite the presence of an army of working poor and the absence of jobs, the myth persists that poverty can be alleviated by vocational training. Job training programs are a boon for investors because the government underwrites the costs of training people to perform the technical tasks required in modern industry. Further, it is the large corporations who obtain government contracts to conduct the training. The job training business has itself become a profitable enterprise.

The rationale for job training programs has been that there are unfilled highly skilled jobs in medicine, teaching and engineering even during high unemployment periods. Hence, training was needed to shift skills to meet the new job market. The rationale has little to do with the actual state of poverty and joblessness. There have been, throughout the abortive war on poverty, far greater numbers of unemployed than vacancies at all levels. The open market just has too few jobs, regardless of level. Corporations that contracted for job training centers (such as the Litton Industries Center in Pleasanton, California) have extracted profits from their training enterprises, and for their subsidiary publishing firms, but have been unable to deliver jobs outside of the army. (The military has been the model of job training. It promises men the opportunity to learn a skill and removes the restless young from the job market only to return them, if it returns them at all, still unable to command a job in civilian society.)

The creation of new jobs for the poor depends, in part, upon the degree to which investment decisions go into meeting a vast backlog of unmet needs in health, housing, urban transportation and education. But new, adequately paid jobs in the public nonmilitary sector depends also upon who is permitted to reap the return on the investment. The problem here is that investment decisions are made in anticipation of profits. Of course, if national security can be made profitable so also can education, health and urban transportation. Yet, the very conditions which assure profit preclude any meaningful impact upon poverty. The example of industry's participation in health services for poor people is instructive. Medical care plans have amounted to a government subsidy of the health insurance and health industry interests. State taxes (paid in regressive proportions by wage and salary earners, and by consumers) guarantee the profits of those corporations which sell health insurance with sky-rocketing medical costs (support for doctors and hospital administrators) built in. Medical plans in New York and California have gone far to expose the inadequacy of available health care. Hospitals and clinics are still understaffed. They are often poorly located to meet the needs of people. Their preventive, diagnostic work and emergency services (needed particularly where there are high rates of infectious diseases and high crime rates) remain among the least adequate services. They do not provide free comprehensive medical and dental care for poor people, let alone reduce poverty. Tax money goes to the insurance and systems planning organizations, to hospital administrations and to the private practitioner. This is yet another way to use public finances to subsidize the affluent. This same pattern is apparent in the workings of industries associated with the Urban Coalition in the fields of housing and education for poor people. In other words, antipoverty programs have been used to perpetuate, even in some cases to increase inequities in wealth.

CULTURE OR MONEY

The myth that the poor are lazy, black, welfare cheaters is often fanned by conservative politicians. In this form, the myth has little credence among the academically respectable community. But well-regarded scholars have contributed to the equally pernicious belief that his life style is to blame for the poor person's failure to rise out of poverty. These academics who attribute the basic causes of poverty to the poor, rather than the affluent, have been sought after by federal program planners. The federal planner's job depends upon his ability to come up with programs which promise four things: to manage the problem at hand, to dispel radical or revolutionary protest, to assure the inviolability of major centers of wealth, and to keep poverty a separately defineable problem—separate from the war in Indochina, from tax loopholes, vertical monopolies, political campaign supports, racism or lobbying. Those who believe that the remedy for poverty is a change in the attitudes and behavior of the poor are useful to the policy planner. Poverty, however, cannot be understood within such narrow confines.

The concept of culture applied to American society would

show a large number of heterogeneous subcultures, many doing at least as well as American middle-class culture in providing for the affectional and identity needs of their members. Some of them have evolved alternative status systems in drug dealing or illegal activities, or in revivalistic religious sects. But within the actual opportunities available, even these show some signs of adaptability. As actually employed in policy, the culture of poor people has become the whipping boy, the obstacle, to their mythical movement into the middle class and, thus, out of poverty.

Poverty subcultures have been studied in ways which defy the very respect for diversity which first gave rise, among ethnographers, to the concept of culture. Culture is an integrated pattern of beliefs and activities—a totality which provides its own meaning to life. But too often poverty subcultures have been studied without any attempt to understand their cultural integrity. Instead poverty cultures have been measured by statistical comparisons with middle-class norms—against crime, drug abuse, fatherless families, low education, high birthrates—which regard alienation, marginality and despair as deficiencies in the motivation of individuals. Sociologists and social planners (Moynihan is the best example) go on to make the following assumptions: 1) whatever the saving graces of such cultures, they cannot make it in our society without changing; 2) such cultures provide a feeding ground of support for nihilistic revolutionaries or angry indigenous leaders; and 3) such radical orientations are dangerous. The diagnosis is similar to W.W. Rostow's international theory of social change in underdeveloped nations. Pacification programs abroad are provided ideological shelter by the view that flirtation with revolutionary change is but a stage to be withstood until natural forces (and technical assistance) produce economic development following the American model. Similarly, such programs as Head Start and New Careers are a remedy, to instill in poor individuals the assets necessary to compete for jobs in middle-class society. Whatever value programs such as these may have, they are only a part of a war on poverty to the extent that they take a certain amount of wealth and power from some hands and place them in the hands of poor people. In this light they have hardly been part of a war on poverty at all.

By this measure, some plans for a guaranteed annual income should be included in a war on poverty. Others should not. In the United States today a family of four can barely meet its needs for minimal participation in the larger society with an income below $9,000. If we were to set that figure as the guaranteed annual income for such a family, it would soon become apparent that the costs would be enormous. In fact, to provide such an income for all those now living on less, while holding productivity constant, we would have to reduce the rest of us to about that level.

The income maintenance issue shows why technical solutions for poverty are inadequate. The technical mechanics of income redistribution have been worked out already. Economist James Tobin's credit income tax plan, for example, would grant a minimum income to every citizen. Taxation rates would mean that the grant would be kept in its entirety by those below the designated poverty line, and kept in gradually decreasing proportions as income rose to a break-even point of perhaps $12,000 for a family of four. Beyond that break even point, about 20 percent of all taxpayers would be returning more than this grant to the treasury. The plan is excellent, for it preserves work incentive and would, in fact, supplement job income for underpaid families. The problem with income maintenance is not the absence of knowledge about what should be done. There are numerous plans like those of Tobin already in existence. What such plans need if they are to be actualized is not more money for research or larger intellectual armies of well-paid income maintenance researchers. Such plans need advocates and political constituencies. We still need professionals who can help their clients organize. We need a movement for social change.

Seymour Melman has argued that a good part of America's economic stagnation lies in the fact that we have become the world's specialists in arms and space technology. These two related fields return little to the overall economy and drain the scientific and engineering talent which might otherwise make an industry economically competitive in more useful items, thereby increasing productivity, jobs and investments in the backlog of unmet community priorities. Melman's view, while quite logical, must be tempered somewhat by ecological constraints. Growth in the GNP requires more consumption and disposal of resources and is not our ultimate solution. This does not undermine the value of his insight that a reordering of priorities is vital for the economy. To Melman's thesis of cutting defense spending, and to the factor of a high-level guaranteed income, we add one further element to a revised war on poverty—the element of community control.

The concept of community has almost lost meaning in mainstream American society, but the need for community is being reasserted in the counterculture, and remnants of community are still alive in certain poor subcultures. A native American Indian knows full well when the legal fictions of municipalities, counties and states deprive him of shared program responsibility with those who are a part of his tribal community. Some government programs serve to destroy what sense of community still survives. To create a federal or state assistance program which violates the culture of an existing community, and which then offers maximum feasible participation instead of community control, is just not good enough. Federal programs like Head Start or New Careers are obviously needed by some communities. The legitimate evaluation is not how many minority youngsters have made it to middle-class achievement standards. They can and should be evaluated by their local boards, or by the parents and participants, on criteria relevant to the community's own goals. Opportunity for sustained control over institutions provides the only regenerative power base by which poor communities can hang on to scarce resources.

A NEW WAR

Here, then, are the elements of a new antipoverty war. They are stark and radical, but no more utopian than any other plan which would do the job. They are predicated upon an assumption that the professional's function is to suggest not what is currently feasible by current political standards, but what must be tried if effects are to be seen.

1. Close all tax shelters and loopholes for personal and corporate incomes. If we include real estate, capital gains,

depletion allowances and foundation supports, this could represent an income of over $40 billion.

2. Reduce defense expenditures by $12 billion annually for five years.

3. Require all contracts for services to the poor in health, education or welfare to go to organizations in which the target community is represented among the governing boards and at all employee levels of the organizations' paid staffs.

4. Raise personal and corporate taxes on all incomes above $20,000.

5. Provide income maintenance supplements to $9,000 for individuals willing to work half-time, to produce less and to consume less. Provide income maintenance of $1,500 for every individual over 18; $2,000 to retired persons over age 60. This should come in the form of a universal allowance which would be negated above a break-even point of approximately $9,000 (for a family of four) where progressive tax increases would take over.

6. Provide a universal child-care allowance of $1,000 per child ($1,500 per adopted child, to counter the charge of encouraging a baby boom). This is critical to the task of avoiding the stigma of charity.

7. Provide grants directly to community-based agencies for the development of alternative institutional services in health care and education, e.g., free clinics and community schools. This includes the right to make mistakes in the type and quality of services selected. Decentralization is important and coordination efforts must be divorced from control functions.

8. Increase support for professional education (medicine, dentistry, teaching, social work, psychology, law and public health) to programs requiring at least two full years of service internship under a community-based agency. Reduce support for other programs.

9. Write into professional and business licensing laws terms for providing poor and minority employment, and reduced fee service for poor people.

10. Provide low-cost educational and therapeutic facilities not only to the poor but to professional and business organizations and to labor unions. Those who have substantial assets and dependable incomes must be helped to deal with the psychological and environmental costs of continual preoccupation with production, income and competition and with the benefits of alternative, reduced-income life styles.

11. Share the sense of community and service with the affluent. This may be done by permitting individuals to order priorities for the expenditure of their tax dollars and by providing individuals, even corporations on the local level, with information on services created by their local taxes.

12. Restrict all campaign giving to tax-deductible individual donations of $100 which an individual may assign to a corporation, union or political group, or to a candidate.

13. Create a national organization from the radical caucus of each professional organization to ascribe to such goals and advocate for them.

The day of looking at the poor as in need of restitution is passing. That view was consistent with a war on poverty which assumed no basic change in wealth, power and values in the society at large. More of the same program will produce more of the same results. Gladwin's summary statement in his recent book, *Poverty U.S.A.*, makes the point:

> ... social reforms necessary to make poverty avoidable and remediable must embrace a larger part of society than just the poor alone. ... these reforms can be implemented only by forces not conceivably available to poor people, however well organized. These reforms must furthermore reallocate power and above all money and the power that flows from a money within our society, or else the poor will remain forever poor.

FURTHER READING

Poverty U.S.A. by Thomas Gladwin (Boston: Little, Brown & Co., 1967). "Advocacy and Democracy: The Long View" by A.F. Guskin and Robert Ross in American Journal of Orthopsychiatry, 41, January 1971, pp. 43-57.

"On Taxing and Redistributing Income" by George McGovern in *New York Review of Books*, May 4, 1972.

Our Depleted Society by Seymour Melman (New York: Dell, 1966).

"The Meaning of the Cybernetic State" by R. Perrucci and Marc Pilisuk in *Triple Revolution Emerging: Social Problems in Depth* (Boston: Little, Brown & Co., 1971).

"Social Work Action for Welfare Rights," unpublished position paper, May 1970.

Culture and Poverty: Critique and Some Proposals by C.A. Valentine (Chicago: University of Chicago Press, 1968).

Notes on Contributors

Jerome Carlin ("Store Front Lawyers in San Francisco") is a lawyer and sociologist turned full-time artist. Author of *Lawyers On Their Own, Lawyer's Ethics* and *Civil Justice and the Poor*, he has had a one-man show of his paintings at the Snow Gallery in San Francisco.

Richard A. Cloward ("Advocacy in the Ghetto," "The Relief of Welfare") is professor at the Columbia School of Social Work. He was a founder of Mobilization for Youth and is its director of research. His latest book is *Regulating the Poor: The Functions of Public Welfare,* co-authored with Frances Fox Piven.

Leon Eisenberg ("Poverty, Professionalism and Politics") is professor of psychiatry at Harvard Medical School and psychiatrist-in-chief at the Massachusetts General Hospital. His research interests are in child development, in particular in the acquisition of problem-solving sets.

Richard M. Elman ("Advocacy in the Ghetto") is a free-lance writer who was formerly research assistant at the Columbia University School of Social Work Research Center. Among his many publications are *The Poorhouse State* and *The Speculators*.

Alvin E. Green ("New Careers in Mental Health Systems: Epilogue to a Survey") is director of Community Studies, Department of Education, The Menninger Foundation. He co-authored, with Louis A. Zurcher, *From Dependency to Dignity*, and his major interests are in community organization and community mental health.

Christopher Green ("Guaranteed Income Plans–Which One is Best?") is assistant professor of economics at North Carolina State University at Raleigh. His present research interests are in the economics of income maintenance and the factors governing the high rate of Negro unemployment. He is author of *Negative Taxes and the Poverty Problem*.

Alan Haber ("New Careers: Issues Beyond Consensus") is one of the founders of the New Left movement in the United States and author of the *Port Huron Statement* which led to the development of Students for a Democratic Society. He was a Fellow of the Institute of Policy Studies and co-editor of *Poverty in America: Book of Readings*, 1964. He currently devotes most of his energies to a cabinet-making shop and to the activities of a commune in Berkeley.

Bruce Jackson ("In the Valley of the Shadows: Kentucky"), associate professor at State University of New York at Buffalo, is author of *Outside the Law: A Thief's Primer* and *Wake Up Dead Man*, a collection and analysis of Texas convict worksongs. He teaches courses on literature, folklore and criminality.

Ed Johnson ("New Careers in Mental Health Systems: Epilogue to a Survey") is a psychiatric nurse who has been a "cottage parent," child-care worker and poverty warrior in a community action program. He also participated in the writing of *From Dependency to Dignity*.

Beverly Leman ("The Business of Urban Reform") is an activist in the women's movement and the antiwar movement. She was managing editor of *Viet-Report*.

Michael Lipsky ("Rent Strikes: Poor Man's Weapon") is associate professor of political science at MIT. He wrote *Protest in City Politics; Rent Strikes, Housing, and the Power of the Poor;* and is co-author of *Riot Commission Politics*, forthcoming from Transaction Books. He is editor of *Law and Order: Police Encounters*, also published by Transaction Books.

S.M. Miller ("Will the War on Poverty Change America?" "Social Action on the Installment Plan," "Poverty Programs and Policy Priorities") is professor of education and sociology at New York University. He has been a government consultant on poverty, social change and school dropouts. He is co-author of *The Future of Inequality, Applied Sociology* and *Social Class and Social Policy*.

Richard Parker ("The Myth of Middle America") is a Junior Fellow at the Center for Democratic Studies at Santa Barbara. He was a former economist for the United Nations Development Program. His articles have appeared in 20 books and journals including *Ramparts, New Republic,* the *New York Times,* and *The Washington Post.* His latest book is *Myth of the Middle Class.*

Marc Pilisuk ("Barely War," "Battlefield Reports–the Record of Attempted Change," "Toward a New War on Inequity") is professor in residence at the School of Public Health, University of California, Berkeley. For further information, see the cover.

Phyllis Pilisuk ("Barely War," "Battlefield Reports–The Record of Attempted Change") is a social scientist and social worker in Berkeley, California.

Frances Fox Piven ("The Relief of Welfare") is a political scientist teaching at Boston University, has authored many articles on urban politics, is currently working on a book titled *Recent Movements of the Poor and Why They Failed,* and is associated with the founding of the welfare rights movement.

Martin Rein ("Will the War on Poverty Change America?", "Social Action on the Installment Plan," "Poverty Programs and Policy Priorities") is a professor in the Department of Urban Studies and Planning at MIT. Author of many works on public policy, poverty, the welfare state and housing, his most recent book is entitled *Social Policy: Issues of Choice and Change.*

Frank Riessman ("Self-Help Among the Poor: New Styles of Social Action") is editor of *Social Policy* and director of the new careers development center and professor of educational sociology at New York University. His publications include *Children Teach Children, New Careers for the Poor* and *The Culturally Deprived Child.*

Michael Stegman ("The New Mythology of Housing") is assistant professor of planning at the University of North Carolina at Chapel Hill.

Peter Wiley ("The Business of Urban Reform") is an editor of the national serviceman's antiwar newsletter *Up Against the Bulkhead* and an organizer of the Stop Our Ships Movement. He formerly served on the editorial board of *Leviathan*.